ACKNOWLEDGEMENTS

Among those who have helped me I would like particularly to mention: Sir Anthony Wagner, Garter King of Arms, for referring me to the writers in *The Complete Peerage* on the point of Richard III's creating John Howard Duke of Norfolk during the lifetime of the previous holder of the title, Prince Richard of York;

Major-General W. D. M. Raeburn, C.B., D.S.O., M.B.E., Resident Governor of the Tower of London, for escorting me to the Wakefield Tower and the Bloody Tower and for giving me his opinion on the un-likelihood that the then Constable of the Tower, Sir Robert Brackenbury, would have allowed access to the Princes except at the direct command of the King;

Mr. F. M. Lind, B.D.S. (Lond.), L.D.S., R.C.S. (Eng.), for reading the evidence of the state of the lower jaw in the skull of Edward V, and suggesting (p. 198) two causes which might have produced the inflamed and septic condition which Professor Wright and Dr. Northcroft said must have been present. The Rev. J. E. T. Cox, Vicar of Little Malvern Priory, for his permission to photograph the windows containing portraits of Edward Prince of Wales and his sisters, and Mr. Roy Smith for producing the prints in a very difficult undertaking.

Finally I must thank my brother for his constant sympathy and his most useful criticism and advice.

The family tree on page 223 is based on that appearing in Henry VI, *parts I, II and III, edited by G. B. Harrison in the Penguin Shakespeare.*

THE PRINCES IN THE TOWER

THE PRINCES
IN THE TOWER

BY

ELIZABETH JENKINS

The sweet fruition of an earthly crown
Marlowe, *Tamburlaine the Great*

BOOK CLUB ASSOCIATES

LONDON

This edition published 1978 by
Book Club Associates
By arrangement with Hamish Hamilton Ltd

Copyright © 1978 by Elizabeth Jenkins

Printed in Great Britain by
Ebenezer Baylis & Son Ltd,
The Trinity Press, Worcester, and London.

ILLUSTRATIONS

Between pages 114 *and* 115

A family tree appears on page 223

INTRODUCTION

THE CULT of Richard III which is so vigorous today takes its rise from various sources. After a view has been very decidedly held for centuries, a reaction usually sets in. Further, in Richard III's case, three serious errors of judgment, largely uncontested for nearly 500 years, are now being amended; one was that he had been proved guilty of the murder of the Princes, whereas nothing that would be accepted as legal evidence against him has ever been produced; another, that he had been guilty of the murder of Prince Edward of Lancaster, of Henry VI and of his own wife, Anne Neville. The first of these charges is disproved by contemporary accounts: of the second, if he were guilty, which is not proved, the responsibility would rest on Edward IV, and of the third, there is not only no evidence of his guilt but considerable circumstantial evidence of his innocence. Thirdly, in the interests of story-value, he was described as hunch-backed, and a repulsive anecdote added that he had been gestated for two years and born with long hair and teeth. These details were supplied by John Rows, a contemporary who produced an illustrated Roll of the Earls of Warwick. The first version, finished before 1485, gave a eulogistic written description of Richard and drawings of him which did not show any deformity. The second version, produced between 1485 and 1491, left out the drawings and added in words the odious description. Careful collation of what contemporary witnesses said has shown that he was of medium height, lean, with one shoulder higher than the other. The very old Countess of Desmond who had once danced with him remembered him as the handsomest man in the room.

These reconsiderations have brought about in some minds a massive swing of the pendulum. The most assertive was Sir Clements Markham, who was obsessed by a maniacal hatred of Henry VII which carried him to the point of declaring that the latter was not, and never had been, Earl of Richmond, though this was a title which descended to him at his posthumous birth, his father Edmund Tudor never having been attainted. Sir Clements Markham attempted to fasten on Henry VII the guilt of the Princes' murder. It must be admitted that both Richard III and Henry VII were thoroughly formidable, and that to be found standing in the way of either of them amounted to a fatal misfortune. It is not a question of whether Henry VII were morally capable of the crime but as to whether he actually committed it. Of the circumstantial evidence against Richard III which is so strong as to be almost conclusive, two very important elements were ignored by Sir Clements Markham in his *Richard III, His Life and Character*, and by Josephine Tey, who wrote an extremely successful novel, *Daughter of Time*, devoted to the exculpation of Richard III. Both leaned heavily on the assertion that there was no general rumour during Richard's lifetime that he had murdered his nephews, it was a piece of propaganda put out by Henry VII. This error was completely exploded in 1936, with the publication of the account, written in December 1483, by an Italian visitor to England, Dominic Mancini (*The Usurpation of Richard III*, translated and edited by C. A. J. Armstrong). Mancini left this country just after Richard III's coronation and he reported that even then people were saying that Edward IV's children were dead or as good as dead. Sir Clements Markham could not have read this work as his book was published in 1906, but it would have been available to Josephine Tey whose novel appeared in 1951. The other grave mistake made by both of them is the dismissing as futile the very important contemporary source, *The Chronicles of Croyland*. Most of this was compiled by the monks of Croyland Abbey, but the parts dealing with the reigns of Edward IV and Richard III are now accepted as the work of Dr. John Russell, Bishop of Lincoln, Lord Chancellor of Richard III, a member of the Council and present at the scenes of court and council he described. Miss Tey's reference to 'even a monk of Croyland', and Sir Clements Markham's to 'the credulous old Croyland monk' are absurdly misapplied.

These two works are the best known of their *genre*, but there are a heap of others of similar inspiration. One feature is common to them all. They describe, often with admirable lucidity, the course of events up to the coronation of Richard III, but when they try to provide an alternative solution to the enigma of the Princes' disappearance, they spin off into space. The chroniclers say the boys were not seen outside the Tower again, but they may have been, it is only the chroniclers who say they were not. Possibly the Queen smuggled them abroad. They may simply have disappeared. Perhaps it was all the work of the Duke of Norfolk? The bones of two children of twelve and ten were found where More said the Princes had been buried, but many murders have been committed in the Tower, and these may be the bones of two other children of those identical ages, whose names have escaped us, who happened to be buried in that spot.

There is one good aspect of all these works. They show what fine traits of character and intelligence Richard possessed, and how excellent a beginning he had made in the short time allowed him to be king. This story was too much overlooked in the past, though Dr. Gairdner* brought it out, but it deserves considerable emphasis and repetition. Once it is

* Gairdner, James, *History of the Life and Reign of Richard III*, 1898.

admitted that Richard committed the crime, it becomes alarmingly clear how much reason he felt he had to do it, and how much the circumstances of his past had contributed to the doing. The story is not the sensational one of the crime of a habitual murderer, but the awe-inspiring one of a capable, strong-minded, dedicated king driven to a dreadful act from which he chose to think there was no escape.

IN 1509 William Dunbar wrote a poem celebrating London. This was fifty years later than the accession of Edward IV, but Dunbar could still praise the clearness of Thames water. He saw it a greenish blue like aquamarine, which he called beryl. White swans were swimming on it, and barges were passing, moved by sail or oar.

Fresh is thy river with his lusty strand!

The strand was gravel as one can see it yet, beside the Tower and on minute beaches under embankments. Dunbar exclaimed at the splendid sight of London Bridge carried across the river on its white pillars, and at the sound of bells ringing from the steeples of city churches. Proceeding eastwards in his mind's eye, he saw the Tower of London itself; he thought, mistakenly, that it had been built by Julius Caesar, and he was so much impressed by the spectacle of its walls and towers and its mounted cannon, he declared it to be the house of victorious Mars.

The Tower stood at what was then the extreme eastern limit of the city, so much so that the city wall came up to it, ending in the Postern Gate, and the curtain wall of the Tower itself continued the city's boundary down to the river shore. The Tower's western windows looked over the city's congested roofs, above which rose the great landmark of St. Paul's cathedral; its eastern ones commanded St. Katherine's Dock and beyond that, the water-meadows of the meandering Thames and empty down-land stretching to the sky-line.

The fortress had been founded by William the Conqueror to keep London in awe. He began the great square central keep which was finished by William Rufus. Of brick, faced with stone and surmounted by four turrets, it has walls fifteen feet thick. On its first floor, a great apartment was used for centuries as a council chamber; on the same floor is the Chapel of St. John, a lovely Norman work contained in an oval of pillars supporting round-headed arches.

The collection of buildings known as the Tower had been added to in successive reigns; in 1460, it consisted, first, of an outer wall girdled by a moat which the river filled; within this was another wall, bearing at regular intervals twelve towers. These towers were of stone and flint; the brick and stone of the central keep had been whitewashed by the aesthetic, extravagant Henry III, and was thenceforward known as the White Tower. Between the White Tower and the river shore was a range of fourteenth century buildings, comprising a great hall with a castellated roof and a castellated block at each end of it. These buildings which have now disappeared were the royal apartments used by the sovereign when he was staying at the Tower. The left-hand block was adjoined by a water gate, flanked by two towers. This was the only access to the Tower by water, and was originally called St. Thomas's Gate as one of the towers contained a chapel dedicated to Thomas à Becket. In later years when it was used for bringing state prisoners into the Tower, to imprisonment or death, it became known as the Traitor's Gate. Though it had always been a fortress and a stronghold for the royal treasures, the Tower in the fifteenth century was used as the second of the two great London palaces. Henry III had not only whitewashed the outer walls of the White Tower, he had painted murals on the walls of St. John's Chapel and filled its windows with coloured glass. In 1398, Richard II had ordered one hundred and five square feet of glass figured with fleurs de lys and the royal arms for the royal apartments, and when he enlarged the Byward Tower, one of the pair of towers guarding the entrance through the outward wall, he decorated its interior with gold and vermilion wall paintings of angels and birds, and floor tiles ornamented with the royal leopards and his own cognizance of the white hart. The shimmering light reflected from the water must have given a special radiance to glass, gilding and ceramics, and the river itself, freighted with the barges of rich men, with rowing boats for passengers and trading vessels making their way up to the wharves, while swans steered between them, did not suggest a scene of gloom and terror.

Dunbar said that the water ran down under the walls of London with shining clearness, and nowhere could he have seen this better than from the Lambeth shore, opposite the Palace of Westminster.

The Palace was a complex of buildings which had been erected in successive eras. Lying along the riverside under the lee of Westminster Abbey, it showed, in the mid-fifteenth century, a prospect of gables, towers, battlements; range above range of steep roofs, arched doorways, innumerable windows, oblong, pointed or round-headed. Great chimneys rose over roofs and turrets. At the base of the walls, thickets and bushes met the water's edge.

The dominating feature of the scene was Westminster Hall, then called the Great Hall, built by William Rufus and altered by Richard II between 1395 and 1400. Richard raised the height and put on the beautiful roof whose springing arches are borne on the backs of flying angels. The Great Hall lies parallel with the river; at right angles to its western end stood St Stephen's Chapel, a lofty, narrow, gothic building with tapering crockets soaring all round its roof. The interior decoration, carried out by Edward III, was famous all over Europe. Thousands of leaves of gold and silver foil, hundreds of pounds' weight of azure, vermilion and green had been employed to cover every surface. The columns that divided and framed its lancet windows were coated with thousands of paterae of gilded gesso; coloured enamels were laid as a transparent glaze over gold and silver. The floor was paved with Purbeck marble.

The royal closet, in which the King's family heard mass, projected into the chapel at first floor level beside the high altar; beneath it was a side chapel dedicated to Our Lady of the Pew, a corruption of Puits. The island on which Westminster Abbey itself was built had once been a marsh and the land between the Abbey and the river was watery still. J. T. Smith, writing in 1807, said that there were then four wells on the site of Westminster Palace.

The analysis of fragments of the windows of St. Stephen's which Smith caused to be made, showing that the stains were extracted from metals, suggests the deep, cold and brilliant colours of the glass. The red came from gold and copper, the orange and yellow from silver, the blue from the silver-white metal, cobalt, the violet from black manganese. The gold leaf, Smith said, 'was of great purity and thicker than that which is now ordinarily employed'.*

At right angles to the chapel, was the Lesser, or White, Hall, used by the King for assemblies for which the Great Hall would have been too vast, and at one end of the White Hall was the two-storey building of which the upper room was the famous Painted Chamber, decorated as his bedchamber by Henry III, and having in one of its walls a quatrefoil squint through which the King could see into an oratory as he lay on a bedstead painted dark green and powdered with gilt stars. This chamber was reached by a newell stone staircase; it had been established on the first floor to avoid damage from disastrous floods of Thames water, one of which had been so deep that men had rowed in wherries over the floor of Westminster Hall. Some description of the Painted Chamber has survived because the White Hall adjoining it was later used for sittings of the House of Lords, and when in 1832 it was thought necessary to enlarge this, the Painted Chamber was broken into, and antiquaries did what they could to record the mural decorations while workmen were knocking the walls to pieces.

The largest area formed an azure background to the coronation of Edward the Confessor. The King stood surrounded by prelates, and silver lettering explained the scene. At other stations on the walls were mailed figures on horseback, their mail and ornaments worked in silver or gilt stucco, in high relief. In the embrasures of the windows, royal figures were standing under gilded canopies; above each canopy an angel with

* Smith, J. T., *Antiquities of Westminster*.

3

outstretched wings arrayed in blue robes trimmed with gilt, held out a crown.

A set of tapestries discovered in the Painted Chamber but not, it is supposed, originally hung there, were of late fourteenth-century workmanship. One showed a king, in robe and crown, giving audience, one a prince and princess going aboard a tall ship, one a fleet loaded with warriors, one was of a landing operation, one the besieging of a city; one conjured up some dreadful, forgotten tale of a knight cutting off a lady's head.* Viewed from the floor against a lofty wall, these thronged scenes in the dim colours of tapestry work made a background of doom-laden ideas, accepted without being altogether understood.

The tempo of existence in the palace was however one of bustling activity. The standard of personal comfort in the royal apartments was high, and much of this had been due to Richard II. He had established private latrines, and fireplaces in the small rooms, whereas before fires burned only in the great chambers. He had also provided bathrooms. In Westminster Palace was a room with two large bronze taps 'for the King's bath, to bring hot and cold water into the bath'. Whatever comfort might be lacking in a domestic system, it was supplied by thorough and efficient personal service. Members of the royal family were surrounded by human agents whose first duty it was to keep them washed, dressed, warmed and fed; but the staff responsible for these services were a minute fraction of the work-force required to maintain the Palace. Most of what was needed in the palace was made within its walls. Masons, tilers and carpenters, blacksmiths and armourers, butchers, bakers, brewers and confectioners, tailors, semptresses, shoemakers, goldsmiths and jewellers, who worked for the king lived within his precincts and received a daily ration. The palace servants included cooks, grooms, stable-boys, gardeners, laundresses, the singing children of the royal chapel, trumpeters, heralds, minstrels. There was another group, in personal attendance on the king: physicians, barbers, the keepers of the king's wardrobe, pages, clerks, scribes, chaplains; and in the rank above these were councillors: bishops, lawyers, statesmen who gave service of a kind even more necessary, who helped the king to continue his task of keeping the whole system in activity, avoiding dangers, consolidating advantages; for the entire scheme of things, which appeared so deep-founded and secure, might, from lack of skill, or treachery, or a reverse of fortune merely, be undermined like a sandcastle by the incoming tide,

>   *and farewell, King!*
>   *Richard II*, iii, 2.

* *History of the Kings' Works*, Vol. I, 1963, Brown, Colvin and Taylor. *Gentleman's Magazine*, 1819, II, p. 390, 1823, II, pp. 99–100, p. 489.

2

THE English royal treasury held many crowns; the oldest and most famous was 'the rich crown' of Edward the Confessor. This was kept by itself in a leather case with two locks. It was set with four great rubies, four smaller rubies, thirty-eight other rubies, twelve sapphires, forty-three emeralds and forty pearls.* This wreath of light set on the king's brow gave a visual magic to the ceremony of coronation. Richard II who spent lavishly on clothes and jewels, had several crowns made for himself. Henry IV, a plain man who needed money sorely for affairs of state, pawned one of these, a circlet loaded with rubies, sapphires and diamonds, one hundred and fifty-one stones in all, to the Mayor of Norwich; he also pawned his own great pinnacled crown, set with pearls, sapphires and rubies, known as 'the crown Harry', to his uncle the Duke of Clarence.†

The garland-like shape of the earlier crowns was retained in some cases to a much later date, but about the middle of the fifteenth century the form was introduced of the circlet with two crossed hoops rising from it; this though less graceful allowed more room for incrustation with gems and created an intenser glitter. The indescribable beauty of the jewels, their radiance and colour, made the crowns a vivid image of the power and majesty they represented and formed a tangible object to strive for, which carried with it a state of wealth, dominion, felicity, which had, in men's opinion, no earthly counterpart. So great was the prize that anyone with a distant claim to it would join the struggle for it.

Edward III's heir, the Black Prince, died before his father, but he was survived by four brothers, the Dukes of Clarence, Gaunt, York and Gloucester. Harding's rhyming Chronicle says of them:

> So high and large they were of all stature
> The least of them was of his person able
> To have foughten with any creature.

These tall and warlike figures loom in the background of the Wars of the Roses, for since the Black Prince's son, Richard II, left no child, descent from one or other of his uncles set in motion every claimant on the scene.

* Palgrave, *Ancient Calendars and Inventories*, Vol. III, p. 2.
† *Archeologia*, Vol. LXXXVI.

The succession was wrenched from the Black Prince's line when John of Gaunt's son deposed Richard II in 1399 and ascended the throne as Henry IV. In 1420, when she was nineteen, Catherine of Valois, a Princess of France, was married to Henry IV's son, the formidable Henry V. She bore his son, Henry VI, the following year and in 1422 she was left a widow.

Henry had wooed her with his sword, but Catherine was eager for the match. Her country was ravaged by the Hundred Years' War begun by Edward III who already owned Normandy because William the Conqueror who had made himself King of England had been Duke of Normandy, and also Maine, Aquitaine and Gascony because these provinces had come to Henry II on his marriage with Eleanor of Aquitaine; but Edward III then claimed the whole kingdom of France because his mother Isabel had been the sole heiress of her father, the French King Philip le Bel. This struggle, ruinous to both England and France, had left the latter exhausted by 1420. Catherine's father, Charles VI, had recurring bouts of total insanity, while her mother, Isabeau of Bavaria, was so vicious the French themselves lost patience and put her under house arrest in the palace of Tours. To a girl with such a background, to be married in splendour to the victor of Agincourt, to be Queen of England, was a glorious prospect. It was not without its drawbacks. After the wedding at Troyes, Henry returned to the task of fighting such of his bride's countrymen as still resisted English dominion. Much of her brief married life was spent with her husband on his military campaigns in France, and some of it by herself in England. In December 1421 she lay in at Windsor Castle of the king's son, the child who became at eight months old King of England, and titular King of France.

In the first few years of widowhood, Catherine occupied the natural position of the infant king's mother. When he was less than a year old, she appeared with him on a state occasion. The London Chronicle says that he 'with glad semblance and merry cheer, on his mother's lap rode through London to Westminster, and on the morrow was so brought into Parliament'.

But the Queen Mother had no official position. The management of the child king was shared between the members of the Council and the attendants whom they appointed. She was not present at his coronation, performed at Westminster in 1429 when he was eight years old, or at his coronation in Paris the following year. It seems that she had a preoccupation of an absorbing kind. Marriage to Henry V had brought many advantages, but not the comforts of home life and the passion she had now conceived for Owen Tudor, her Clerk of the Wardrobe, promised her a happiness she had not yet found.

Tudor had been a favourite squire of Henry V; he was debonair, good-natured and outstandingly handsome. His connection with Catherine

6

is assumed to have been a secret marriage, because the marriage, though not proved, was never denied. It is supposed to have begun in 1425, and must have been carried on with remarkable discretion, though some suspicion seems to have been aroused, because in 1428 the Council published an edict saying that heavy penalties would be incurred by anyone who married a Queen Dowager, or any lady dowered in lands belonging to the Crown, without the consent of the King and his Council.

Catherine had been awarded several manors reserved for the use of dowager queens, among them Hadham and Hatfield. She bore three sons to Owen Tudor without public comment; Edmund of Hadham in 1430 and Jasper of Hatfield in 1431. The third was born, perhaps prematurely, since the place was so awkward, in Westminster Palace itself. This child was at once carried out to the Abbey of Westminster and put into the Abbot's care. He was brought up in the community and became a monk.

It was not till 1436, after the birth of a daughter who lived only a few days, that the Council took official notice of the Queen Dowager's private life. Owen Tudor was imprisoned, though he soon escaped, owing to his geniality with the jailers; her two sons, the six year old Edmund and the five year old Jasper, were handed over to Katherine de la Pole who was Abbess of Barking. This convent and its grounds stood west of the Tower of London. On the south shore of the Thames almost opposite the Tower, in full view of the convent though separated from it by the broad flood, was Bermondsey Abbey, a beautiful set of fourteenth-century gothic buildings enclosing a large garden. This Abbey had some obligations to give hospitality to members of the royal family. Very ill after the birth of her last child, Catherine was taken there in the autumn of 1436. Her will, made in the form of a letter to Henry VI, now fifteen years old, asked him to have her means used for the payment of her debts, for legacies to her servants and masses for her soul. It made no mention of her second husband or his children, it only begged the King to act 'according to his noble discretion' and her 'intents'. On January 11, 1437, Henry sent her a New Year's gift of a crucifix set with pearls and sapphires resting on a tablet of solid gold. His mother lived long enough to receive it; she died two days afterwards.

3

HENRY V's conquests in France did not long outlast his death. The struggle to maintain them was disastrous to English and French alike. A peace party in England headed by the Marquess of Suffolk arranged for a truce to be cemented by the marriage of Henry VI, now twenty-three, with the fifteen year old Margaret, daughter of the Count of Anjou. England was seething with discontent. Twenty years of fatal incompetence by the government, the poverty of the Crown owing to the pillaging of the King's resources by everyone about him, the brutal lawlessness of barons and knights who commanded armies of retainers and a countryside frightened and demoralized by disbanded soldiers returned from the French war, had brought the nation to a state in which numbers of responsible people would be prepared to support any faction that could promise firm and equitable control.

Against this background, the characters of Henry VI and Margaret of Anjou pursued an inevitable course. The King's deeply spiritual nature, his complete unselfishness, his humility, his tenderness towards mankind were, unfortunately, divorced from any practical capacity whatever. His occupation of the throne was a sheer calamity, but even so his qualities inspired, in some parts of the nation, an affection and loyalty which were never entirely lost. He suffered two attacks of complete mental aberration, but his normal condition was one of a holy simple-mindedness, which made him a prey to anyone he trusted.

Margaret was a very beautiful girl, high-spirited and imperious. Her untamed energies were concentrated on supporting and maintaining the King's position as an absolute monarch. She would not or could not understand the force of the complaints against the gross abuses that position was fostering, or that to try to remedy them was the surest way of protecting her husband's throne.

The outstanding difficulty of the government in 1444 was the dire poverty to which plunderers, high and low, had reduced the Crown; but the *Short English Chronicle* says: 'In that year Queen Margaret came into England with great royalty, at the King's cost.' Fifty-six English ships had been chartered to convey her and her retinue, but the bride herself was so poorly found, that on her arrival at Southampton Lord Suffolk, who had

8

arranged the match, felt it necessary to send to London for a dressmaker, that she might make her entry into London with credit. Payment was made to a valet, 'sent from Southampton by command of the Marquess of Suffolk with three horses for Margaret Chamberlayne, tire-maker, to bring her into the presence of the Lady Queen, for divers affairs touching the said Lady Queen.'

What she had lacked in clothes and properties, Margaret amply made up in beauty and temperament. From Henry VI's childhood until his present age, there had been no court, but one now formed itself about the brilliant young queen. She appears to have been loyal and affectionate to the King, but it was only too natural that she should need a male friend other than a husband whose condition, though in the religious sphere it was almost that of mysticism, in practical affairs was verging on feeble-mindedness. Unfortunately, Margaret's first favourite, John de la Pole, Marquess (and later Duke) of Suffolk, and Edmund Beaufort, Duke of Somerset, who succeeded him in her affections, both aroused the nation's furious anger as promoters and sharers of the robbery of the King's revenues. This had got to such a pitch that though taxes were heavy, the King's income would not allow him to maintain a suitable household. Suffolk and Somerset were also held accountable for the loss of Henry V's conquests in France. Suffolk had arranged Henry VI's marriage with Margaret of Anjou as the means of making a truce, and not only had he stipulated for no dowry with her, he had promised to restore Anjou and Maine to the French as part of the marriage treaty. The public indignation was reflected even a hundred years later in Hall's *Chronicle**
(p. 204): 'as who should say, this new affinity excelled riches and surmounted gold and precious stones'. Her father, Count René of Anjou, called himself King of Sicily, Naples and Jerusalem, though, Hall said, 'he had not with them a penny of profit or a foot of land,' and, 'for all his long style, had too short a purse to send his daughter honourably to her spouse.' As Hall put it, 'Anjou, Mans and Maine were the very stays and backstands to the Duchy of Normandy,' and when these were ceded, Normandy was easily taken. In 1453 when the famous John Talbot, Earl of Shrewsbury, was killed at Castillon, the English were finally turned out of France.

For them to persevere in attempting to subdue the land by war and destruction would not only have been unforgivable, it had become impossible, and though their failure in the French war was what the nation blamed them for most bitterly, Suffolk and Somerset might well have failed in it if they had been able and honest men like Shrewsbury. Their criminal offence was the exploiting of the good-hearted, simple king, helping themselves and their creatures to his revenues and using their

* Hall, Edward, *The Union of the Noble and Illustre Families of Lancastre and York*, (ed. H. Ellis, 1809).

9

enormous powers to subvert the law, so that they and their protégés might raven on the possessions of their weaker neighbours. Early in 1450, the Commons brought charges against Suffolk which dealt with his conduct of the French war but also accused him of appropriating taxes to his own use, and declared that among other offences, he had first ordered the Sheriff of Lincoln not to prosecute a man who had committed several murders, and then got the King to pardon the Sheriff for failure to do his duty. They stated that Suffolk had controlled the appointment lists of sheriffs long since, either for the sake of money bribes to himself, or to ensure that those elected would be favourable to his interests. Those whom he could not count on were set aside, with the result, as the Commons laid before the King, 'that he hath, by his might and help of his adherents, disherited, impoverished and destroyed many of your true lieges . . . he hath purchased many great possessions . . . and done great, outrageous extortions and murders.'*

That Suffolk wrote verses to the Queen under her cognomen of the marguerite:

> My heart is set and all my whole intent
> To serve this flower in my most humble wise,

shows the closeness of the bond between two persons who valued each other exceedingly but did not in the least value the English nation, and regarded all attempts to restrain their criminal practices as crimes against themselves.

Suffolk met his defeat at the hands of Parliament and the King, to save him from being tried for his offences, passed a sentence on him of five years' banishment. Suffolk, attempting to make his way to France, was captured on the high seas by enraged malcontents and beheaded on deck with five strokes of a rusty sword.

This act of rough justice left the Duke of Somerset in control of the King and Queen. His record and his subsequent conduct were no better than Suffolk's, and in July 1450 a Kentish rising advanced on London under a man calling himself Jack Cade. The insurgents issued a proclamation of grievances which underlined the charges of corruption brought against Suffolk six months before. This gave a detailed picture of the thievery in the King's circle; it castigated 'the insatiable, false and of-nought brought-up certain persons, daily and nightly about his highness'. When financial reform was attempted, these people would say 'it were great reproof to the King to take again that he hath given, so that they will not suffer him to have his own good, but they ask it from him, or else they take bribes of others . . . to get it for them.'

The rebellion looked as though it might be dangerous, but the rebels were thrown back in an encounter and the rising died down with the death

* *The XV Century*, E. F. Jacob, p. 493.

from wounds of Cade himself. Its demands, so plainly just, were totally ignored, but the outbreak, abortive though it was, gave his opportunity to the most important figure who had yet appeared upon the scene.

Richard, Duke of York, was formidable to the Lancastrian king because he was descended from two sons of Edward III, one of them, the Duke of Clarence, being older than John of Gaunt, Duke of Lancaster, the ancestor of Henry VI, so that it might be argued York had a better claim to the crown than the present king. At all events he was a prominent member of that circle, all of whom had claims of some kind to the succession, among whom, it was asserted, Parliament had the right to choose who should wear the crown.

York's wife, Cicely Neville, was the daughter of Ralph Neville, Earl of Westmorland, by his second wife; and that wife had been Joanna Beaufort, John of Gaunt's daughter by his mistress Catherine Swinford, whose children by the Duke had been legitimized by Act of Parliament.

Cicely Neville was said to have been very beautiful; loyal adherents called her the Rose of Raby, as Raby Castle was her father's seat, but in her husband's castle of Fotheringhay, she gave herself such royal airs, the people called her Proud Cis.

York was the greatest landowner in the country after the King. He possessed vast estates on the Welsh marches, the earldom of Ulster with rights over Connaught, Trim and Clare, the earldoms of Rutland and Cambridge as well as all the lands belonging to the Dukedom of York. Though he had the Plantagenet's blood, their warlike character and their wealth, he had not inherited their physical appearance, the height and fairness, the oval face, domed eyebrows and long nose. York was short and dark. Of his four surviving sons, Edward born in 1442, Edmund in 1443, George in 1449 and Richard in 1452, the first three had the Plantagenet looks; only Richard took after his father, with dark colouring and a small frame.

York had commanded the English forces in France during the last phase of the French war, and as his Duchess was always with him, their eldest son Edward was born at Rouen. This strong and beautiful child was afterwards hailed by a delighted people as the Rose of Rouen.

York's indignation at the abuses of Suffolk and Somerset had very early aroused the Queen's vindictiveness. For the first thirteen years of her marriage, Margaret was childless and she saw in York not only an enemy but a possible claimant to the throne. Her hatred was fanned by York's surviving rival, Somerset. The Duke of Somerset was as arrogantly dishonest as Suffolk had been and since he was yet another of the descendants of John of Gaunt he also was a possible claimant to the throne which gave him a further reason for wishing ill to York. In his case however the Queen did not count this against him. The mutual devotion of Somerset and herself may well have been innocent but it was shown so plainly, it was inevitably a cause of scandal.

The Queen had caused the King to deprive York of the command in France and to confer this on Somerset, while appointing York King's Lieutenant in Ireland; this post he filled with great success, for the Irish trusted and liked him, but by removing him from the centre of affairs, it had the effect of banishment. The popular fury culminating in Cade's rebellion, however, gave him his chance. In August 1450 he returned to England to head a movement demanding reforms, and having proved that nothing would influence Margaret and her party except armed force, in January 1452, accompanied by 4,000 of his own retainers, he confronted the King on Blackheath and demanded that Somerset should be imprisoned pending an investigation. The King promised this and York disbanded his force; but the Queen at once persuaded the King that Somerset ought not to be put under arrest, and York, without the protection of his men, when summoned to the King's tent, found that he was treated as a prisoner, and brought face to face with Somerset himself. He was forced to attend the King to St. Paul's Cathedral and swear an oath never to take up arms against him again. From the way he was treated, it was clear that he stood in considerable danger, but this was averted by the rumour that an extraordinary rescue was imminent. His son, the ten year old Edward, was now reported to be coming up to London to his father's aid with eleven thousand men. The troops were no doubt to be commanded by experienced soldiers, but they were not the less formidable because an energetic child was riding at their head. They did not engage, the rumour of their approach gave the Duke of York the protection he needed. The episode was the first of many instances of young children's playing a part in the affairs of the coming era.

York was safe from personal harm, but the Queen and Somerset managed to exclude him from the Council. The year 1453, however, was one fraught for them with stress and gloom. It was the one in which King Henry had the first of his periods of total insanity, but before this descended on him the King performed an act of characteristic kindness. His step-father Owen Tudor was already receiving an annuity from the Privy Purse; Henry now sent for his two half brothers, Edmund Tudor aged twenty-three and Jasper Tudor, twenty-two. The former he made Earl of Richmond, the latter Earl of Pembroke. Though the King, the fountain of honour, can ennoble people whatever their antecedents, these bestowals by Henry VI are taken to prove that the King himself accepted the validity of his mother's second marriage.

The final collapse of the English power in France and the loss of all the English conquests except Calais unleashed a fresh outburst of fury against the Queen and Somerset and in August the King suffered a complete mental collapse. He could not speak, he could not move without help, he was unconscious of the presence of anyone. In October the Queen bore a son. Her situation demanded pity, for when she carried the child to the King, Henry appeared not to see him, remaining in fixed, sightless melancholy. Her passionate delight was marred by acute suffering. It was widely believed that the child was Somerset's.

The Queen and Somerset at first tried to keep secret the King's condition; when this was no longer possible, Margaret demanded to be made Regent, with 'the whole governance of the realm' and power to appoint ministers. This, naturally, was refused, and Parliament appointed York as Protector. The Duke made a beginning of financial reform. Acts of Resumption had been urged by previous Parliaments, to oblige those who had received lavish gifts from the Crown to give them back in consideration of a modest settlement; York continued this policy and some Parliamentary control was obtained over the endowed revenues of the Crown.* Somerset was imprisoned in the Tower, but nevertheless his agent caused alarm by going about the streets in the Tower's immediate neighbourhood, engaging all the available lodgings and putting the Duke's armed retainers into them.

In February 1455, the King made a temporary recovery of his wits; he welcomed his fourteen months old son and was delighted to hear that the child had been christened Edward after the Confessor. York was deprived of his authority and Somerset was released from the Tower. Among the events which took place in this period of the King's recovery, one was of distant, far-reaching and very great importance. The death of John of Gaunt's second wife only allowed him to marry his mistress Catherine Swinford two years before his death; his children by her were therefore illegitimate, and had been called Beaufort after the Castle where they were born. Of the children, Joanna Beaufort was the mother of the second family of Ralph Neville, Earl of Westmorland, Henry Beaufort became the astute and magnificent Cardinal, John Beaufort was created Marquess of Somerset. His son, John Beaufort, created Duke of Somerset, died in 1444, and was succeeded as Duke of Somerset by his brother Edmund, the friend and supporter of Margaret of Anjou. Edmund's two sons lost their lives at the Yorkists' hands in 1464 and 1471, and the residual heiress of the Somersets was John, Duke of Somerset's only child, the Lady Margaret Beaufort, whose future importance was not suspected in 1455. In this year, a child of twelve, she was married by the King to Edmund Tudor.

The importance of the Beauforts was conjectural; it lay, not in the position they had made for themselves as wealthy and powerful members of the aristocracy, but in whether they had a valid claim, through John of Gaunt, to the crown. Richard II, to gratify his uncle, had passed an edict saying that though born out of wedlock, the Beauforts were legitimate.

* Jacob, *op. cit.*, p. 502.

Henry IV, who as John of Gaunt's only legitimate son, had a strong interest in the matter, had caused Parliament to amend this by saying that though allowed to be legitimate, the Beauforts were not capable of succession. The contention was afterwards raised that one Parliament could not legally tamper with a patent issued by another, and that as the Beauforts had once been declared legitimate with no qualifying clause, they were, *ipso facto*, capable of succession. Opinion on this point is still divided. It hardly arose in 1455 when Edmund Tudor, as Hall described him, 'that goodly gentleman and beautiful person,' was married to the small, dry, serious-minded little girl. In spite of her self-possession and her highly intellectual cast of mind, the child had a nascent capacity for emotion, but whether or not the handsome, charming husband brought it to bear, the marriage lasted only eighteen months. Edmund Tudor died in 1456, and the following year when she was fourteen his widow was brought to bed of his posthumous son, who was called Henry after his godfather the King. The Lady Margaret was married twice again, to Lord Henry Stafford, and to Thomas Lord Stanley, Earl of Derby, but she bore no more children. For dynastic purposes, the one was enough. The blood of Edward III had been safely conveyed through this small vessel. Henry Tudor became King Henry VII.

Meantime, in 1455, York and his allies decided that matters must now come to the arbitrement of force. Retiring to his estates on the Welsh marches he summoned a large army of his retainers and returned across England into Hertfordshire. There he confronted the King and his much smaller army, at St. Albans. The battle was a decisive victory for the Yorkists, with the supreme advantage of the death of Somerset. The King, who had been wounded in the neck by an arrow, was brought back to London with every sign of respect by York, who was again appointed Protector to govern in the King's name. Henry was reunited with his Queen; he underwent another attack of derangement which, this time, lasted for only six months, for he recovered in February 1456. Margaret arranged for him, though still very weak, to appear in the House of Lords and relieve York of his office. It was thought that the King would have been glad enough to continue under York's protection, and that for this reason the Queen removed her husband from London and established the seat of affairs at Coventry. In 1459 she made a tour of Cheshire, the County Palatine that was an appanage of the Prince of Wales. Here she feverishly sought to kindle loyalty by taking the six year old Edward of Lancaster about, and making him distribute silver badges of his cognizance, the White Swan.

Ludlow, the Duke of York's castle in Shropshire, was one of the fortresses commanding the Welsh marches. It stood among wooded hills on steep ground overlooking a tributary of the Severn. It was a favourite home of the Duke and Duchess, and five years before, when Edward and

Edmund were twelve and ten, they had been living there in a household appointed for them by their father, who had obtained for them the titles of Earl of March and Earl of Rutland from Henry VI; a letter written by them to their father in 1454 thanks him for their green gowns and asks that they may have also 'some fine bonnets', and complains of the behaviour to them of the governor of the castle, Sir Richard Croft. The letter is signed: 'Your humble sons, E. Marche, E. Rutland.' In 1459 York and his family arrived at the castle accompanied by York's brother-in-law the Earl of Salisbury and a member of the Yorkist alliance even more important than he.

Richard Neville, Lord Salisbury's son, had married Ann Beauchamp; she was richly dowered at the time of the wedding, but the unexpected death of her brother left her heiress to the Warwick earldom and its lands and Richard Neville became Earl of Warwick. A gifted soldier with a flamboyant personality, his possessions were now wider than those of his father, and nearly as extensive as his uncle York's. The confederation of York, Salisbury and Warwick was so powerful, in wealth and in estates from which armed men could be recruited, and the public discontents were so alarming, that it shows how deeply rooted in the English mind was the idea of the sacredness of kingship, that so many people supported the Lancastrian party for so long.

Salisbury had been obliged to fight an action to get from Middleham to Ludlow and this re-started the war. The King's army advanced on Ludlow and several of Warwick's troops deserted in the night and went over to the King's side. The royal army carried the castle by storm. York made his escape to Ireland with his son Rutland, the Duchess of York with the younger sons, George and Richard, was handed over to the supervision of her sister, the Duchess of Buckingham, whose husband was a Lancastrian supporter, while Edward joined forces with Warwick and Salisbury and made his way to the coast, from where he crossed the channel to the refuge of Calais, of which strategic post Warwick was the captain. The Lancastrian victory was only temporary. Edward and Warwick came back from Calais with a new army. They marched on London, and the city authorities let them in. With this extremely important base secured, they went up to meet the King's army at Northampton. The battle which resulted was a decisive Yorkist victory; the Queen with the young Prince fled to Scotland, and once more with every demonstration of respect, the helpless King was escorted back to London, but not, this time, to give his name to a government by the Duke of York. The latter thought that the way was now open to his hitherto undeclared ambition.

He landed from Ireland in September 1460 and advanced on London with banners bearing the royal arms and trumpets sounding. He entered the Great Hall of Westminster Palace where the Lords were assembled and when the Archbishop of Canterbury asked him if he wished to wait on the King, York replied that he knew of no one who ought not, rather, to wait on him. Then he came forward and laid his hand on the marble chair, the King's Bench. The Lords were taken aback by so drastic a step. York saw their hesitation and for the time being withdrew; but it was decided by those who wished to see his reforming programme carried out, that while the King should retain the crown for his lifetime, his heirs should be York and York's sons, and that York should be created immediately Prince of Wales, Duke of Cornwall and Earl of Chester. These were the titles of Margaret's son, Prince Edward of Lancaster. By assuming them, no less than by laying his hand on the marble chair, York had signed his own death-warrant.

From her refuge at the court of Scotland, the Queen had come down to Hull and was collecting a force of northerners to whom she promised, as the price of their support, that they should be allowed to sack and pillage all the English towns through which they passed.

York had sent away Edward to control disorder on the Welsh marches and he himself went up to his castle of Sandal in Yorkshire to oppose the Queen. Rashly issuing from his stronghold in answer to her vituperative taunts, York, outnumbered and outmanœuvred, met the royalist army outside the neighbouring town of Wakefield. He and his son Rutland were killed, Salisbury was captured and beheaded. Rutland, a fair, girlish-looking youth of seventeen, begged Lord Clifford to spare his life; but Clifford's father, the twelfth Baron Clifford, had been killed by York himself at St. Albans. Clifford shouted to the terrified boy: 'Thy father killed my father and so will I thee.' When he had exacted this bloody reprisal, Clifford hacked the head from the corpse of the Duke of York, and impaling it on his spear, carried it into Queen Margaret's presence. The hideous object gave her no dismay. The Duke had demanded a crown, he should have one, she said. A crown made of paper was lodged on the head, and the head fastened above the Micklegate Bar. The grinning trophy was dramatically placed; this gate, an archway between two castellated turrets, was the one by which kings traditionally entered the city of York. Rutland's head and Salisbury's were put up alongside, Margaret commanding that plenty of space should be left between the three for those of Edward and Warwick.

The Lancastrian forces now began a descent southwards and the pillage Margaret had promised to her northern army was carried out on the panic-stricken districts through which they passed. Their reign of terror encouraged the criminal population, who rushed out of their lairs and joined the orgy of robbery, murder and burning. Margaret had expected that as her victorious rout of manslayers and free-booters approached London, they would be reinforced by an army from Wales led by Jasper Tudor, but Edward, who had showed military enthusiasm at ten, now, at eighteen, proved himself a general of exceptional ability, fast-moving and capable of great striking power. He advanced rapidly into Hereford and defeated the Lancastrians at Mortimer's Cross. Among the prisoners was old Owen Tudor who was beheaded in the market place. He could not believe that his luck had run out at last, and expected a reprieve till the executioner was ripping off the collar of his doublet; nor had his powers of fascination waned after death; an old woman got hold of his head, wept over it and set it up with candles burning round it.

This battle checked any further advance from Wales; it also provided Edward with his favourite cognizance. On the morning of February 3, 1461, a parhelion was seen in the sky, a sun with a reflected sun on each side of it. 'The sun in splendour', a gold orb surrounded by gold rays, became his personal device.

While Edward was putting down resistance in Wales, Warwick marched north into Hertfordshire to check the Queen's approach to London. The enemies met once again at St. Albans, and at the second battle on this terrain, Margaret was victorious and Warwick fled. The Yorkist nobles who fell into her hands she had condemned at a court-martial at which her eight year old son was made to sit as president. His mother arranged for him to be present at the beheadings afterwards.

The intoxicating effects of the victory would seem to have blinded Margaret and her advisers to the urgent necessity of pressing on at once to secure London. This failure gave Edward his chance. Joining forces with Warwick and his reconstituted army, he entered the city on February 26, 1461.

The horror inspired by Margaret's northern rabble and the deep desire of the people of London, whose livelihood depended on it, for a stable government that would protect and foster commerce, overcame for the majority of the citizens, the academic question as to which of two descendants of Edward III should wear the crown. Their welcome for Edward was that aroused by the right man appearing at the right moment. The French chronicler Chastillon had said that Henry VI 'was no more than a shadow on a wall'; Edward, with his tall and powerful physique, his geniality, his easy-going but unshakeable confidence, appeared to have every quality which the feeble Henry and his ferocious queen so conspicuously lacked. Armstrong says,* it was a guiding principle of the Yorkist period, to identify the personal with the public capacity of the Prince. No monarch could have been better fitted by nature to carry this out. The Yorkist princes 'presented in their own persons the popularly understood image of royalty'. Gregory's *Chronicle* states that at Edward's taking over of the city, people began to say: 'Let us walk in a new wine-yard and let us make a gay garden in the month of March with this fair white rose and herb, the Earl of March.' A song was made for the hour:

* *Inauguration Ceremonies of the Yorkist Kings*, C. A. J. Armstrong, *Transactions of the Royal Historical Society*, 4th Series, XXX, 1948.

Now is the Rose of Rouen grown to great honour
Therefor sing we everyone, yblessed be that flower . . .
Had not the Rose of Rouen been, all England had been dour,
Yblessed be the time God ever spread that flower.

Edward put up for the time at his mother's house, Baynard's Castle.
This stood a little to the right of the spot where the Fleet Ditch ran into
the Thames. Rising up sheer out of the water like a Venetian palace it had
a façade striped with narrow turrets, with a hexagonal tower at each end.
Behind the water-front, buildings enclosed a courtyard. It had been
rebuilt by Humphrey Duke of Gloucester in 1428, and on his attainder
it had fallen to the King, who gave it to the Duke of York. From 1457
onwards York had used it as his town house. It was to be the scene of
famous events. At present, news was brought there to Edward that a large
crowd assembled in St. John's Fields, Clerkenwell, when it was demanded
of them by Warwick's brother, the Bishop of Exeter, if they would have
Edward to their king, had shouted yea, yea!

Edward went in a procession to St. Paul's where a Te Deum was sung,
and then to the Palace of Westminster, where he seated himself in the
marble chair his father had only touched. He did not arrange for his
coronation until he had delivered the decisive blow to the Lancastrian
forces in the north. The city of London advanced him a loan for the
enterprise and the bloodiest battle of the war was fought at Towton in
Yorkshire, on March 29, 1461. Snow storms often strangely occur at the
end of March, and on this Palm Sunday the air was darkened by driving
snow which came in the faces of the Lancastrians. The enormous numbers
of the slain included, it is said, two-thirds of the peerage. Among them
Lord Clifford was killed. The Yorkist victory was decisive and complete.
Margaret fled with her husband and her son to Scotland, where the royal
family were prepared to welcome them as a means of harassing the English.
Margaret secured their firm alliance by ceding to Scotland the border
town of Berwick, and Scotland was expected to provide a base for a
Scottish-French-Lancastrian invasion of England. Some of the noble
families of Wales supported the Yorkists but the Tudor and the Beaufort
spheres of influence were on the Lancastrian side. The solid support of
the Yorkists lay in the Midlands and the South, and in the supremely
valuable city of London, where there was more to be gained by stable
government than anywhere else. Each faction was inspired by deep-seated
motives which had nothing to do with mere legality. Hereditary loyalty
and the demand for economic stability were sometimes combined in one
person; where they fought each other, the struggle was deadly.

Though Edward would not have gained the all-important support of
the city of London unless his rule had promised material advantages, his
claim to the crown was backed by every consideration which could give

it weight.* He had received the support of electors in St. John's Fields; he had won the great battle of Towton, and as he said himself in a later pronouncement: 'more evident proof and declaration of truth and right and God's will may not be had than by . . . reason, authority, and victory in battles.' His hereditary claim, which had been asserted by his father, was arguably better than that of Henry VI. The date which had been decided for his coronation was June 28, 1461, and this date was finally adopted; but at first there was some argument, because this Sunday was the Feast of the Holy Innocents, commemorating Herod's massacre of the young children. The horror aroused by the idea of child-murder was so great, that for centuries it had been felt that the day would be unlucky for any project undertaken on it. This feeling had ebbed in the mondaine world of the 1460's, but enough of it remained for the objection to be put forward, although it was not sustained.

Two days before the ceremony, Edward entered London and the impact he made was reflected in the song:

The Rose came to London, full royally riding;

On the Sunday, he went to the part of Westminster Hall where the Court of Chancery sat. Here he put on robes and a cap of estate, a velvet headgear with a band of ermine, and took his seat on the Marble Chair with a sceptre in his hand, awaiting the arrival of the procession which was to conduct him the few paces from Westminster Hall to the Abbey. There he was crowned with 'the rich crown of St. Edward' and another sceptre, that of the Confessor, was placed in his hand. On Monday, St. Peter's Day, the King wore his crown again, at mass in Westminster Abbey, the Church dedicated to St. Peter. Tuesday was St. Paul's Day, and he wore the crown a third time at mass in St. Paul's Cathedral. At this ceremony, the London Chronicle says: 'An angel came down and censed the King.'

For several hundred years, men had imagined the presence of these super-natural beings, radiant, inhuman, with the power to fly. The thirteenth-century carvings on the Triforium Arch in Westminster Abbey show two angels with feathered wings and robes pleated by airy movement, swinging censors. Richard II had placed the arches of the roof of West-minster Hall on the backs of angels with wings outspread, and numerous churches show roof beams supported by flocks of crowned angels with outstretched wings. Angels were also represented by human beings taking part in public ceremonies. Gregory's *Chronicle* says that when the nine year old Henry VI was received in London on St. Valentine's Day, 1432, at the Little Conduit there was a show of the Trinity, 'full of angels, singing heavenly songs'. The *London Chronicle* gives no details about the youth, robed and winged, who, it would seem, came down from some stage or scaffold to cense the King in St. Paul's, but the spectacle must have been

* Armstrong, *op. cit.*

B

19

a thrilling episode in a solemn, crowded scene, where some of the spectators may have believed it to be supernatural.

After the battle of Towton, Edward had ordered the removal of the heads of his father, brother and uncle from the Micklegate Bar, and had had them buried, with their bodies, at Pontefract, the nearest castle to York. A funeral trophy to the Duke of York was set up in St. Paul's, 'powdered with silver roses and golden suns' the two chief emblems of Edward and his house. Eighty pounds' worth of wax candles burned about it and it was guarded by four hundred and twenty gilded angels. This took place in 1463, but the month after his coronation Edward performed a small act of piety to his father's memory. The Duke of York, in spite of enormous resources, would seem to have suffered from time to time from the shortage of hard cash which was endemic in the Middle Ages, before the Spaniards flooded the scene with gold and silver coins from the New World. York, besides, was owed £20,000 by the government of Henry VI, and had been asked to 'forbear' pressing for payment. Sir John Fastolf, the Paston family's wealthy patron, had obliged the Duke by lending money on one of the Duke's jewels. This was a brooch, 'with a great pointed diamond set upon a rose enamelled white'. A pointed diamond was one set, as Italian jewellers called it, 'in punta'. The jewel was cut to a point at one end and mounted on its flat base, projecting like the pistil of a flower. This beautiful ornament was in the form of the Yorkist family emblem. In July 1461, Edward redeemed it.

4

THE long-standing alliance between the French and the Scots, by which the French hoped to embarrass England, as England tried to embarrass France by an alliance with Burgundy, made Scotland a natural refuge for Margaret with her helpless husband and eight year old son. The far north of England was Lancastrian in sympathy, as were the remoter western districts of Wales, and the greatest of the northern families, the Percys, was hostile to their rival in power, the Nevilles. Though Edward had achieved the crown, he was not in entirely secure possession of it; he could count only on the support of London, the Midlands and the south-east of England. Since it was essential that he should not be absent long from the centre of government, the subjugation of the threatening north must be left to other hands, and in 1461, Warwick was given this command and created Warden of the Eastern and Western Marches towards Scotland. It was his initial support of the Yorkist cause which earned him the title of King-Maker, but whereas the Duke of York might have been victorious without Warwick's help, Edward, in the first two years of his reign, could scarcely have maintained the conquest without it. From 1461 to 1463, the great northern fortresses of Bamburgh, Dunstanburgh and Alnwick were besieged by Warwick, subjugated, manned by lords presumably loyal to York, and lost again because when Margaret landed in 1462, with a small contingent of French helpers, the castellans opened their gates to her. In 1463, supported this time by a large Scots army, she laid siege to the border castle of Norham. Warwick and his brother, Lord Montagu, raised the siege. The Queen fled with her son to France. Henry VI, defenceless and alone, was taken into the protection of the Bishop of St. Andrews. The main body of the northern Lancastrians was defeated by Montagu in May 1464, at a battle fought in a meadow beside Hexham; the great numbers of those killed in battle and executed, were a crushing blow to Lancastrian resistance. The garrison of Alnwick and Dunstanburgh capitulated. After a heroic resistance, Bamburgh was subdued. On this, the first occasion of a castle's being broken up by artillery, parts of the walls were blasted into the sea, and the commander, Sir Ralph Grey, was stunned by a piece of masonry falling from a stone ceiling; before he recovered consciousness, the garrison had surrendered.

Edward meantime had left the conquest of the north to Warwick and Montagu with every confidence. In 1461 he had made a progress into the west, partly to assert his power in Wales, and partly to show himself to the people, an undertaking that always gained him applause and valuable support. The *London Chronicle* gives a panoramic view of the countryside and the King's cavalcade moving through it. Setting out on August 14, 1461, 'in harvest the King rode to Canterbury and so to Sandwich and so along by the sea side to Hampton and so into the marches of Wales and then to Bristol where he was royally received with great solemnity, and so about, in divers places of the land.' In September, the Yorkist Sir William Herbert reduced Pembroke Castle where Jasper Tudor, Earl of Pembroke, was taking care of his nephew, the five year old Henry Tudor. Jasper apparently had confidence in William Herbert and his wife; attainted, he fled abroad but he did not take the child with him. His title was cancelled by his attainder, and bestowed on William Herbert, together with Pembroke Castle. Here, for the next ten years, Herbert and his Countess brought up Henry Tudor kindly among their own children. The latter's title of Earl of Richmond which he had inherited from his father, was, however, taken away from him, Edward re-creating it for his brother George, the twelve year old Duke of Clarence.

In 1464, the King had been on the throne for three years, troubled but undislodged. The question of his marriage was now of urgent political importance. He must strengthen himself by a valuable alliance; above all, he must produce a family of children, so that, whatever the chances of infant mortality, there should be one child that was the undoubted heir to its father's throne. Extremely handsome, of outstanding capacity, in control of a country whose high potential wealth it was clear he would consolidate, Edward was entitled to look for an illustrious match. Of those nearest home, France and Burgundy were the most obviously attractive. There were good arguments in favour of either. Burgundy was an invaluable commercial ally; its greatest industry was cloth-making and England's chief export was wool; a strengthening of Burgundy by a marriage alliance with England would trim the power of France, an advantage to England in any circumstances. But France also was a trading ally; the French market absorbed a wide range of English goods, and a French alliance cemented by a marriage promised one unique advantage: it would finally prevent Margaret of Anjou from invading England with a French army at her back.

Margaret's powers of creating a formidable resistance had for the last two years been concentrated in the wild regions of the north, and Warwick, Warden of the Eastern and Western Marches towards Scotland, had been left to deal with her. It was natural that he should see in the strongest light, the advantage of a French marriage treaty, that would prevent her from ever summoning such French aid as would make her victory not only likely but almost certain. But there were other reasons why he inclined to the splendour of a French alliance. Louis XI who had ascended the French throne in 1461, understood, from the wealth, the power, the hereditary importance of Warwick, that he was the English noble who must have the preponderating influence on the English King. He courted Warwick with consummate skill, and made the English Earl believe there was nothing the French King would not do to gain his friendship. The offered alliance was extremely attractive to Warwick. However powerful he were, Warwick could not be king. It was touch and go whether the English people would allow Edward permanently to replace Henry VI, and Edward's claim was a sound one. Warwick had no claim at all. With his pride, his arrogance, his ambition, he must, all his life, be content with a place second to that of his first cousin. That place, therefore, must be as magnificent as possible. The King of France would contribute to this end more effectively than the Duke of Burgundy.

Louis' daughter was a child of three and the king would not consider any engagement for her, but his wife's sister, the daughter of the Duke of Savoy, was a marriageable age and though not a princess of the royal house, her close connection with the king made her as eligible as if she were, and Warwick prepared to lay before King Edward the advantages of the French match.

5

HENRY V's brother, Lord John of Lancaster, Duke of Bedford, had had a famous career. After his brother's death he had been Regent of France and Protector of England for the child Henry VI. He had been very successful in his military operations in France until Joan of Arc raised the siege of Orleans. When she fell into Burgundian hands in 1431 Bedford, in close alliance with the Burgundians, bought her from them, and had her burned alive. As a part of his Burgundian alliance he had married the Duke of Burgundy's sister Anne. After her death he married Jacquetta of Luxembourg, sister of the Count of St. Pol, a small Burgundian principality. Jacquetta was a dowerless lady with no claims to so great a match except the very strong one of personal attractions. The Duke died at Rouen two years later and his widow was of course chargeable to the English Crown. She was escorted to England in state, given a dower and the manor of Grafton in Northamptonshire.

One of the English knights who had accompanied her retinue was Sir Richard Woodville, a handsome man with an outstanding talent for making his way that he was to hand on to his children. The Duchess of Bedford married him secretly in 1436, but unlike Catherine de Valois, she could not keep her secret. As the marriage was in direct contravention of the edict which forbade ladies enjoying crown lands to marry without the consent of the King's Council, her income was forefeited; but Richard Woodville was able to gain the favour of John of Gaunt's son, Cardinal Beaufort, the immensely wealthy priest and statesman, who spent some of his fortune in completing the building of Winchester Cathedral where his tomb is standing.

The Cardinal procured Woodville's pardon and the restitution of his wife's income, and from that time Woodville's advance was steady. He was created Baron Rivers in 1448, Knight of the Garter and Privy Councillor in 1450. Of his numerous tribe of children, five sons and seven daughters, the two most famous, Elizabeth and Antony, were born in 1437 and 1442.

The Woodville family presently aroused a contempt and hatred which a modern trend tries to write off as merely the result of jealousy and spite, inspired by the fact that one of them was able to marry the King of

England; but as the hatred became one of the facts of history, and as the people who felt it were the ones who lived at the same time as the Woodvilles and had actually to put up with them, it should be treated seriously and accounted for as far as possible.

Since the Norman Conquest, the English have been taught that it is their duty to act as milch-kine to needy and overbearing foreigners. This partly explains their scant respect for foreign titles, and why they can hear, unmoved, that English dukes are not thought grand enough to be included in the Almanach de Gotha. The widowed Duchess of Bedford who, like many widows whose first husbands had been more distinguished than their second, continued to be known by her former style, seems never to have enjoyed public respect. The Burgundians were indignant when the Duke of Bedford married her, thinking that he was insulting the memory of their Duke's late sister, and her clandestine marriage to Sir Richard Woodville did nothing to improve her reputation. She could prove that she fetched her descent from Charlemagne, but this was of little interest to the English, and the other line of descent of which her family boasted was not likely to reconcile them either. The family of Luxembourg altered the roll of their pedigree to make it appear that they were descended from a water spirit called Melusine. This being was wedded by Raymonde, Count of Poitou, and erected for him by magic the castle of Lusignan. She bore him a train of deformed children, events only too possible in ordinary human life, but the marriage was happy, except for the exacerbating promise she exacted from her husband to let her be in complete retirement on Saturdays. The Count, goaded by the suspicions of his friends, one Saturday looked through the keyhole of his wife's apartment and saw her in her bath—but not her; from the waist downwards she was a huge and horrible serpent. Betrayed and discovered, she told him she must leave him but promised that she would always reappear to warn the family of a coming death. Thereupon she vanished.*

The idea of a woman, half of whose body is that of a monstrous serpent, seems so repulsive it is strange that the Luxembourg family should go to the pains of forgery to claim such a descent. If Elizabeth Woodville's forbears had said they were descended from a naiad, there would have been, as far as she herself was concerned, some aesthetic fitness in the tale. Fair, cold, and graceful, she would have looked the part. The Duchess of Bedford was a friend of Queen Margaret and Elizabeth was given a post as one of the Queen's ladies in waiting. At seventeen she had already made some mark. Sir Hugh John, a knight in the train of Richard Duke of York, was enamoured of her and very eager to have her as his wife. He was humble himself but he had two highly distinguished patrons to speak for him. The Duke of York wrote to Elizabeth on his knight's behalf, saying: 'Ye, for the great womanhood and gentleness

* Baring Gould, S., *Curious Myths of the Middle Ages*, 1869.

approved and known in your person, his heart wholly have.' This letter being of no avail, it was followed by one from the Earl of Warwick, earnestly advancing Sir Hugh's suit because of 'the great love and affection he hath to your person, as well for the great soberness and wisdom that he found in you, as for your great and praised beauty and womanly demeaning.'* Warwick spoke, as York had spoken, of the knight's great worship and renowned manhood, and promised, as York had promised, to be good lord to them both in the event of the marriage. What neither of the nobles undertook to say was that Sir Hugh John's estate was great enough to tempt an ambitious and penniless young beauty. Perhaps they took it for granted that, since she was one of the twelve children of poorly provided parents, and so could bring no riches, she was not entitled to demand any. The two letters are very interesting as they both give the same impression of Elizabeth's characteristic charm. This was more vividly presented by Hall many years later when he drew a contrast between her and Margaret of Anjou. The Lancastrians, he said, were loyal 'for the love they bore the king, but more for the fear they had of the Queen, whose countenance was so fearful and whose look was so terrible, that to all men against whom she took a small displeasure, her frowning was their undoing and her indignation was their death.' Afterwards, when he speaks of Elizabeth Woodville, he notes 'her lovely looking and feminine smiling (neither too wanton nor too humble)', but matched with intelligence, 'her tongue so eloquent and her wit so pregnant'.

In trying to form a visual impression, it is disconcerting to find that the portrait in Queens' College, Cambridge, which should have been an authentic likeness, has none of the characteristics common to three miniature paintings in manuscripts and the superb picture in Edward IV's family group in the stained glass window in the North Transept of Canterbury Cathedral. In the portrait in Queens' College the hair is drawn back under a pot-shaped cap worn at the back of the head, and its colour can hardly be determined except that it is not dark. The eyes have normally opened eyelids. In the three miniature paintings, the hair is worn long and flowing and is coloured bright gold. The most characteristic trait is that of the eyes with their half-lowered, swollen-looking lids. This is so marked in all three cases, it looks almost like caricature. In the Canterbury window, the work of a master, one can see the feature in terms of actual likeness. The eyes have the ex-ophthalmic look which is said to be a sexual attraction, the heavy eyelids are slightly cast down. The grace and remoteness of the figure are astonishing.

The strangely charming girl was justified by events in her refusal of Sir Hugh John, so were her parents in not having forced her to accept him. In the early 1450's, she made a hundred times a better match with

* Agnes Strickland, *Elizabeth Woodville, Lives of the Queens of England*, 1870.

Sir John Gray, a Lancastrian knight, possessor of the manor of Bradgate in Leicestershire and heir to Lord Ferrers of Groby. Bradgate, five miles from the town of Leicester, stood on a rocky slope among beautiful wooded hills with a stream running below its walls. As its châtellaine, she seemed to be established, with the two boys born of the marriage, Richard and Thomas, for a lifetime of quiet prosperity and peace.

Meantime her father, her mother and her eighteen year old brother Antony were in high favour with the Lancastrian court. In 1460, when Warwick was Captain of Calais, it was feared by the Council that he, his father Lord Salisbury and Edward, then Earl of March, were planning to use Calais as the base for an invasion of the south coast of England. To counter this danger, Lord Rivers was sent to Sandwich to collect a fleet and to keep the look-out. Warwick's spies told him that Rivers was in lodgings at Sandwich, he, his wife and Antony Woodville. One of Warwick's captains, Sir John Dinham, executed a night raid on Sandwich, captured the fleet, and, surprising Rivers, his wife and son in their beds, carried them on board. When they arrived at Calais it was nightfall again, and the prisoners were brought before the Earls 'with eight score torches'. As adherents of Henry VI, Rivers and his son had used some very abusive words about the Earls of March and Warwick. This was to be expected in a supporter of the opposite faction, and from a Percy or a Beaufort the words would have been swallowed till they could be avenged. From such creatures as the Woodvilles, it was felt to be insupportable. First addressing Rivers, 'my Lord of Salisbury rated him, calling him knave's son; that such as he should be so rude as to call him and these other lords traitors, for they should be found the king's true liegemen when such as he should be found a traitor. And my Lord of Warwick rated him and said, His father was but a little squire, brought up with King Henry V, and since made himself by marriage, and also made a Lord, and it was not his part to have held such language to those who were of king's blood! And my Lord March rated him likewise. And Sir Antony Woodville was likewise rated for his language, by all the three Lords.'* The party were held until they had paid a ransom.

The most interesting feature of this story is its date. Four years before Edward's marriage to Elizabeth Woodville her father and her brother, relying on the support of the Lancastrian party, were notorious for their insolence to their betters.

Elizabeth's husband had barely succeeded his father as Lord Ferrers when he was killed, leading a victorious charge, at the second battle of St. Albans, leaving her a widow with orphan sons of four and three years old. Her situation was very wretched, for as her husband had been killed in action against the ultimately triumphant Yorkists, the Bradgate inheritance was confiscated, and she, the destitute widow of a rebel, was

* Paston, *Letters, 1422–1509*, ed. J. Gairdner, 1900, no. 346, Jan. 28, 1460.

obliged to return with her two children to her parents' house at Grafton.

The forest of Whittlebury in the neighbourhood of Grafton was a royal chase. The story of Elizabeth's waylaying Edward as he was hunting and appealing to him for the return of her late husband's estate, and of his falling under the enchantment of her strange beauty, can at this time of day be neither proved nor disproved. The oak tree was still standing in the nineteenth century under which it was said that she had appeared before the king, a small child in either hand, to plead for their inheritance. The events are made more probable if less dramatic by evidence that in spite of the offence given by the Rivers which provoked their abduction by Sir John Dinham, and the fact that the family had been entirely Lancastrian in sympathies, Edward had been reconciled to the fascinating if time-worn Duchess of Bedford to the extent of restoring her dower to her which had once again been forfeited on the grounds of treason. Edward's general policy, from good nature as well as ability to reign, was always to be reconciled to enemies where he could and to exert savage severity only when his patience had been abused past bearing. Whatever might be in doubt as to the affair's antecedents, the culmination was unmistakable. The young man of twenty-two, florid, of great virility and strength, a womanizer who, as Hall said, 'loved well both to look at and to feel fair damozels,' was drawn by an unslaked craving for the fair, cold, nymph-like creature, whose very coolness invested her with a spiritual as well as a physical desirability. An Italian version of the courtship said that he threatened her with the point of a dagger at her throat; if so, she was no doubt too *rusée* to be much frightened; but Hall commented on 'the confidence that he had in her perfect constancy and the trust that he had in her constant chastity,' and Mancini, writing in 1483, put down what was the general opinion of one of her attractions: 'that she remained unperturbed and determined to die rather than live unchastely,' and that Edward 'coveted her the more, who could not be overcome in her constancy even by an infatuated king.'*

Whatever the compulsion, the result was an amazing triumph. The widow, of no great place, no wealth, no influence, mother of the two sons of a dead rebel, and five years older than the King, was to be made Queen of England. The month of April passed, and on May 1, the loveliest of days even when it is cold, 'privily in a morning he married her at Grafton, where he had first fantasied her visage.'

Fabyan says† the marriage was solemnized 'early in the morning'. No one was present except the bridegroom and the bride, the Duchess of Bedford, the priest, two gentlewomen, 'and a young man to help the

* Mancini, Dominic, *The Usurpation of Richard III*, ed. and translated, C. A. J. Armstrong.

† *New Chronicles of England and France*, p. 654.

priest sing'. When the rite was finished, the King 'went to bed and so tarried three or four hours'. Then he left Grafton and came back to his lodging at Stony Stratford as if he had been out hunting, and went to bed again to sleep off his fatigues. From this lodging he sent a formal message to Lord Rivers that he meant to come over to Grafton and visit him. Here he was received openly, 'with all honour', and here he stayed four days, 'in which season', Fabyan says, 'he nightly to her bed was brought, in so secret a manner that almost none but her mother was of counsel.' The anxious scheming had almost achieved its end, but the family could not be satisfied until the marriage was given public recognition. This must of course wait on the King's decision of what would be a suitable moment for the declaration.

May, June, July went by, so did August and the first three weeks of September, with no knowledge of the affair outside the household at Grafton. Edward's inaction was not, it would seem, due to timidity at the prospect of making so startling and unwelcome a disclosure to his lords, but to an inherent easy-goingness, based on solid self-confidence. The news would cause some displeasure, and why should he incur the nuisance of this before he must? It was no trouble to him to maintain pleasant relations with Warwick, with his Council, with his family, while preparing to blow them at the moon.

On September 28, 1464, a meeting of the King's Great Council was held at Reading Abbey. This was a favourite royal resort. The Abbey was one of the wealthiest in the kingdom; the comfort and luxury it afforded were of such a high order that Henry VIII took it over as a royal palace at the Reformation, and once the King was at Windsor the route up the Thames by barge was easy. At this council meeting Edward explained the coinage he was introducing; this included 'five new monies of gold'— recoinages of the gold noble worth ten shillings, the half noble of five shillings, the gold farthing (or fourthing) of half a crown, and the new, beautiful gold coins with, on the reverse, a feathered angel standing with a spear over a prostrate dragon, the angel worth six shillings and eightpence and the angelet, of half the value. At some point in the proceedings, the inevitable topic was introduced—the King was begged to marry. The moment had now come. The King said that he intended to marry to please himself. He uttered the name of Dame Elizabeth Grey, and there were exclamations that though she was virtuous and beautiful, she was not a suitable wife for the King of England. Edward then said that he was already married to her.

There can seldom have been a more astounding revelation; but, as it has been said, Edward's strong card was the fact that the marriage had already taken place. Argument was useless; but this secret step had been a very strong action, particularly as regards Warwick. It was not only a breach of confidence towards a cousin, who, however inclined

29

to domineer, had been his warmest supporter; it was utterly treacherous, since for the last five months, Warwick had been allowed to negotiate with Louis XI for a French marriage. By this abrupt and rude disclosure, made without a hint of warning to Warwick, so that the Earl was as much astonished as everybody else, Warwick was, for the time at least, deprived of his status in French eyes as the all-powerful minister of the English king. He never forgave the affront. Warkworth's *Chronicle* says of him and Edward: 'They were accorded together diverse times, but they never loved together after.'

The following day, September 29, Michaelmas Day, Elizabeth, having been by some means brought to Reading Abbey, was presented by the King to his Council as their Queen. She was then led by the hand of the fifteen year old George, Duke of Clarence, into the Abbey Church where she was publicly declared Queen and attended mass. Agnes Strickland* who had examined an illumination in the Collection of Royal Manuscripts in the British Museum, says that the Queen is depicted in a crown with crossed arches, her pale yellow hair streaming down her back. 'She is very fair, her eye-lids are cast down with an affected look of modesty which gives a sinister expression to her face.' Her dress is of striped blue and gold with a broad ermine hem. 'The Queen is represented entering the Abbey Church of Reading, led by a youth just the age of Clarence . . . She is received by the Abbot whose face is very expressive . . . The royal barges are seen waiting in a bend of the river.'

The marriage was of course a topic of the first importance in the courts of Europe, where it aroused surprise, annoyance and contempt. Edward's foreign correspondent Lord Wenlock wrote to the Franco-Burgundian agent Jean de Lannoy: 'We must be patient, despite ourselves.'†

The beautiful Queen with the heavy-lidded eyes might have an air of legendary grace, but she was grasping, and she began to show her power at once. It was said of her that she gained her way with the King by feminine gentleness, humbleness and modesty; but she gained it. There was no place for her in Edward's regal sphere such as Margaret of Anjou had occupied in that of Henry VI, but in private matters her influence was almost unbounded. Her immediate and lasting concern was the aggrandizement of her own family—her father, her five brothers and her six sisters. Within two years of her marriage, the King, giving Sir Walter Blount a solatium of a thousand marks, deprived him of the highly valuable office of Lord Treasurer and bestowed it on Lord Rivers. Her brother Antony Woodville was already married to Lord Scales' heiress, and, as Stow said, 'by her he was Lord Scales'; but in 1466 he was given the Garter and the Lordship of the Isle of Wight with

* *op. cit.*
† *Edward IV*, Charles Ross, 1974, p. 92.

the castle of Carisbrooke. The month following that of her own recognition, October 1464, the Queen got her sister Margaret married to Lord Maltravers, heir to the Earl of Arundel. In January 1465, the richest of all the prizes was obtained; the Queen was able to procure for her brother, John Woodville, a youth of twenty, a marriage to the very wealthy Dowager Duchess of Norfolk. The latter's age is variously stated as between seventy and eighty, but it was obviously that of an old woman, and the marriage was termed by William Worcester: 'maritagium diabolicum'. The Duchess was Warwick's aunt, and four years later John Woodville paid for this indecency with his head. This was unfortunate enough, but in 1465 the Queen forced on a marriage whose consequences to her were to prove utterly disastrous. The first Duke of Buckingham had been killed in 1460 at the battle of Northampton, leaving as his heir his five year old grandson, Henry Stafford the second duke. On Edward IV's accession the following year, the child became a ward of the Crown, and was brought up for some years in the household of Edward IV's sister, the Duchess of Exeter. His uncle, Thomas of Gloucester, had married the Bohun heiress, and some of the lands she had brought to the marriage, instead of remaining in the Stafford family, were settled by Edward IV on his queen; not only was this an injury, but in 1465, at the age of eleven, the young Duke of Buckingham was married off to the Queen's sister, a child of similar age, the portionless Katherine Woodville. Mancini explains Buckingham's hostility to the Woodville family by saying that he, 'of the highest nobility, had his own reasons for detesting the Queen's kin, for when he was younger he had been forced to marry the Queen's sister, whom he scorned to wed on account of her humble origin.'*

The marriages in 1466 of the Queen's sisters, Anne to Viscount Bourchier, heir to the Earl of Essex, Eleanor to Anthony Grey, heir to the Earl of Kent, Jacquetta to Lord Strange of Knockyn and Mary to Lord Herbert's heir, beyond deepening the general discontent, had no such formidable consequences.

The advancement of her relatives was a constant preoccupation with the Queen, but her chief concern was with the source of all her power, to maintain her influence over her husband. In this she was very largely successful until almost the end of his life; she bore him ten children, the last one within three years of his death, and though he soon turned to other women and acquired a reputation for lechery, this did not diminish her own status; but the early months after the announcement of the marriage may well have been the happiest of her life. The tremendous ambition had been achieved and it had brought her everything she desired. The King was passionately in love with her and the obstacles

* Mancini, op. cit.

and dangers inherent in her position had not had time to show themselves. After the recognition in the Abbey church, the King and Queen spent several weeks at Reading Abbey.* A parliament was sitting at York and on November 26, the King sent Warwick up to adjourn it, saying it was impossible for him to go to York at present. On November 30, the King and Queen were at Windsor. On December 8, the King took her to spend the first Christmas of their marriage at Eltham Palace, in Kent. This, lying in its own park between Shooters Hill and Greenwich, had been built by Edward II's son, the short-lived John of Eltham. Henry III had enlarged it and Edward IV himself was to do a great deal of work on it; between 1475 and 1483 he was to build the Great Hall, with twenty-two lofty, narrow windows and two bay windows at the dais end, and an arched doorway wreathed by his device of the White Rose of York placed on a sunburst—*Le Rose en Soleil*. The palace as he inherited it contained three courts; the garden entry was on the south; a wide moat surrounded the whole, and before the north gateway this became a stretch of water one hundred and fifteen feet wide. Over this, Edward built the beautiful stone bridge with four groined arches.

The secret wedding had been aptly performed early on the morning of the first of May, but winter has its own scene for romantic excitement, the spare beauty of a park in December, the bare branches, the red-gold sun, the grass stiff with rime.

> O, the rising of the sun
> The running of the deer,
> The playing of the merry organ,
> Sweet singing in the choir.

At Eltham the King commanded the Exchequer to pay 'to our right entirely well beloved wife the Queen, for the expenses of her chamber, wardrobe and stable, against this feast of Christmas coming, £466 .13 . 4.'†

In January the King and Queen returned to Westminster. When the Great Council was summoned, lands of four thousand marks a year were bestowed on her, and a little while afterwards the manors of Shene and Greenwich.

---

* Scofield, *op. cit.*, Vol. I, p. 365.
† Scofield, C. S., *The Life and Reign of Edward IV*, Vol. I, 1923.

6

MANCINI reported that the Lord Mayor of London had said that if Elizabeth Woodville were crowned queen, 'it would cost 10,000 men,' such was the estimate, however exaggerated, of public disapproval. Meantime, the court ceremonials went on in a high style. Antony Woodville, Lord Scales, wrote a letter to the Champion of the Duke of Burgundy, saying that, just after Easter, the ladies surrounding 'my sovereign lady, to whom I am right humble servant, subject and brother' had given him a collar enamelled with forget-me-nots (the flower *Souvenance*), and a letter tied with a gold thread, telling him that he ought to undertake some emprise 'worthy of the time'. The letter proved to be a request for a joust to be held, and when the King had read it, he gave permission for the tournament to take place. Antony Woodville now sent the letter and the collar to the Champion, asking him to accept them as a challenge. The Duke of Burgundy did not, for the present, authorize his champion to accept the challenge, but he complied with another request. Edward had asked him to send some of the Duchess of Bedford's high-born Burgundian relatives to impart an air of family grandeur to her daughter's coronation, and the Duke despatched the Duchess's uncle, Count James de St. Pol and one hundred knights with their servants. The knights, who would have been useful if the Lord Mayor's apprehensions had turned out to be well founded, were paid fifty nobles apiece by the King, who gave the Count de St. Pol himself three hundred nobles.*

The coronation had been arranged for Whit Sunday, May 26. The Queen was at Richmond, at her palace of Sheen; as she was, according to tradition, to make her coronation procession from the Tower to Westminster, her journey to the Tower must take her across the Thames by London Bridge. This famous highway was entered on the south side by a road that ran a little way across the river between dwelling houses and was then defended by a building over an arch, known as the Great Stone Gate. The roadway ran clear again for a short space and beyond a few more houses rose what was still called the New Stone Gate, leading on to the drawbridge which, when raised, allowed tall-masted vessels to come up or down stream. The New Stone Arch presented a square

* Agnes Strickland, *op. cit.*, p. 13.

appearance, its flanking towers being no higher than the arch itself. Beyond it, almost in the centre of the bridge, was a fourteenth-century chapel, its castellated roof surmounted by a pinnacle. The chapel was built on two floors, each lighted by lofty stained glass windows. One floor was entered at street level; the lower one gave on to the starling at the base of a pier, so that sailors could come in without mounting the bridge. All the space on both sides of the bridge, between the New Stone Gate and the chapel and the chapel and the further shore, was lined with dwelling houses and with shops whose owners lived above them. The bridge formed almost a separate community; it was a thriving commercial centre, and of unique importance as the only bridge connecting the city and the south side of the river.

The preparations to receive the Queen as she crossed the bridge on her way to the Tower were energetic and brilliant. The drawbridge was fumigated, a measure against the reek from traitors' rotting heads, stuck up on poles above the New Stone Gate for ravens, crows and gulls to peck at. The road over the bridge was sprinkled with forty-five loads of sand. At the bridge's centre a stage had been put up, where eight images, six dressed as women, two as angels, appeared in a tableau of welcome. Their hands were gloves stuffed with flock, their wigs were dyed with saffron. Crude and garish they may have been, in their robes of green, red and gold paper, but the angels' wings were of astonishing beauty; between them, they displayed nine hundred peacocks' feathers.*

The Queen spent the night in the Palace of Westminster before the coronation ceremony. The Records of the Skinners' Fraternity contain a miniature of her in what were said to be her coronation robes. Against a pale green ground flourished with pale pink roses and deeper pink carnations, she appears in a blue mantle lined with ermine above a scarlet robe with an ermine bodice. The painting shows the characteristic traits of long, unbound fair hair beneath a crown, an oval face and heavy, drooping eyelids.†

In the procession from Westminster Palace to the Abbey, the bride was preceded by the Duke of Clarence, the Duke of Norfolk and the Earl of Arundel. A train of noble ladies in red, trimmed with white fur, followed them. Among the throng, the eleven year old Duke of Buckingham was 'borne upon a squire's shoulder', and the young Duchess of Buckingham, also 'borne on shoulder'. Since it was thought advisable to carry children of eleven, the crowds must have been very great.

The Queen came into the Abbey under a canopy of cloth of gold, borne on four gilded spears, a bell of silver-gilt hanging at each corner. She held in one hand the sceptre of St. Edward, the sceptre of the realm

* *Coronation of Elizabeth Woodville*, George Smith, 1935.
† Lambert, John J., *Records of the Skinners of London*, 1933.

in the other. Her train was carried by the Dowager Duchess of Buckingham. She was followed by two of the King's sisters, the Duchess of Suffolk and the as yet unwedded Margaret of York. With them came the person for whom the splendid ceremony was almost as great a triumph as it was for the Queen herself, the Duchess of Bedford.

The rites were elaborate and long, and it was the office of the Abbot of Westminster, two days before the coronation, to inform the Queen 'of divers observances' that she must 'do and keep in the coronation', and throughout the ceremony itself to be always at her side, 'for to inform her of her governance'.* The Queen was no doubt able to perform with dignity and grace all the actions required of her; what she found unbearable was the weight of the crown. During the mass, it was noticed that the Duchess of Bedford 'held the crown on her head', supporting some of the weight of it in her two hands.

When the crowning had been performed, the procession returned, bearing the Queen through the Great Hall, to her chamber in the Palace. Here she was 're-vested in a surcoat of purple' and the massive jewelled crown was replaced by a coronet. Before she reappeared, Clarence, Norfolk and Arundel rode on horseback into Westminster Hall, which was already crowded with people coming to attend the banquet or to look on. The three nobles, their horses 'trapped to the ground', Norfolk's and Arundel's in cloth of gold, Clarence's in crimson, 'garnished with spangles of gold', manœuvred them about the hall 'to avoid the people against the coming in of the Queen into the hall'. Clarence dismounted at one point; while the Earl of Oxford presented the Queen with a ewer of water for her ceremonial washing, the Duke of Clarence held the basin; a function of high distinction and importance.

Walter Halyday, the Marshall of the King's Minstrels, had been given twenty pounds to distribute as 'largesse and reward for the King's and all the minstrels to the number of a hundred persons and more, attendant upon certain lords in the Coronation of the Queen'. Between the courses of the banquet, 'the King's minstrels and the minstrels of other lords' were 'playing and piping on their instruments great and small before the Queen full melodiously and in the most solemn wise'.

At the bringing in of the courses the three nobles rode their horses about the hall as before. The long and stately banquet proceeded, the fair-haired Queen in purple its beautiful centrepiece; but though she had been relieved of the weight of the crown, she still found the lesser weight of the coronet oppressive. 'At any time when she ate, she herself took off the crown, and when she had done, she put it on again.'†

Mancini says that though both the King's brothers were 'sorely

* Quoted by G. Smith, *op. cit.*, from a fifteenth-century MS, 'The Manner and the Form of the Coronation of the Kings and Queens of England'.
† George Smith, *op. cit.*

35

displeased' at his marriage, Clarence had 'vented his wrath more conspicuously in his bitter denunciation of the Queen's obscure family'. He had, however, been cowed by the King into a semblance of courtesy. He had led the Queen by the hand into the Abbey Church at Reading, he had on this day knelt before her with the laver, now he was riding about the hall in her service on a horse draped with horse cloths that came to the ground. Even on a fine day in early summer the light is variable in so large and lofty a building as Westminster Hall. From the dais under the great window on which the chief table was set, the Queen would scarcely have made out Clarence's face above the glimmering trappings of his horse.

The previous winter, in 1464, the King had enlarged the Queen's apartments in Westminster Palace. His accounts said: 'building for the Queen a withdrawing-chamber and a wardrobe',* but in addition to this suite and her share of the Royal lodgings in the Tower, it was considered that she required a town establishment of her own; and she was now given Ormonde's Inn, a stone-built house which, Stow says, was afterwards pulled down and the site used for shops. It faced on to Knight-Rider St., a road lying parallel with Carter Lane, where the King's wardrobe stood, between Carter Lane and the Thames shore, a district in the shadow of St. Paul's.

* *History of the Kings' Works*, Brown, Colvin, Taylor, H. M. Stationery Office.

7

A HOUSEHOLD had been formed for her. Her chamberlain was Lord
Berners, a relative of Archbishop Bourchier who had crowned both
Edward and Elizabeth. Sir Humphrey Bourchier was another of her
officials, with her relative James Haute. Her brother John Woodville was
her Master of the Horse. Anne Lady Bourchier and her sister-in-law
Lady Scales with three other ladies were her ladies in waiting. She had
besides seven damsels and two women attendants, and three minstrels.
Her confessor was Edward Storey, Chancellor of Cambridge University,
her resident physician Dr. Domenico de Serego. Another resident was
John Giles, Master Scholar, whose services were necessary, for there
were now living in the Queen's household the King's wards, the young
Duke of Buckingham and his brother, Humphrey Stafford.*

Living in this state, with her cold beauty and her reserved bearing,
she must have commanded a considerable degree of respect from those
who surrounded the king, and it is surprising that the general opinion
of the marriage should have been so unfavourable as it was reported to
be by the chroniclers of succeeeding reigns. Polydore Vergil, Fabyan,
Warkworth and Hall were writing in the era of Henry VII and Henry VIII
and a Lancastrian bias was to be expected, but it would not have served
any useful purpose wantonly to malign the marriage of Edward IV,
since Elizabeth Woodville's daughter, gracious and generally beloved,
was the wife of Henry VII and the mother of Henry VIII. The consensus
of the chroniclers' opinions was clearly based on a well grounded tradition,
though naturally this lost nothing in the repetition. Polydore Vergil,
writing his history at the behest of Henry VII, said that people imputed
the marriage to King Edward's dishonour 'as the thing whereunto he
was led by blind affection and not by rule of reason'. Grafton commenting
on the secrecy with which the marriage was performed, said that 'for
the baseness of stock that the lady was of, he would no prince nor king
to have known of it, no, not so much as her own father'. Fabyan in *The
Great Chronicle* lays much of the public dislike to the degree of favour
shown to the Queen's family. 'Then were the children of the said Lord
Rivers hugely exalted and set in great honour, . . . to sundry great

* Scofield, C. S., *The Life and Reign of Edward IV*, Vol. I, p. 377.

promotions . . . and thus kindled the sparkle of envy, which by continuance grew to so great a blaze and flame of fire.'

The situation of the Queen and her relatives was exposed to criticism and abuse, but they would seem to have taken no pains to mitigate this by moderation and tact. One of the worst known instances of the impudent, savage and lawless greed of powerful nobles which the disturbed era of the Hundred Years War had engendered, was the treatment experienced by John Paston when he had inherited from Sir John Fastolfe Caister Castle and the manors of Drayton and Cotton. The Duke of Norfolk took Caister by force and the family only recovered it after his death, and Lord Moleyns attacked Drayton, where, in the words of John Paston's complaint to the King, he brought 'riotous people to the number of 1,000 persons . . . with guns, pans of fire, long crooks to draw down houses, ladders and picks with which they ruined the walls and long trees with which they broke up gates and doors and so came into the said mansion and ruined down the walls of the chamber where the said wife of your said beseecher was and bare her out at the gates and cut asunder the posts of the house and let them fall and broke up all the chambers and coffers of the said mansion and bore away stuff, array and money'. Edward IV himself began a policy of curtailing the military powers of the nobles, the one completed by Henry VII; but Edward did not put it consistently into practice as occasions might always arise when he needed the nobles' military support himself. He would not, for instance, offend the Duke of Norfolk. Though it required superior resources and driving power to begin this rapine, once the field was open, lesser men might come in and take what they could. Lord Scales had written to the Burgundian champion in terms of mincing delicacy and circumspection, but two months after his sister's coronation, he declared at a supper party on July 26, 1465, that he would ride home and 'enter two fair manors in his county', the estates he had gained through his wife, Lady Scales, lying in Norfolk. John Wyke who was present and heard him say so, wrote to John Paston: 'I suppose it be to enter into Castor and Cotton, wherefor, make good watch betime.' Lord Scales did not after all attempt armed robbery in this high style; he would scarcely be able to summon a following on the scale of Lord Moleyns, but the brag over the wine of a supper party showed what he would have done if he could; this underlying greed for wealth and power was, however, more discreetly concealed than that of his sister the Queen, his father Lord Rivers the Lord Treasurer, his mother the Dowager Duchess of Bedford and his two nephews, the gay, extravagant young Thomas Grey whom the King had made Marquess of Dorset, and his younger brother Lord Richard Grey. These members of the Woodville clan were worldly and enthusiastic partakers of their good fortune. Lord Scales was the only one to earn a word of praise from Mancini, who called him 'a kind, serious and just man'. He had some of the cool-bloodedness of his miraculously successful sister, and a calmness, a taste for reading, an interest in the cult of chivalry and a leaning towards going on pilgrimages, made him not less, but more formidable than his extravert relatives.

8

THE children of Richard Duke of York had formed an affectionate family circle. In 1460, after their father's defeat at Ludlow and his own retreat to Calais, Edward sent to Thomas Bourchier, Archbishop of Canterbury, asking him to shelter his younger brothers. George and Richard, aged eleven and eight, were accordingly taken into the Archbishop's household. When Edward and Warwick had won the battle of Northampton, the Duke of York returned from Ireland and sent for the Duchess to join him at Hereford. Before she set off, she asked John Paston's steward, Christopher Hanson, if her sons George and Richard and their sister Margaret might stay, meanwhile, in the Paston's London house. Hanson wrote to his master: 'I granted them in your name to lie here till Michaelmas'. He said: 'She hath left here both the sons and the daughter', and he added: 'The Lord of March cometh every day to see them.'*

When Edward was crowned in 1461, the two boys were treated with every sign of brotherly fondness. George was created Duke of Clarence and Richard Duke of Gloucester; they both underwent the long, elaborate ritual that made them Knights of the Bath. In the case of the nine year old Richard, arrangements had to be made for his living in the family of some nobleman, a boarding-out that was regularly a part of the upbringing of children of good birth. The Earl of Warwick's family was the obvious choice for the reception of the King's younger brother and Richard was received as an inmate of the Earl's household, which was for the most part settled in Middleham Castle in a district of the bare and beautiful Yorkshire moors, that is bounded by the Ure and the Cover, racing tumultuously over their rocky beds. Here he underwent the rigorous training of a noble youth, first and foremost in arms, but also in hunting, hawking, dancing, music and the highly formalized code of manners that regulated the lives of the great. The Countess of Warwick must have been kind to him, to judge from Richard's after-kindness to her. There were only two surviving children of the Warwick family, Isabel aged eight and Anne aged five. The girls were Richard's second cousins; thirteen years later Anne became his wife. The reasonable assumption

* Paston, *Letters*, ed. Gairdner, 1900, no. 357, Oct. 12, 1490.

40

is that he admired the Earl of Warwick and was happy with the Countess and her daughters, but his over-riding affection, his total commitment was to his King and brother. He showed this unswervingly throughout the whole of Edward's life and when he chose his motto it was *Loyaulté me lie*.

He was many hundred leagues away from London, but Edward did not lose touch with him; he was all the time developing Richard's capacity as a useful servant of the Crown. A precocious, intense and solemn boy, with the mental ability of his family, he was able to take advantage of these openings. To be Admiral of England at the age of ten, can have meant only a titular dignity, but to be, at twelve, Commissioner of Array for nine counties, responsible for the recruitment of a statutory number of men at arms, involved work that, under the necessary guidance, would have been within the powers of a very intelligent and able boy. By 1464 when he was twelve, his loyalties were engaged, to the King, to the Earl who was the King's most powerful supporter and to the Earl's family who gave him a home. Then, in October of this year came the thunderbolt —the news that the King had been secretly married to Elizabeth Woodville.

Kings' marriages, as matters of great public concern, were usually matters of prolonged public discussion. That the King of England could have been actually married six months before, with no one's having heard a word of it, must have come as a severe shock to the King's young brother. Nor was that all; however much courtesy and discretion were practised, it could not be long before the young Prince realized that the family with whom he was living on affectionate terms had been deeply angered by his brother's act. His allegiance was his brother's, unalterably, but the situation must have been painful to a nature both secretive and highly-strung.

The following May the Queen was crowned. Richard was at Court, and whether he had seen her before or not, this was the first time he saw her as his brother's wife, a beautiful woman whose smooth manner and drooping eyelids did not always conceal her haughtiness and arrogance. What she saw in him she appears to have disliked; a slight boy with dark eyes and hair and one shoulder higher than the other, of reserved bearing with an unmistakable strength of personality. It was said by the chroniclers that the Queen from the outset regarded the King's family with suspicion and dislike as persons liable to absorb some of the royal gifts and bounties, all of which she was resolutely determined to secure for her own clan, her five brothers, Antony, Edward, Lionel, Richard, John, her seven sisters and her two sons, Thomas and Richard, within a year or two of the same age as the young Duke of Gloucester. The latter, with the censoriousness of youth, was not likely to have been anything but harsh in his private judgment of the Queen and her relatives. His brother

41

Clarence, of an altogether different temperament, was equally hostile. Clarence, Mancini said, vented his dislike of the marriage more openly than Richard. That was to be expected. Clarence was extravert, shallow, and such discretion as he had was used for deceit and treachery. The drawing of him in the Latin version of the Rows Roll is extremely interesting.* An elegant, lively figure, he stands in armour, a surcoat over it bearing the royal arms, on his fair hair an ermine-trimmed cap of maintenance surmounted by a coronet. He balances an upturned sword in his right hand and on his left a model of Warwick Castle, since by the time the drawing was made he had married one of Warwick's daughters. The debonair grace and jaunty smile match the picture of him left in words. Completely the opposite of his brother Richard, he was a continual liability to his brother who was king. Hereditary monarchy has many and great advantages; its disadvantage is the power it gives to the monarch's immediate relatives whether they are fit to exercise it or not. Clarence, egotistical and weakminded, could never reconcile himself to not being king. From the earliest years of Edward's reign he was a *mauvais sujet*; that he had charm made him a dangerous one. It was natural enough that he inspired a perverse affection in a sister who took his part against all comers. Margaret of York when Duchess of Burgundy was prepared to advance the interests of her favourite brother against those of Edward himself; but Edward also had an affection for Clarence which it required years of proved treachery and treason on the latter's part finally to overcome. For the time being, however, whatever the feelings of Clarence and Gloucester towards the Queen, they were strictly bound to treat her with deferential courtesy.

This year, 1465, the King received a guest who was most congenial to him, whose company he heartily enjoyed. Thomas FitzGerald, Earl of Desmond, the Deputy Lieutenant of Ireland, the most influential of the Anglo-Irish nobility, has been described as a man of Renaissance cultivation with Irish charm. On one of the occasions during his visit when the King took him hunting, he asked Desmond what Desmond thought of the Queen? In the candour of private masculine conversation, Desmond said though she was beautiful and virtuous, Edward would have done better to choose a bride who would have brought him an alliance, and he might do well to consider divorcing her and making a more advantageous match. Edward, with the recklessness men sometimes show in telling women what they themselves regard as humorous, a recklessness which would be unbelievable if instances of it were not so frequent, repeated Desmond's remarks to the Queen. Elizabeth Woodville was said to be always mild in her manner to the King; no doubt she received the information with her lowered eyelids and faint smile; but the careless injury was deep and deeply felt. The one aspect of herself

* Rows, John, *History of the Earls of Warwick*, ed. Courthorpe, 1845-59.

which she could not alter or modify was her undistinguished origin. If this were, ultimately, to be considered grounds for putting her down from the high station of which she was still in the first enjoyment, she would have no defence. Without any marital offence, wives of kings were sometimes put away, as matters of state convenience. In 1465, the second year only of marriage to a husband whose infatuation with her had astonished Europe, she cannot have felt herself in actual danger; the mere fact that Edward had repeated the story to her was proof that he considered it a joke; but the advice was not only an affront to her dignity: that was bad enough: far worse, and far more dangerous for the Earl of Desmond, it was, in itself, a threat to her security. She bided her time.

The next year, in February 1466, the Queen gave birth to the King's first child by her. Edward was much interested in astrology and suffered the disappointments of people who seek enlightenment from it through incompetent practitioners. The physician, Dr. Dominic de Serego, had foretold that the child would be a boy. When the doctor went to the door of the Queen's bedchamber to learn the result, one of the ladies called out sharply: 'Whatever the Queen's Grace hath here within, sure 'tis a fool that standeth without.' Concluding from this that the child was a girl, Dr. Dominic avoided the King's presence. The Princess Elizabeth proved however in the long run to be the most important of all Edward's children. As it was, she was welcome to a father who was greatly in love with her mother, and princesses were only less valuable than princes: they were the means of alliances. A new font had been set up in St. Stephen's Chapel for the christening and despite previous discontents, the Earl of Warwick stood godfather. The Queen's churching, a few days later, was described by a visitor from Bohemia, Gabriel Tetzel. The procession from Westminster Palace to the Abbey was headed by priests bearing sacred relics and boys carrying lights, singing. Then came a great company of ladies, trumpeters, pipers and players of stringed instruments; then two and forty of the King's own minstrels; after them heralds and pursuivants, followed by sixty lords and knights. Then came the Queen, walking under a canopy carried by two dukes. Her mother followed her and threescore other ladies.*

After the service in the Abbey, Tetzel was conducted through a banqueting hall in the Palace where a rout of guests were sitting down to dinner, to a private apartment, very richly furnished. Here he was bestowed in an alcove from which he could watch the scene. The Queen sat at table in a golden chair. While she ate, the ladies, her mother among them, knelt on the floor in front of her. Throughout the repast, she kept a haughty silence. So far as it rested with her, no one should have cause to remember that her previous existence had not been passed in a royal family. She adopted as her own one of Margaret of Anjou's badges, a

* Scofield, *op. cit.*, Vol. I, p. 399.

flower between two buds. Later in the year she continued a benefaction which had been taken in hand by her royal predecessor. Twenty-two years before, Henry VI had begun one of the most beautiful buildings of the age, the lofty, narrow chapel of fairy-like gothic decoration, of King's College at Cambridge, which was continued by Edward IV, Richard III, and Henry VII, and completed by Henry VIII. Margaret of Anjou had lent her support to the founding of a college in the same university and Elizabeth Woodville followed her in the project. The college was called Queens' College in memory of them both.

In 1466 a celebration took place which was chiefly interesting because of the Duke of Gloucester's presence. George Neville, Warwick's brother, was already Bishop of Exeter and Lord Chancellor. In 1465 he was consecrated Archbishop of York and in the following year his enthronement was celebrated by a splendid banquet held at Cawood Castle, a stronghold belonging to the Archbishopric twenty miles south of the city of York. Leland printed the bill of fare* saying he drew it from 'an old paper roll'. Sixty-two cooks had been employed to prepare birds, fishes, meats in enormous profusion. Peacocks were served among the dishes of game, and one was borne in, its bill gilded and its tail spread. The puddings, thirteen thousand in number, included jellies, plain and particoloured, tarts, hot custards and cold custards, one 'great custard, planted', scattered with spangles of foil, wafers, 'sugared delicates' and groups of allegorical figures made of coloured sugar. Three hundred tuns of ale were broached, one hundred tuns of wine, a pipe of hippocras. There was 'damask water to wash in after dinner', rosewater distilled from the highly scented damask rose. The mass of the diners were seated in the great hall but the most distinguished ones sat in a separate chamber and at the top table here sat 'the Duke of Gloucester the King's brother'; on his right was his sister the Duchess of Suffolk, on his left the Countesses of Westmorland and Northumberland, and 'two of Lord Warwick's daughters'. Warwick had but two, Isabel who was now thirteen and Anne who was ten. Lord Warwick himself acted as steward on this great occasion and the young Duke of Gloucester was treated as one of an intimate family party. His relations with the Earl, however disquieted, had not arrived at any open breach. The following year, in 1467, he sat with Lord Warwick on a legal commission to hear cases at York.

Warwick would no doubt have been personally glad of Richard's allegiance but he had already seen that he could not detach the younger brother from his loyalty to the elder. Richard was an important piece on the chessboard but he was not and never would be the disloyal Prince whom Warwick needed as an ally against the King. This rôle was admirably filled by Clarence. Discontented as the latter was, grudging and resentful, he particularly hated the Woodvilles for the personal favour they enjoyed

* *Collectanea*, Vol. VI, pp. 1–14.

and for the wealth and influence they had achieved. The Queen's father Lord Rivers held the immensely profitable position of Lord Treasurer. Antony Woodville, Lord Scales, possessed of an heiress' lands, was governor of the Isle of Wight; the Queen's youngest brother John had acquired an enormous fortune by marrying the ancient Duchess of Norfolk, her six sisters were matched with some of the most eligible partners in the kingdom. Wherever Clarence looked, the prospect was a sickening one, but he was not the only nobleman who found it so. Lord Warwick detested the Woodvilles, as supporters of the King against himself, when he ought to have commanded all the King's gratitude and allegiance, and as greedy upstarts who were a menace to the continuing prosperity of the Nevilles. That Warwick's own family had benefited immensely by royal patronage and wealthy marriages, was a different matter. The Nevilles were the Nevilles: the Woodvilles were nobodies. Lord Warwick's landed possessions were vast, his power of raising and maintaining a private army was thoroughly formidable, and he was discontented. When he made overtures to Clarence they were, inevitably, accepted. When Warwick suggested that the Prince should marry his elder daughter Isabel, Clarence was pleased. Not only were Isabel and her sister heiresses of the great Warwick estates, an alliance with their father might bring him within reach of the crown. So Edward thought. When he heard of the proposed match he forbade it, but the prohibition made the situation the more dangerous.

In July of this year, the Queen was brought to bed of another daughter, the Princess Mary. Throughout the eighteen years of her marriage to the King, she bore ten children. Her cold beauty and grace would seem to have kept their power over Edward unimpaired; he was easily attracted by other women and made his approaches freely; but this cheerful sensuality did not weaken the hold on him of the cool, elegant and sinister woman he married, on whom he begot children until he was within three years of his death.

Warwick had invariably tried to promote an English alliance with France, which was tantamount to one against Burgundy, and Edward's evident leaning towards Burgundy angered him, as it not only worked against his political bias, it showed the French King that in England, Warwick was no longer 'le conduiseur du royaulme'. In the spring of 1467, the Earl went on a private mission to Louis XI. He knew that the latter, alarmed at the rumour that Edward intended to betroth his sister Margaret to the Duke of Burgundy's son and heir, Charles the Bold, would be glad to discuss some means of reducing the injurious effect to France of the match, if it took place. Meanwhile the challenge to a joust which Lord Scales had issued to the Duke of Burgundy's champion on his sister's coronation was at last accepted, and the day after Warwick had embarked for France, the Duke of Burgundy's illegitimate son, the Bastard of

Burgundy, arrived in state to contest the issue. Parliament was to meet in four days' time, and it would be Archbishop George Neville's duty as Lord Chancellor to make the opening address. The Archbishop was so much angered and alarmed by the welcome given to the Burgundians, who had been invited by the King to attend the opening, that, with his brother Lord Warwick absent, he felt unable to face the occasion and sent word to say he was too ill to attend. His place was taken by the Bishop of Lincoln.

Edward was already suspicious of the Archbishop. He had forbidden the marriage of Clarence and Isabel Neville, but he had heard that, notwithstanding, the Archbishop was negotiating in the Papal court for the dispensation which the marriage of second cousins would require. The refusal to attend the opening of Parliament where he had a highly important duty to perform angered Edward past bearing. He acted with a promptness and severity that was the more characteristic for being unexpected. Accompanied by Lord Herbert he went the short distance from Westminster Palace to York Place, the Archbishop of York's London house on the shore of the Thames below Charing Cross (the house which Henry VIII took from Wolsey and made into Whitehall Palace). Arrived at York Place the King sent for the Archbishop and told him to give the Great Seal into his hands. Unable to refuse, the Archbishop did as he was told and the King returned carrying the Great Seal with him; having by this act dismissed the Archbishop from his post as Lord Chancellor.

Three days afterwards the joust took place in the lists at Smithfield. The Bastard and Lord Scales both distinguished themselves but the proceedings were cut short by news of the death of Duke Philip which recalled the Bastard and his retinue to Burgundy. Charles the Bold was now Duke of Burgundy and negotiations for the marriage between him and Margaret of York were concluded. The wedding was to take place the next year, in 1468.

9

In this year, 1468, Edward appointed as Deputy Lieutenant of Ireland, James Tiptoft, Earl of Worcester, a highly cultivated, Italianate Englishman, of great practical competence, and a cruel brute. Some part of what followed on this appointment has been disputed. What is indisputable is that the Earl of Desmond was accused by a section of the Anglo-Irish community of being too favourable towards the native Irish, to an extent which made possible a charge of treason, on which Worcester had him executed on St. Valentine's Day, 1468. His lands were sequestrated and seventy years later his grandson addressed a memorial to the Privy Council of Henry VIII, petitioning to have restored to him the manor of Dungarvan. This memorial made public for the first time the story which the Desmond family had kept in their memories; that before Worcester's departure, the Queen had made known to him that she wished for Desmond's death; that she had, early one morning while the King still slept, stolen the signet ring out of his purse and had used it to seal an order for Desmond's execution, which she had prepared and which she had conveyed to Worcester before he set sail for Ireland. The worst feature of the case was that Worcester also caused to be put to death the two youngest of Desmond's seven sons, boys who were still in their school-room. This appalling deed, which had not been commanded him but which, if it took place, must have arisen from some access of fury (else why should he execute the youngest sons only?), is mentioned in 'The Register of the Mayors of Dublin'. 'This year the Earl of Desmond and his two sons were executed by the Earl of Worcester at Drogheda.'* The usual outcome of a story that arouses fierce anger and pity is that it creates a popular version of itself, both passionate and convincing but not necessarily true. Fabyan in *The Great Chronicle* says that Worcester, who was cruel and merciless, put to death two of the Earl of Desmond's sons, 'which were so tender of age that one of them, having a boil or sore on his neck said unto the executioner: Gentle good father, beware of the sore in my neck.'

It was said that Edward was displeased when he heard of Desmond's execution, but whether this meant that he was angry that his authority

* R. J. Mitchell, *John Tiptoft, Earl of Worcester*.

had been abused, or that he regretted that so likeable a man had been found a traitor, is not clear; but Worcester had plenary powers to deal with the Irish situation, and the King never withdrew his favour from him. When he recalled Worcester from Ireland it was to help with trouble at home. No word appears to be on record that he said anything about the murder of two boys, the elder of whom was thirteen years old. If the story were true of the Queen's procuring Desmond's death, old sins have long shadows.

In the greatest scandal of 1468, however, the Queen and her family were implicated to the hilt. Sir Thomas Cook was a very wealthy draper, a Master of the Drapers' Company, who had been Lord Mayor of London, and whom Edward had made a Knight of the Bath at the Queen's coronation. He had built himself a country house in Essex, Gidea Hall, which had a large farm attached to it. He owned considerable property in London, including four brew-houses, and his town house in Broad Street was 'a great place'. Fabyan at eighteen had been one of Cook's apprentices at the time of the affair, and described him as 'singularly witted and well-reasoned'. Cook had in his Broad Street house a tapestry, 'wrought in most richest wise with gold, of the whole story of the Siege of Jerusalem'; Fabyan had heard Cook's foreman say that it cost his master £800. As tapestries were woven, ordinarily, of woollen thread, the addition of a great deal of gold thread made a work of most unusual beauty and sumptuousness. The Duchess of Bedford hankered after it and wished to buy it 'at her price and pleasure'. Her offer was not high enough and Cook refused it; possibly he did not wish, in any case, to sell. This was the background of a shocking story.*

In the spring of 1468, a man named Cornelius was captured, who turned out to be an agent for Margaret of Anjou. When he had his feet burned, he accused Lord Warwick's servant Hawkins of being his fellow conspirator. The Duke of Exeter had imported the first rack used in England; it had been placed in the Tower and was known as the Duke of Exeter's Daughter. Hawkins was the first prisoner to be tortured on it, and he uttered the names of Warwick's friend Lord Wenlock, and of some London citizens, among them Sir Thomas Cook. Edward dismissed any idea of Warwick's being implicated, and released Wenlock; but Cook was thrown into prison to await trial.

At this point, Margaret of York was about to set out on her bridal journey. She asked the King to release Cook on bail, because he had guaranteed the bond that secured her dowry of 200,000 gold crowns. Edward obliged the sister from whom he was now parting; Cook was bailed, while the King, the Queen, the Dukes of Clarence and Gloucester and the Earl of Warwick, escorted the bride with a great train to Margate and saw her on board. After her departure Cook was re-arrested and

* Robert Fabyan, *The New Chronicles of England and France*, ed. H. Ellis, 1811.

while he was again awaiting trial, the Queen's father Lord Rivers the Lord Treasurer and her cousin Sir John Fogg, Treasurer of the Royal Household, under pretence of searching for evidence of treason, sent their servants to ransack Gidea Hall and the house in Broad Street. Knowing that their masters would bear them out, the servants ran amok. In the London house they drank as much wine as they could hold and broached the rest to waste. They carried away two hundred broadcloths, plate and jewels to the value of £700 and the gold-worked tapestry which had excited the feverish cupidity of the Duchess of Bedford.

Cook was brought to trial before Sir John Markham, Lord Chief Justice of the King's Bench, a judge celebrated for his impartiality. The jury found that Cook was not guilty, either of treason or misprision:— having knowledge of treason without disclosing it. This jury was dismissed and another empanelled; but even they, though clearly, as Ross says, 'acting under extreme pressure',* would convict Cook of misprision only. On this verdict, he was sentenced to an enormous fine and returned to prison until it should be paid. An independent enquiry was set up, to estimate the loss he had suffered through robbery at the town house— the ravaging of Gidea Hall was not considered—so that it might be set off against the fine. Cook claimed that his losses in the town house were £14,000. This left him still liable to a fine of £8,000; but this was not all. The Queen revived an ancient demand known as Queen's Gold which allowed her to claim £100 for every £1,000 exacted by the King. In spite of their successful looting, the Queen and her parents were highly dissatisfied with the verdict. If Sir Thomas Cook had been executed for treason, the whole of his fortune would have been forfeit to the Crown, and they could have relied on further pickings. They were so much enraged against Sir John Markahm, it was said that they importuned the King to dismiss him, and Edward did in fact deprive him of office the following year.

Edward was very much influenced by his wife and her relations; however unfaithful he were in a casual fashion, he had a lasting attachment to the Queen; he was sick of the domination of Lord Warwick and he enjoyed the society of the Woodvilles; they were congenial to him and as they owed everything to his favour and goodwill, they were unfailingly sympathetic and obliging. The comfort of such situations depends on each side's being to some extent influenced by the other, and he probably allowed them all more scope than they should have had. But Edward was an able king and he would not have acted with criminal irresponsibility at the demands, however vehement, of the Queen and her parents. He had spent time and trouble in cultivating good relations with the London merchants, and apart from the important consideration that he gained £8,000 from it, this treatment of Cook was not favourable to his material interests.

* Ross, *op. cit.*, p. 101.

49

But Jacob says: 'the King dismissed Lord Chief Justice Markham for being, as he thought, too lenient'.* He ascribes the King's act to a genuine professional opinion. Markham had heard the case twice, his judgment must have been right and the King's wrong; but there were grounds for Edward's being highly uneasy at the suspicion of anyone's being concerned in the schemes of Margaret of Anjou. Cook was the second time in prison awaiting trial, when in July 1468, Louis XI, always ready for a covert injury to the English, and incensed by the marriage, the previous month, of Charles of Burgundy and Margaret of York, provided the means for Jasper Tudor to attempt an invasion on the west coast of Wales. It was a force of only three ships and fifty men at arms, but as Wales had never submitted to the Yorkists, there was a chance that a spark might result in a conflagration. Jasper Tudor meant to enter Harlech Castle, where the garrison was Lancastrian in its sympathies; but Lord Herbert held him off. Even so, Jasper Tudor turned his force northwards and had sacked and burned the town of Denbigh before Lord Herbert overtook him and drove him back to the sea. Edward already felt that he might be menaced by Warwick, and the actual landing of a Lancastrian expedition in Wales made him thoroughly alive to the danger of a serious invasion, and likely to view with extreme severity any person even suspected of complicity with Margaret of Anjou. His dismissal of Sir John Markham was grossly unjust, and his own greed for Sir Thomas Cook's money was no doubt a disreputable element in the case, but there was, on his part, some idea of political sense in his action. The Woodville party were inspired by naked, shameless rapacity. The affair brought them an increase of their evil reputation and they could not afford it.

* Jacob, *The XVth Century*, p. 459.

10

ENMITY between Warwick and the King was not so far public, but Fabyan said: 'Many murmurous tales ran in the city atween the Earl of Warwick and the Queen's blood'. In the spring of 1469, however, risings were breaking out in the Midlands and the North. They were ascribed to three ring-leaders, Robin of Redesdale, Robin of Holderness and John Amend-all, who may all have been the same man, Sir John Coyners, a relation of Warwick. The rebels had put out a petition for the redress of grievances, heavy taxation, military service out of their own districts, depredations of great lords that went unchecked, but it was thought that the risings might be the *avant-garde* of a formidable movement for the house of Lancaster. Edward went north with a small army and what amounted to a family party. He had with him the Duke of Gloucester as an able military assistant, also his father-in-law Lord Rivers and his brothers-in-law, Lord Scales and John Woodville. The Queen accompanied them and the expedition appears to have begun more as a progress than a military operation; but when Edward saw the dimensions of the revolt, the Queen left the northern route and retired to Norwich. She had this year borne her third daughter, the Princess Cecily, who was to be considered the most beautiful of a band of beautiful sisters.

As soon as the King had left London, Warwick made the ominous announcement that his daughter Isabel was to be married to the Duke of Clarence. The Countess of Warwick and her daughter had already been conveyed to Calais. Here Warwick and Clarence joined them, and on July 11 the marriage was performed by Archbishop Neville before a distinguished company and against the King's express command.

Edward found when he reached the Midlands that the rebellion was a great deal more serious than he had supposed and that the rebels' army was much larger than his own. He received a deputation from the rebels, saying they intended no harm to the King but strongly advising him to part from the Woodvilles. He therefore dispersed them; Lord Rivers and John Woodville went to the family house at Grafton, and from there made their way westwards towards Wales. Lord Scales joined his sister the Queen at Norwich, where the Mayor, hearing of her intended approach, became much alarmed. The Recorder of Norwich who had

C

experience of such matters, was in London, and the Mayor wrote to him for his advice. The Recorder said that the local dignitaries must be warned that the Queen would 'require to be received and attended as worthily as ever was Queen before her'.*

Meanwhile Warwick and Clarence had returned to England with an army and London had admitted them within the walls, for they said they had come to help the King, and Warwick was so popular with the citizens because of his lavish hospitality: anyone who knew a member of his household might come every day to his kitchens and carry away as much boiled and roast meat as they could stick on a dagger—the authorities were afraid that to exclude him might provoke a riot.

It was evident that the trouble was partly aroused by and directed against the Woodvilles and this was blazoned by a manifesto, issued by Warwick before he and Clarence had left Calais; it was attached to a copy of the rebels' petition and it demanded a stop to the 'deceivable, covetous rule and guiding of certain seducious persons—Lord Rivers, the Duchess of Bedford his wife, the Lord Scales, Sir John Woodville and his brothers, Sir John Fogge—their mischievous rule, opinion and assent', which, said the manifesto, has caused 'Our Sovereign and his realm to fall into great poverty and misery, disturbing the ministration of the laws, only entending to their own promotion and enriching'. Lord Rivers, the Duchess of Bedford his wife and their sons had caused the King to bestow livelihood and possession on them 'above their deserts and degrees, . . . to the utter impoverishing of us, his true Commons and subjects, and to the great enriching of themselves', while their large retinues of servants committed 'great murders, robberies, rapes, oppressions and extortions', which were 'daily done' and remained unpunished. Had the manifesto gone on to give examples, the sufferings of Sir Thomas Cook at the hands of Lord Rivers and Sir John Fogge would have borne a foremost place.

Edward finding himself outnumbered had fallen back on Nottingham and sent for reinforcements. The strongest of these was to come from Lord Herbert, who had been given the title of Earl of Pembroke which had been taken from Jasper Tudor, and was now advancing from Wales in the King's support; but at Edgecot in Oxfordshire, his army was caught between Warwick's and the other insurgents, and defeated. Pembroke was taken prisoner and Warwick had him executed at Northampton the following day. News of this reached Edward outside the town, and his men disbanded themselves and fled. Warwick had received word of the King's approach and Archbishop Neville was sent out to take him.

The Wheel of Fortune was a favourite image of the Middle Ages. The last time the King and the Archbishop had had an important meeting, the King had taken the Great Seal out of the Archbishop's hands. The

* MacGibbon, D., *Elizabeth Woodville*, 1938.

52

latter now escorted Edward, courteously but as a prisoner, to Warwick Castle.

Warwick's execution of Lord Pembroke had been altogether illegal, since Pembroke had not been in arms against the king whom Warwick still acknowledged; but Pembroke had been in high favour with Edward and had succeeded to the power and influence in Wales, carried by the office of Chamberlain and Chief Justice of South Wales, which Warwick had meant to occupy himself, but he now committed an act of savagery far more relishing. His men discovered Lord Rivers and John Woodville on the farther shore of the Severn, and brought them in to the Earl at Coventry. Rivers had been named foremost among the 'seducious persons' whose greed and impudence had been outrageous to honest men, and his son John had also been mentioned by name. The latter had the particular claim to Warwick's anger that, of all the marriages made for the benefit of the Queen's penniless relations, that of the wealthy and venerable Dowager Duchess of Norfolk to the nineteen year old John Woodville had reached the very limit of what was preposterous and disgraceful; and the ancient Duchess who had been treated in this undignified manner was Warwick's aunt. The Earl had the father and son beheaded outside the walls of Coventry.

Warwick intended to destroy as many of the Woodvilles as he could. While the King was still under house-arrest in Warwick Castle, a man of Warwick's named Thomas Wake brought to the Castle, 'an image of lead made like a man at arms, containing the length of a man's finger and broken in the middle and made fast with wire', which he showed to the King and to several lords present with him, trying to make the King believe that the Duchess of Bedford had used it in the practice 'of witchcraft and sorcery', against him, whereas, the Duchess said in the petition she afterwards addressed to the King: 'neither she, nor none for her or by her, ever saw it, God knoweth'.* The marriage which the Duchess's daughter had made was so ambitious and triumphant that the suspicion of its having been brought about by witchcraft had naturally been voiced though not taken seriously; but a definite accusation against the Duchess of Bedford was alarming; less than thirty years before, Eleanor Cobham, Duchess of Gloucester, and aunt by marriage of Henry VI, had been tried and convicted of witchcraft; it was said, among other charges, that she had used potions to win the Duke's love. She was sentenced to walk barefoot through the London streets carrying a wax taper and then imprisoned for life. As Lingard says, Edward rightly dismissed the accusations against his mother-in-law.

The popularity of Warwick with the Londoners had been the reason for admitting him within the city gates, in case rioting in his favour should break out, but the civic authorities now found that disturbances

* Lingard, *History of England*, Vol. IV, p. 164.

arose from the very fact of his admission. The law had broken down. Edward IV was under arrest and Henry VI was still in the Tower. Rioting in the streets and attacks on foreign merchants made a serious situation. Charles the Bold sent a message promising to support the city if it remained faithful to the Burgundian alliance—in other words, if it rejected the French alliance personified by Warwick. The Earl thought it best to remove Edward to distant Yorkshire, to Warwick's own castle of Middleham, where the formidably attractive king would be out of communication with London and in the region where the Nevilles relied on their strongest support. Edward's conduct during these months, from his capture to his final enlargement, has been described as consummately able. He remained calm, affable and co-operative; he did not provoke by a show of anger or defiance, nor did he attempt to call up the armed support he could have summoned, which would have resulted in another outbreak of civil war. He waited. Warwick would not dare to put him to death and it remained to be seen how much support Warwick would be able to command. It turned out, as Edward must shrewdly have supposed, that this was next to none. In his later years, Edward surprised onlookers by how much he knew about the inhabitants of his kingdom, their commitments, their resources and dispositions. He was exceptionally fitted to form an estimate of the nation's temper. He seems to have had now a well-founded confidence that however he might have aroused discontent, the people as a whole did not want to dismiss him and return to the régime of Henry VI, of which Warwick would be the chief manipulator. It was a policy of masterly inactivity, possible only to a man who combined easy self-confidence with an iron will. The test came with a providential outbreak on the northern border on behalf of Henry VI; it was necessary to deal with it at once and Warwick found that without the King's authority he could not muster men. Warwick's treatment of the King was obviously hostile: if Edward regained his power, anyone who supported Warwick might be found guilty of treason; this consideration paralysed Edward's subjects. Warwick was obliged to free the King from house arrest at Middleham and allow him to come to York; here, in the second greatest city of his realm, attended in dignity and splendour and, so far as could be seen, master of his own actions, he became once more the head of his state. An army was readily raised and the rising of the Nevilles of Brancepeth put down without difficulty. From this demonstration of his power, Edward moved on, unresisted. He went to the neighbouring castle of Pontefract and from there he summoned the Duke of Gloucester, their brother-in-law the Duke of Suffolk and all the members of the Privy Council. In October the King decided the time had come for his return to London. Unopposed and accompanied by the Duke of Gloucester and the Lords of the Council, he set out with his train. Archbishop Neville followed. When the entourage had got as far south as Hertfordshire, the

Archbishop turned aside to his manor, The Moor. Here he was joined by the Earl of Oxford. They decided that for the sake of their own prestige, they must form part of the King's triumphant entry into London, and they rode forward quickly to overtake the cavalcade; but three miles on the way, they were met by a messenger of the King's; the King told them that when he wanted them, he would send for them. They turned about and rode back to The Moor.

The King meanwhile entered London, a city which rejoiced to see him back. He was welcomed by the Lord Mayor and aldermen in scarlet, by the city guilds in blue. He adopted at once a policy of conciliation. In the face of the behaviour of Warwick and Clarence it was difficult for onlookers to have confidence that this could last. John Paston wrote: 'The King himself hath good language of the Lords of Clarence, of Warwick . . . saying they be his best friends, but his household men have other language.'* Edward did not attempt to penalize either of the rebels, but he took away from Warwick the offices in Wales which the latter had grasped on Pembroke's death, and gave them to the Duke of Gloucester. At seventeen, Richard was now Chief Justice and Chamberlain of South Wales till the majority of Pembroke's heir, and in his own right, Chief Justice of North Wales, Chief Steward and Surveyor of the Principality of Wales, and the Earldom of March. The death of Lord Rivers had left vacant the office of Constable of England, and this also the King conferred on Richard. When this office had been bestowed on Rivers, it had been done with reversion to his son, Lord Scales. Edward sometimes took back a position or a peerage which he had given or promised, according to what the great game of chess he was always playing seemed to him to require. When he did this, something else was given to the deprived person. Scales had now inherited his father's earldom and was henceforward Lord Rivers.

In view of the fact that Edward was afterwards accused of harsh dealing with Clarence, it can only be said that every time he pardoned his brother, it was giving him opportunity to offend again. In 1470, Warwick and Clarence either fomented fresh rebellion in Lincolnshire or else they decided to make use of disturbances already at work. The King's Master of the Horse, Sir Thomas Burgh, of Gainsborough in Lincolnshire, suffered as the Paston family had suffered. His manor was attacked by a gang of his enemies: Robert Lord Welles, the latter's son Sir Robert Welles and his brother-in-law Sir Thomas Dymmock. These with their men robbed the house of its contents, burned it down and chased the owner out of the county. Edward had been too slow in dealing with Robert of Redesdale, but he acted promptly now. Early in March he set out for Lincoln, sending for reinforcements from Coventry to join him at Grantham. It was spread about that the King had recalled the pardons granted

* Paston, *Letters*, Vol. V, no. 63.

after the last rebellion and that he was coming north on a punitive expedition. Sir Robert Welles issued a proclamation to the county of Lincoln to assemble at Ranby Haw to resist the King who was coming to destroy them.

Warwick and Clarence were moving up to Yorkshire with an army ostensibly to support the King, while the force under Sir Robert Welles was moving on the east.

Edward had summoned Lord Welles and Sir Thomas Dymmock to appear before the Privy Council in London, and as his movement north had been so rapid, the prisoners were sent after him. He thus had Lord Welles in his hands, and he caused him to write to his son Robert, demanding his submission, for if he refused, both Lord Welles and Sir Thomas Dymmock would lose their heads. Robert Welles, whose army formed one-half of the pincer movement Warwick had planned to entrap Edward, now retreated towards Stamford. Edward came upon them and found them disposed to fight. Supposing that his conditions had been flouted, he ordered the immediate execution of Welles and Dymmock and then rushed upon the engagement known as Lose-Coatfield, for the panic-stricken rebels dropped their clothes and weapons as they fled. In this struggle some of the soldiers had been giving as their battle cry— A Warwick! A Clarence!—some had actually been wearing Clarence's livery. The confession of Sir Robert Welles was merely a confirmation: 'I have well understood . . . from my Lord of Clarence, as of Warwick, that they intended to make a great rising . . . to the intent to make the Duke of Clarence King, and so it was oft and largely noised in our host.'[*] With this in his possession, Edward sent to Warwick and Clarence, commanding their presence. They replied that they would not come without safeguards and a guarantee of pardon. Edward told messengers to tell them that he would treat them as a sovereign ought, even with favour and pity if they obeyed him. If they did not obey his summons this time they should get their deserts. The messengers begged the King not to charge them with such a message as this, and Garter King at Arms was despatched with it.[†] Clarence and Warwick then began a flight, northward to Manchester, where they hoped for aid from Lord Stanley, and when this was refused, down the whole length of England to the south coast of Devonshire where they embarked at Dartmouth. At Warwick Castle they had taken up the Countess of Warwick and her daughters. The young and frail Duchess of Clarence was pregnant and near her delivery. They proceeded up the Channel to Calais. Warwick was still Captain of this important fortress, but when he reached the harbour on April 16, instead of the immediate admittance he had expected, his vessel was fired on. He dropped anchor and learned that the day before,

* *Excerpta Historica*, p. 284.
† Scofield, *op. cit.*, Vol. I, p. 516.

messages had been received from Edward IV, forbidding the deputy Captain, Lord Wenlock, to allow him entrance. The Duchess of Clarence was now in labour. The Rows Roll says that the Countess of Warwick was 'glad to be with women that travailed of child', that 'she was full comfortable and plenteous then of all thing that should be helping to them'. She now had to manage the confinement of her own daughter, on shipboard, without any of the medicines or properties she would have provided for another woman. Warwick sent a boat, asking Lord Wenlock to let them have some wine, and it returned with two casks. Isabel was delivered at last of a dead boy and the infant was dropped into the sea. The event recalls the words Pericles* speaks to his queen Thaisa, delivered of a child on board ship:

> A terrible child-bed hast thou had, my dear,
> No light, no fire, the elements forgot thee,

and though Pericles is speaking to his dead wife, the words might have been spoken by Clarence of the dead child:

> Nor have I time
> To give thee, hallowed, to thy grave, but straight
> Must cast thee, scarcely coffined, in the ooze.

From this time, Clarence's fortunes were on the wane.

* *Pericles*, Act III, sc. i.

II

WARWICK and Clarence had escaped but twenty of their men were captured and brought in to Southampton. The Earl of Worcester had been recalled from Ireland to deal with a critical situation, and to his powers as Constable of England the King now added that of trying treason cases without a jury; Worcester's opinion of the prisoner's guilt was all that was needed to condemn him to the horrors of a traitor's death. Worcester's sheer brutality was made the more abhorrent by his intellectual sophistication and his Italian culture. In Rhodes the Turks had the custom of impaling prisoners alive, and Worcester impaled the twenty prisoners taken at Southampton, but historians disagree as to whether the impalement were before or after death. Warkworth's Chronicle of the First Thirteen Years of King Edward IV,* says that the prisoners were 'hanged, drawn and quartered, and headed and after that they [were] hanged up by the legs and a stake made sharp at both ends, whereof one end was put in at the buttocks and the other end their heads were put upon'. Warkworth at least believed that the victim was not only dead but decapitated before the impalement was carried out, but the fact that this was said to be done 'to aghast the king's rebels' and that for this, 'he fell in indignation with the common people', who were, after all, accustomed to the sight of rebels' quartered limbs displayed in public places, and above all that Worcester himself was nearly lynched on his way to execution some months later, leaves the matter in a horrible uncertainty.

Warwick's anger at his loss of influence over Edward was unquenchable; as the writer of 'A remarkable fragment of an old English Chronicle'† put it: 'He withdrew himself from the amity of . . . King Edward the IV, . . . inasmuch as his insatiable mind could not be content; and yet before him there was none in England of half the possessions that he had, . . . and yet he desired more . . . he enticed so the Duke of Clarence that he followed all his counsel.' The defeat at Edward's hands now urged him to a *volte-face* so surprising as to be unbelievable, except that it was true. He had lost all chance of exerting power through Edward and he now

* *Chronicle of Edward IV*, John Warkworth, ed. J. O. Halliwell, 1839.
† *Thomas Sprott*, ed. Thomas Hearne, 1719.

saw that there was no prospect of success through Clarence; the alliance of his daughter Isabel had been expended in vain; but he had a second daughter, the fifteen year old Anne. He conceived the extraordinary but brilliant idea of allying himself with Margaret of Anjou, marrying Anne to her son, the nineteen year old Prince Edward of Lancaster, and throwing all his might into the project of wrecking Edward IV and restoring Henry VI. That Margaret of Anjou abhorred his very name was a difficulty that required the skill of a master-hand to overcome. Seeing in this project a chance to join England to France by the strongest ties and at the same time effectually and finally to separate England from Burgundy, Louis XI was ready to bring his consummate abilities to the work. The Queen of Henry VI had for the last ten years been leading a poverty-stricken but heroic existence at the court of her father, René of Anjou, her spirits kept up by the never-dying blaze of her anger, her hatred, her dauntless courage and her passionate devotion to her son. In her small entourage she had her faithful adherent Sir John Fortescue who had been Henry VI's Lord Chief Justice and proscribed by Edward IV as a Lancastrian in 1461, when he went into exile with Margaret of Anjou. He took on the work of tutor to the young Edward of Lancaster and wrote for him his treatise on the laws of England, explaining and supporting the English legal system, with a most humane and enlightened protest against the cruelty and the defective sense of extracting evidence under torture, of which the practice was at that time more widely developed in France than in England. Edward of Lancaster had not greatly benefited by this wise and inspired teacher. At sixteen he was said to be an arrogant youth who talked of nothing but making war and cutting off heads. His mother, after all, had ordained his being present at beheadings when he was eight years old.

These combustible elements were united by Louis XI's unequalled talents for intrigue. Margaret of Anjou kept Warwick on his knees for a quarter of an hour before she allowed the question of an alliance to be broached. She at last consented that her son and Anne Neville should be married and that Warwick, with the support of the King of France behind him, should undertake the re-conquest of England for the house of Lancaster. She only stipulated that her son should not be entrusted to Warwick until the work had been done; the Prince was to remain with her in France until the path had been made clear to his father's throne. Louis XI for his part exacted an undertaking that as soon as Warwick had gained effective control of English resources, he should equip a force to aid in the invasion of Burgundy. The member of the party left altogether unsatisfied was Clarence, who had committed himself to avowed treason for the chance of gaining his brother's throne and was now told that all Warwick could promise him was that he should succeed to it if there were no male heirs to Edward and Anne. In this state of disillusion and bitterness he received an overture which was to make him a very undependable support to the Earl of Warwick. An unnamed lady was sent into France by Edward himself; she entreated Clarence to return to his allegiance to his king and to the family bond with his brother.

The men of Kent had always been ready for revolt, and Warwick opened communications with his party in England through Kentish seamen. He sent a manifesto into England saying he was coming to reform abuses, but he did not say in which king's behalf he would be acting. He was anxious that some disturbance should be made in the north that Edward might be drawn there with his army while Warwick himself beached his invading force on the south-east coast. The third Earl of Northumberland had been killed at the battle of Towton, and Edward had bestowed the earldom on Warwick's brother John Neville; but in 1469, wishing to establish a powerful magnate in the north who would wield the influence of a hereditary ruler and co-operate with the Duke of Gloucester in keeping the whole vast area loyal to the crown, he had reinstated Northumberland's son Henry Percy as the fourth Earl and had made John Neville in recompense Marquis Montagu. Neville denied that the award was a just recompense and though he had maintained his loyalty to the king in spite of Warwick's defection, that loyalty was now badly shaken. This danger however did not immediately show itself. Warwick's ruse to draw the King northwards succeeded; the earl's brother-in-law, Lord Fitzhugh of Ravensworth, raised an insurrection in Yorkshire and there were sporadic disturbances near Carlisle. John Paston wrote: 'so many folks be up in the north' that the King was obliged to go himself to settle matters. Edward spent the month of August putting down a rebellion which was not formidable but which had served Warwick's turn. The latter's fleet had been blockaded in the mouth of the Seine by Burgundian vessels, but equinoctial gales were rising, and the blockade was dispersed by a storm; on the evening of September 13, he and Clarence landed with their forces at Plymouth. They now openly announced themselves as supporters of Henry VI, and began their march on London.

As soon as the news was spread of their arrival, bands of Kentish men stormed up to London and began pillaging and looting in Southwark on the south shore of the Thames. Flemish and Dutch traders and tavern keepers, as prosperous and peaceful foreigners, were their natural targets. The King turned south to meet Warwick's force which was increasing daily, but he knew that Montagu was collecting an army and he paused at Doncaster for Montagu to join him. While he was in his bed, news came that Montagu had deserted the King's cause and was coming with his men to take him. Edward had barely time to save himself by flight. With Richard of Gloucester, Antony Lord Rivers, and his chamberlain and friend William Lord Hastings, and, Commines says, with seven or eight hundred men, without any clothes but what they were to have fought in, no money in their pockets, of whom not one in twenty knew where they were going, he made his way across Lincolnshire to Norfolk; at Lynn he commandeered a fleet of fishing vessels and they set sail for the Low Countries where they arrived on October 11. Edward was penniless and had to reward the captain of the fishing fleet by giving him his own rich, furred gown; but they were received with great hospitality by the governor of Holland, the Lord of Gruthuyse, whom Edward knew already, and who gave them shelter, clothes and money and kept them in his house in the Hague. Though Edward's sister the Duchess of Burgundy was near at hand, she could not immediately welcome her brothers; her husband was at first obliged to be extremely cautious. Menaced as he was by France, he dared not give a Lancastrian English government any excuse for attacking him. Warwick had promised Louis XI that he would mount an invasion of Burgundy as soon as he was in control of England and only lack of money prevented him from doing it. But the threat of an imminent French invasion convinced Charles that his own safety would best be served by putting Edward back on his throne. At the end of December he received the English king and his party.

When Warwick and Clarence landed on September 13, the Queen was in London without her husband or her brother and eight months gone with child. She had had a chamber in the royal partments in the Tower re-decorated for her lying-in.* When the birth of the Princess Mary had been expected in 1467, the Queen had ordered a new feather bed with bolsters and cushions, furnishings of crimson damask and ells of washable fabric: fustian, a thick-twilled cotton, holland, an unbleached linen, and the fine linen cloth imported from Brittany called cloth of Rennes.† Her preparations for this occasion were no doubt on a similar scale of lavish comfort and elegance. She obviously had confidence in her midwife Marjorie Cobbe and wanted to retain her services. In April of the previous year, 1469, the Calendar of Patent Rolls recorded: Grant to John Cobbe and Marjorie his wife, the midwife of the King's consort Elizabeth Queen of England, £10 yearly for the life of Marjorie. Mrs. Cobbe was not in the walk of life of the ordinary *sage-femme*. Her husband had some education and knowledge of affairs. In 1468, he had sat on a commission with Walter Moyle, Knight, to enquire into a dispute about land tenure.‡

The Queen had intended, in the King's absence, to remain in the royal apartments of the Tower, and had ordered supplies of food to be brought there, but by the end of September matters wore too dangerous an air for her to feel secure, even in the palace that was also a fortress. When the

* Sharpe, R. R., *Memorials of London and the Kingdom*, 1894.
† Scofield, *op. cit.*, Vol. I, p. 482.
‡ *Calendar of the Patent Rolls*, 1468, pp. 70–71.

men of Kent heard that Warwick and Clarence had landed, Fabyan says: 'they began to wax wild and assembled themselves in great companies and so came into the outer parts of the city of London' . . . They came up to Southwark on the south shore of the Thames and let prisoners out of the gaols to swell their numbers. On the opposite shore they swarmed into 'Ratcliffe, St. Katherine's, and other places, and robbed and spoiled the Flemings and all the beer houses whereas they came'. These localities were immediately to the east of the Tower, the rioting could have been seen from some of its upper casements.

The previous year, on August 12, Warwick had beheaded Elizabeth Woodville's father Lord Rivers and her youngest brother John. Announcing that one of the objects of his mission was to put down the Woodvilles, he had executed two of them without any form of trial. On October 1, news was received of the King's flight from Lynn and that Warwick and Clarence were approaching London. 'In that night', Stow says, the Queen 'had stolen secretly out of the Tower of London by water to Westminster and there taken sanctuary'.* She brought with her, her mother and her three daughters, Elizabeth aged five, Mary, four and Cecily, one.

On two occasions, of which this was the first, Elizabeth Woodville took shelter in sanctuary. The second time she sought it in the house of the Abbot of Westminster; any place that was under the Abbot's protection was deemed to be sanctuary, but the Abbot's house was not the building known as The Sanctuary. This was a square keep built of ragstone, so massive that when Dr. Stukely the antiquarian watched it being demolished in 1750, he wondered if the workmen would ever get it down. It stood beside St. Margaret's Church, between the graveyard and the west door of the Abbey, and is commemorated in the name of the street, Broad Sanctuary, that joins St. Margaret's Church to Parliament Square.† The tower consisted of two storeys, of which the upper one was a church; on one of the outer walls a turret contained the staircase that led up to it. High up in this wall were two narrow lancet cindows. The roof was crowned by a belfry, added by Edward III. Fugitives who gained the shelter of the keep were safe because no one would be so impious as to drag them out, and also because the walls were impregnable. What they had to bear once they were inside was the extreme hardship of existence in this stone walled, stone floored hold; the coming and going of people bringing them supplies was permitted, but the fugitives themselves dared not come out by daylight.

That it was to this retreat that the Queen fled with her children and her mother, under cover of the autumn night, and not to the Abbot's house, seems clear for several reasons. For all she knew, her situation at Warwick's hands was acutely dangerous; he had put her father and brother to death

* Stow, John, *Annals, or a General Chronicle of England*, 1615.
† *Archeologia*, Vol. I, p. 35.

and stigmatized her husband as a usurper, and though he was accompanied by her brother-in-law, she had long since been an enemy of the Duke of Clarence. In this crisis, she would seek the strongest shelter she could find, whatever its privations. Secondly, Holinshed* describes her plight as one of severe deprivation: he says that the Queen in Sanctuary was 'in great penury, forsaken of all her friends'; but that she 'driven in distress, forsook not that simple refuge which had hard hap forced upon her and, [a king's wife] wanted in her necessity, such things as mean men's wives had in superfluity'. Thirdly, Edward afterwards bestowed rewards on the butcher William Gould who, while the Queen was in sanctuary, brought beef and mutton 'for her sustentation of her household'. The very handsome rewards imply that the Queen would have been in desperate straits without his help, and neither this, nor Holinshed's description, are consistent with her having been the guest, however unwelcome, of the Abbot of Westminster. Finally, Mancini, writing in 1483, at least twenty years earlier than the earliest of the chroniclers, in making a resumé of the past events, rays: 'The place of refuge at Westminster Abbey stood close to the royal palace, and is called by the English a sanctuary'. In this sanctuary, he said, the Queen had given birth to her child.†

That her actual flight was into the sanctuary tower seems certain; the confusion between writers, some of whom speak of her as having been sheltered by the Abbot, might be owing to her having later ventured herself and her party into the Abbot's dwelling. Finally, Warwick having, naturally, heard of the Queen's flight with her family, issued a proclamation, forbidding any one to 'defoul or distrouble' churches or sanctuaries, mentioning by name the sanctuaries of Westminster and St. Martin le Grand, and ordering that they should 'not vex, spoil, rob, indomage or hurt . . . any inhabitant or sojournant within the holy places'.

The conduct of the invaders was not harsh, they could not afford it to be. It was always uncertain, in the last resort, how much support either York or Lancaster would be able to command. Warwick had not only to restore a king who, whatever sympathy he might command, was notoriously unfit to rule; he was also about to recall a French Queen who was abominated. Margaret in her attempts to achieve supreme power had instigated the Irish to harass the Duke of York when he was King's Lieutenant in Ireland; she had given Berwick to the Scots; in 1457 she had encouraged the French general De Brézé to land on the south coast and burn Sandwich to the ground, and for their support in 1460 she had told her northern followers that they might pillage and burn all the English towns they passed through on the way to London. Their trail of murder, robbery and fire-raising had gained for Margaret the savage,

* Holinshed, Raphael, *History of England*, Vol. III, p. 300, edn 1807.
† Mancini, *op. cit.*

unquenchable hatred that is born of fear. As well as all this, Warwick was pledged to Louis XI to force the English government to equip and send an army to help France against Burgundy; this would be highly unpopular; it would require the voting of very large sums of money and oblige men to serve out of their own country in support of a policy which a great many people objected to in any case, since the wealthy merchants and the majority of those who earned their living by commerce wanted to maintain trading relations with Burgundy. Warwick was therefore in no position to begin exacting reprisals from Yorkist supporters, except in one case, where he received an overwhelming measure of popular support. Worcester was deprived of the office of Constable and John de Vere, thirteenth Earl of Oxford, was appointed in his place. It therefore fell to Oxford to convict Worcester of treason, by the same summary methods which Worcester had employed in convicting Oxford's father and elder brother. Worcester was sentenced to be executed on October 17, but the hostile crowds were so great, the guards could not bring him to Tower Hill. They were obliged to take him into the Fleet prison for the night and bring him out to execution the next day.

Warwick's first act of all was to release King Henry VI from the Tower where he had been kept for the past five years; he had had the attendance of two servants and Edward had paid fees to a chaplain to go every day to the Tower and perform divine service 'before Henry, late de facto et non de jure King of England'.* It was not the Yorkist policy to ill treat him but he suffered as helpless beings are apt to suffer when the authorities do not keep a constant watch over the people who have charge of them. He was sometimes roughly handled, when he would say only: 'Forsooth and forsooth, ye do wrong to strike an annointed king', but while his humility and patience were inexhaustible, he seems sometimes to have shown a surprising degree of dignity and sense. When someone, allowed to visit him, spoke of the transference of the crown, Henry said: 'My father was king, his father also was king, I myself have worn the crown forty years from my cradle; you have all sworn fealty to me as your sovereign and your fathers have done the like to mine. How then can my right be disputed?'

He was discovered by his rescuers, 'not so cleanly kept as should seem such a prince'.† Archbishop Neville now installed himself in the Tower and took charge of King Henry. Fabyan says‡ that Henry 'was taken from the lodging where he lay and was then lodged in the King's Lodging'. This was of course in the royal apartments and Shairp says that he was put into the splendid chamber the Queen had prepared for her lying-in.

Warwick himself now appeared before him. The last time Henry had

* Pell Records, *Issues of the Exchequer*, p. 491.
† Warkworth, John, *op. cit.*
‡ Fabyan, Robert, *op. cit.*, p. 659.

seen him, the Earl had been in charge of the escort that had brought him to the Tower, an old straw hat on his head and his feet bound to the stirrups that the gaping crowds might understand he was a prisoner. Now Warwick knelt before him and did him homage. A long blue velvet gown was produced and King Henry was dressed in it and led in procession to St. Paul's. After some days in the Bishop of London's palace beside St. Paul's Churchyard, he was removed to the Palace of Westminster.

Here, he heard from his Council of the plight of 'Elizabeth, late calling herself Queen', and he sanctioned an order so characteristic of himself, it may have been his own: 'Our right trusty and well beloved Lady Scrope' was commanded to attend on her, and on October 30, a warrant was issued, to pay Lady Scrope ten pounds, 'to have of our gift by way of reward for the cause above said'.* Two days later, the child was born. It was Edward IV's eagerly awaited son.

Whether Mrs. Cobbe attended the confinement, whether the royal physicain Dr. Serigo attended it, there is no evidence (Agnes Strickland says they did, and this has been copied by other writers; but Miss Strickland's references—to what she calls *Fleetwood s Chronicle*: i.e. 'The Arrival of Edward IV,' sometimes called *Fleetwood's Book*, because the only existing manuscript was made by Stow from one in the possession of Sir William Fleetwood, Recorder of London in the reign of Queen Elizabeth, and to vol. XII of Rymer's *Fœdera*—are entirely fallacious; neither work contains a word of the matter), but as King Henry meant the greatest kindness by appointing Lady Scrope to take care of Elizabeth Woodville, it must be argued that Lady Scrope had the power to summon whatever was necessary in medical attention and supplies.

The baby, it was said, was christened as plainly as if he had been a poor man's son; that is to say, no rich retinue attended him, bearing presents of gold plate; but he was christened in Westminster Abbey by the sub-prior and he had the Abbot of Westminster for his godfather. He was given the name of his father, Edward.

* Scofield, C. L., *English Historical Review*, Jan. 1909.

12

EDWARD with his brother Gloucester and his brother-in-law Antony Rivers was a few months only in his sister's court, but his stay had an important consequence beside the over-riding one of providing him with a base from which to regain his throne. The Duchess of Burgundy had a humble but exceptionally able protégé, at this time living in Bruges but shortly to become an inmate of her household for the next five years. William Caxton who had begun life apprenticed to a mercer, a dealer in silks and costly materials, had risen by intelligence and business ability to the position of Governor of the English Merchants in the Low Countries, in which he negotiated commercial treaties with the Duke of Burgundy. Caxton's interest in books was at first that of a reader merely. At the time of Edward's arrival at the Duchess's court, he was working on a translation into English of the French collection of stories about the Trojan war, *Le Recueil des Histoires de Troy*. He had shown, he said, the first five or six quires to the Duchess, and the cultivated daughter of Richard Duke of York had found fault with some of the mercer's use of English; he corrected his errors under her guidance and she heartily encouraged him to finish the work. He entered her household on some footing of usefulness to her in 1471 and remained there, receiving a salary, till 1475, but by 1474 he had taken a step of indescribable importance. He had found, in Cologne, a printing press in operation. The invention had been available for some years, and it had not made the immediate, widespread progress that might have been expected, but Caxton was engaged in copying out the *Recuyell of the Histories of Troy*, and, as he said in the epilogue to the third book, his pen was worn, his eyes dimmed and his hand aching from the task. At this point of physical fatigue, it came to him that the printing press was an inspired solution. In 1473 he set up a press of his own in Bruges, under the management of Colard Mansion, a distinguished scrivener and illuminator practising in the city. Caxton's first printed book, *The Recuyell of the Histories of Troy*, was produced on this press in 1475.

Margaret of York was a young woman of great force of character. She made a favourable impression on her husband's subjects; she was not only a kind stepmother to the son and daughter of his previous

66

marriage; though living among the comforts and pleasures of one of the richest and most luxurious courts in Europe, she took a keen interest in works of charity. The illuminated manuscript, *Les Oeuvres de Miséricorde*, shows her in a series of minatures, giving loaves and wine to the poor, a gown to a naked man, money to beggars, visiting a prisoner who peers from behind a grill, standing at the bedside of a sick man, attending a funeral and praying in her oratory. It seems reasonable to believe that the little figures representing the Duchess convey an actual impression of her; they are all exactly like each other and seem to be based on the portrait ascribed to an anonymous Franco-Flemish artist.* She is shown in all of them in the steeple-shaped hennin and the necklace made of enamelled marguerites, from which hang a row of pendants forming alternatively the letters C and M. It is very interesting that the face in the *portrait d'apparat* bears a distinct resemblance to that of Richard III in the stained glass picture in the parish church of Penrith, on one of Richard's northern estates.† The brother and sister have the same wedge-shape of face with a large, well-formed nose. Richard III was said to be slight though strong; the Duchess is drawn in the miniatures with a slender figure of great elegance.

It was ironic that illuminated manuscripts should be coming to their full perfection just as printed books were about to supersede them. The Netherland illuminators reached a degree of graphic minuteness, of stereoscopic detail and depth and brilliance of colour which gives the person who examines their work a sense almost of clairvoyance of the scenes and figures of the fifteenth century. When Edward saw the beautiful manuscript works which his sister could show him, it seems that he determined to commission some for himself when he should be able to do so. The interest which led to his future patronage of Caxton in England began with their acquaintance at this time, and the enlightened ordinance of Richard III, that books brought into England should pay no duty, may have owed something to the deep pleasure the young Duke of Gloucester found in beautiful illuminations and the idea of printing while he was at his sister's court in a temporary eclipse.

The Duchess, loyal as she was to her husband's family, never ceased to be passionately interested in the fortunes of her own; at this time of her eldest and her youngest brothers' being with her, she was making strenuous efforts to heal the injurious family wound made by the disloyalty of her favourite brother of all. She sent continual messages to the Duke of Clarence, urging him to return to the family allegiance. Nothing had any influence on Clarence except self-interest, but his sister's vehement pleadings may have helped to convince him that self-interest demanded his abandoning Warwick's cause and returning to his brother's.

* Ross, *Edward IV*, p. 177.
† Cheetham, Anthony, *Life and Times of Richard III*, p. 199.

Meanwhile Edward with ceaseless vigilance was watching and waiting the moment for his return to England. If Clarence could be detached from Warwick, the latter's power would be considerably reduced. The Earl of Northumberland with his great resources could be relied on to support Edward, for if Warwick remained in power, Northumberland's earldom might be taken from him and given back to Montagu. Edward always had the sympathy of the merchant class, and the Hanseatic League of German towns, a powerful body existing to promote commerce between the countries of Europe, undertook to provide him with fourteen ships, to carry him back to England and to remain at his service for fifteen days after his landing. The English merchants in Bruges made him small loans. Charles of Burgundy continued, in public, the cautious policy to which fear of a combined French and Lancastrian offensive had driven him, and issued a statement forbidding his subjects to give Edward any aid; but in secret he himself gave Edward 50,000 florins and ordered three Dutch ships to be made ready for his use.*

The following spring, March 11, 1471, Edward sailed for England with thirty-six ships, and 1,600 men, and landed on the east coast in the estuary of the Humber. With so small an army, the enterprise was a gamble that might well have failed, but a kind of supernatural luck, characteristic of the fortunes of the House of York, attended on his doings. Northumberland did not obstruct the king's southward march, but nor did Montagu, to whose interest it would have been. The news of the landing reached London, and Archbishop Neville who was in charge of King Henry VI, tried to rally support for him by showing him to the London populace. Edward gained immensely from the people's seeing him—'The Rose of Rouen came royally riding', but to exhibit the pathetic figure of Henry VI was, as Fabyan said, worse than useless: 'The said King Henry was conveyed from the palace of Paul's [the palace of the Bishop of London] through Cheap and Cornhill and so about to his said lodging again by Candlewick St. and Watling St., being accompanied with the Archbishop of York, which held him all that way by the hand.' This spectacle, said Fabyan, 'was more like a play than the showing of a prince to win men's hearts'.

Meanwhile Edward, accompanied by Gloucester, and an army that gathered recruits as it came on, reached the outskirts of Coventry, where Warwick lay. Edward, in a proclamation in which he declared himself King, offered Warwick a pardon so far as his life was concerned, or, alternatively, challenged him to a pitched battle. Warwick, expecting the armies of Clarence, Northumberland and Montagu to converge on Coventry, and also that Margaret of Anjou, her son and an army provided by Louis XI would land on the south coast at any moment, contemptuously refused Edward's offers.

* Ross, *op. cit.*, p. 160.

But Clarence, coming up with his men, was met by Edward and Gloucester between Coventry and Banbury. Edward, relying perhaps on the mediations of his sister, took the risk of leaving his army and accompanied only by Gloucester, rode forward to meet Clarence who also approached with a few followers only, The three princes dismounted; Clarence knelt and Edward raised and kissed him; Gloucester also embraced him, and Edward then empowered him to take Warwick the offer of more than his life, a pardon on very favourable terms. It was another instance of Edward's singular good fortune, that this overture, sincerely made as it was, should be angrily rejected. Warwick had now been reinforced by the arrival of Lord Montagu's army and one under Lord Oxford, an unswerving Lancastrian. Warwick determined, first to repudiate all offers of reconciliation, and secondly to choose his own time to attack. He lay still in the shelter of the walls of Coventry.

Edward saw that in this paralysis of the enemy, the road to London was now open to him. On April 11, he and his two brothers entered the city in a triumphant cavalcade, while the streets were filled with crowds shouting their welcome. Edward went first to St. Paul's where he 'made an offering'; then he went the few paces to the Bishop of London's palace, where he gave orders that King Henry VI and Archbishop Neville should be removed to the Tower. The behaviour of Henry VI makes it easy to understand why, in the preceding centuries, it had been considered that there was something sacred about lunatics. The poor, simple-witted king said to the flourishing, triumphant king: 'I am right glad of your arrival, my cousin. I know that my life will be safe in your hands.'

Edward then rode down Ludgate Hill, through Fleet Street and the Strand till he came to Westminster. In the Abbey, the Cardinal Archbishop, Thomas Bourchier, placed the crown on his head in a brief, symbolic gesture. Then the King entered the Sanctuary, whether it were the stone keep or by this time the guest apartments of the Abbot of Westminster; here he was re-united with his wife and his three little girls, and saw for the first time his six month old son and heir.

> The young Prince he beheld and in his arms did bear.
> Thus his bale turnèd him to bliss.
> After sorrow, joy, the course of this world is.
> (Wright, *Political Poems and Songs*, II 274)

The family party—the King, the Queen, her mother, their four children—then removed to Baynard's Castle, its towers reflected in the Thames, its chambers made ready to receive them on this glorious day. It was the town house of the old Duchess of York, though it was naturally at the disposal of her son the King; Proud Cis had been bitterly opposed to his marriage with Elizabeth Woodville, but after the cataclysmic events of the past year, the renaissance of the House of York, the return to the fold of Clarence, and above all, the fact that the Queen had borne a son, the family reunion may have been one in which all dissatisfactions were overcome by relief and triumph.

13

WARWICK, within the walls of Coventry, had heard that since he had been unable to mount his promised invasion of Burgundy, Louis XI had signed a truce with Charles the Bold. He was therefore deprived of his great supporter, the King of France; but he was also expecting the imminent arrival of Margaret of Anjou. Both considerations perhaps moved him to action.

In the absence of other means of communication, swift-riding scouts discovered the enemy's movements and raced back with the intelligence to their commanders. On April 13, Edward heard that Warwick had come out of Coventry and had already passed through St. Albans on his way to London. Edward set out with an army to meet him; with him, he brought King Henry VI. If Warwick should gain the day and enter London, at least he would not be able to use King Henry as a figurehead. The opposing forces came into each other's neighbourhood at Barnet, on the outskirts of Hertfordshire. Under cover of darkness, Edward encamped nearer to Warwick than the latter's soldiers knew. Their gunners fired cannon at intervals all through the night, but the balls overshot the king's men. The battle was joined at daybreak in misty air; it developed a revolving movement, for the Yorkist ranks gave way on the left and Warwick's ranks yielded to pressure on the right. This caused Lord Oxford's troops to come face to face with their own comrades where they had expected to find the enemy. Oxford's men wore his blazon, 'a star with streams'. In the poor light, Warwick's men mistook this for Edward's 'sun in splendour' and fired on them. Shouts of 'treason'! spread confusion and panic. Warwick knew that his brother Montagu was dead already and he decided on flight. He made for Barnet woods, and falling into the hands of Yorkist soldiers, was killed and 'spoiled naked' of his rich armour before Edward's messenger could reach the scene with the king's orders to spare his life. The value of the victory was great, it was the last battle but one of the civil war, but the value of Warwick's death, which Edward had tried honestly to prevent, was inestimable. No pardon, no apparent reconciliation, would have brought lasting safety. The life of 'the over-mighty subject' would always have threatened the life of the king.

Henry was escorted back to London and the Tower.

Margaret of Anjou had for long hesitated to set sail with her son and their army until she was sure that Warwick was in control of England, but the urgings of Louis XI had caused her at last to decide on her departure; then, contrary winds had kept her fast in Honfleur. When they ceased, she came out to sea, and her fleet, carrying the Prince Edward of Lancaster, and his wife Anne Neville, landed at Weymouth on the evening of the day on which Warwick had been killed, fighting for them. The Countess of Warwick had arrived in another ship, and joined them.

When the dire news reached them, the widow fled across Dorset into Hampshire and took sanctuary in Beaulieu Abbey; her daughter Anne remained with her young husband. The party turned inland to Cerne Abbey and here the Duke of Somerset met them, assuring the frantic Queen that all was not lost, that in the west, at least, they could rally massive support. They were now joined by contingents from Devon and Cornwall; they set out for Bath and Bristol, attracting reinforcements on the way, and at Bristol itself they were welcomed and refreshed.

Edward was already collecting recruits from fifteen counties; he had assembled a large army and his artillery train, but he could not at first make out in which direction Margaret of Anjou was about to move: towards London or into Somerset or towards the Severn. The last possibility was the most threatening. Beyond the Severn lay Wales, where she could join forces with Jasper Tudor and advance into Cheshire and Lancashire, both counties with strong Lancastrian sympathies. Once across the Severn, she might spirit up a chain of formidable local risings.

Edward heard from his scouts that she was making for the Severn; but where was she to cross? Many English rivers, rushing over stony beds and around great boulders, are so shallow, a boy could ford them. The Severn is wide and deep and men in armour cannot swim. There were three places where an army might cross: the bridge at Gloucester, a ford at Tewkesbury and another bridge at Worcester. Edward was occupying a vantage point between Bristol and Malmesbury when he found that Margaret's force was making rapidly for Gloucester. He sent fleet messengers, whose pace was much faster than an army's telling the Governor of Gloucester Castle to shut the city gates on the Queen's men and to deny them the Severn bridge. The Governor might have faltered between two such opposing powers, but news of the King's very great army near at hand encouraged him. He barred the city gates and Margaret's army went on by forced marches to Tewkesbury. Edward, taking an upland route, pursued her, making quicker progress than her troops could achieve in the rough wooded ground pitted with deep lanes on the floor of the Severn valley. When they reached the ford, her exhausted soldiers lay down on the ground and declared they could go no further. Before they had gathered strength enough to continue their advance, Edward arrived within three miles of them. It was open to Margaret's army, when able to move, either to press on across the ford and so into Wales, where Edward would of course pursue them, or to stand their ground and fight. The decision for the latter was Somerset's, against the judgment of his colleagues and of Margaret herself. 'Taking his will for reason', the Duke overbore all opposition. Next morning the battle was joined. Each army was drawn up in three parts; of the Yorkist forces, Gloucester led the van, Edward himself commanded the centre and William Lord Hastings the rear. The three opposing contingents were commanded by the Duke of Somerset, Prince Edward of Lancaster aided by Lord Wenlock, and the Earl of Devonshire. Somerset was beaten by Gloucester's onslaught, and the Duke lost his head. Coming upon Lord Wenlock, he shouted that the latter was a traitor who had not supported him, and killed Wenlock with a blow on the head from his battle-axe. This precipitated a general flight of the centre. In the mêlée Prince Edward turned and fled. All contemporary accounts say that he was slain flying from the field, contradicting Hall's much later story that he was brought a prisoner to Edward's tent, and cut down by Gloucester in cold blood. If Gloucester had killed him, the deed, though savagely cruel, would not have been treachery. As it was, the young man would seem to have fallen a victim to treachery of the cruellest kind. Warkworth says the Prince, crying for help to 'his brother-in-law, the Duke of Clarence', was pursued and killed by Clarence's men.

The flying Lancastrians were driven across a stretch of park-land, known from that time as Bloody Meadow; numbers were slain on the trampled grass, and numbers more were stampeded to drowning in the Avon that flows across the fields to make a wide confluence with the Severn.

The Abbey Church stands near the waterside and a crowd of the defeated soldiers rushed into it to claim sanctuary. Edward in person pursued them to the doors, where he was met by the Abbot who begged him to respect the privileges of the holy place. This the King at first promised to do; the greater number of the fugitives were the common soldiers whom it was his usual policy to spare; but while the Abbot was speaking to him at the west door the King realized that among those inside were some of the rebels' ringleaders: the Duke of Somerset, Sir John Langstrother whom Warwick had made Lord Treasurer after he had executed Rivers, and ten other leading Lancastrians.

This great and decisive victory had taxed the King and his army to the uttermost. He had brought his men to the scene, enduring hunger, thirst and the exhaustion of forced marching in armour over unshaded uplands under the May sun. In his gilded mail, a gold crown on his helmet, he had fought in the thick of the battle with heroic bravery and endurance, most ably seconded by his younger brother. Now that the hard-fought fight was won, he was in no mood for leniency which, by sparing the ringleaders, might mean that the whole gigantic task would have, presently, to be undertaken all over again. Despite his promise to the Abbot, he ordered the ringleaders to be haled out. His defender, the writer of *History of the Arrival of King Edward IV*,* says that Tewkesbury Abbey, without either a royal charter or a papal bull, had no claims to be a sanctuary. The following day, a court martial held by the Duke of Gloucester, condemned them on a charge of high treason and they were beheaded in Tewkesbury market place.

Margaret of Anjou with her young daughter-in-law had gone for shelter sixteen miles away to Little Malvern Priory. Here she was brought the dreadful news of her son's death. From the time of her arrival in England as the bride of Henry VI, she had been recognized as high-spirited and imperious to an overpowering degree. Haughty and savage, vindictive and courageous, it was her maniacal determination that had kept the Lancastrian cause alive, so that Prince Edward of Lancaster might one day succeed to his feeble father's throne. No enemy, no crisis had ever found her anything but passionate and ferocious. Now, she sent word to Edward that she was 'at his commandment'.

The victory at Tewkesbury was decisive, but it was not quite the end of Lancastrian resistance. An illegitimate cousin of the Nevilles, known as the Bastard of Faulconbridge, had been given command of the ships in the Channel by Warwick, to intercept any aid that might be sent to Edward from Burgundy. He now landed his men at Sandwich, marched through Kent, receiving an accession of support at Canterbury, and came up to London Bridge from which he was repulsed by the London citizens.

Elizabeth Woodville, a second time threatened with danger, in the absence of her husband, had left Baynard's Castle with her children and retired into the Tower. Before, she had been frightened out of this fortress by the approach of Warwick and Clarence, who had declared that they were coming to restore King Henry VI; as the wife of a usurper, she had felt herself in great danger and had fled into sanctuary. Now, Warwick was dead, Clarence reconciled and her husband victorious; she had received his gauntlet by a messenger as a sign that the victory of Tewkesbury was his; the future was bright but the immediate present was somewhat dangerous; the Tower was the safest place, and she returned to the royal apartments there, with her three daughters and her invaluable baby son. With her, this time, was her brother Antony Rivers; unlike his brother-in-law, he was not a distinguished soldier but he had had some military experience, and his presence must have afforded some comfort. To those in the Tower, the sounds of Faulconbridge's approach were plainly heard. Fabyan says, that when his 'riotous and evil-disposed

* *History of the Arrival of King Edward IV*, ed. John Bruce, 1838.

74

company of shipmen and others', had been refused entry to the city, 'they set upon divers parts thereof, as Bishopsgate, Aldgate, London Bridge and along the waterside, and shot guns and arrows and fired the gates with cruel malice . . . and fought so fiercely that they won the bulwarks at Aldgate and entered a certain way within the gate'.

At this very time, across the city on the western wall, a Lancastrian knight was in the prison of Newgate. He had been excluded by name from a general pardon issued by Edward IV in 1468, and was wiling away the tedium and wretchedness of imprisonment by writing one of the great books in the English language. Sir Thomas Malory was working on material supplied by French and English texts of the past two centuries, but when he drew the scenes of Arthur's court, he imagined the Tower, the Palace of Westminster, the Thames, of his own time. As he finished the book 'in the 9th year of the reign of King Edward IV—' i.e. between March 4, 1469, and March 4, 1470, some of his descriptions, though not of actual events, are vivid, illustrations of the contemporary scene. His knights are in the plate armour worn by those of Edward IV, and it might have been said of Tewkesbury, 'they came in so fiercely, that the strokes resounded again from the wood and the water'. The chronicler's account of the Bastard's men shooting guns and arrows at the gates in the wall just west of the Tower is illuminated by Malory's saying: 'Sir Modred, . . . a short tale to make . . . went and laid a mighty siege about the Tower of London and made many great assaults thereat and threw many great engines unto them, and shot great guns' (*Morte d'Arthur*, Bk XXI, chap. 1). This was on another occasion when there was a queen in the Tower. Guinevere had taken refuge there.

The butcher William Gould who had supplied the Queen's party with beef and mutton while she was in sanctuary, had prepared to victual the Tower for her also. The King said in an ordinance decreeing a reward to him, that 'after our field of Tewkesbury, at her being in the Tower, he brought one hundred oxen into a meadow beside our Tower for the killing of the same, whereat the Kentish men and other at times our rebels, shipmen, took of the said beasts fifty and led away . . . to his great hurt and damage'.* What Edward called 'the meadow beside our Tower', would seem to be the stretch of field outside the Postern gate, lying behind the Tower and extending to the range of open fields called Stepney.

The two attempts of the Bastard's men—at crossing London Bridge, and at descending on the west part of the city by landing at Kingston on Thames—might have proved dangerous by encouraging a discontented rabble within the walls, who, as the author of *The Arrival* says, 'would have been right glad of a common robbery, that they might put their hands in rich men's coffers'; but they were repulsed by the citizens at

* Ellis, *Original Letters*, I, Vol. II, p. 140.

the first one, and gave up the second before they had brought it to anything. Their assault on the gates in the eastern wall was finally driven off
by a force of the city train bands under the Recorder of London and
by the garrison led out by the Lieutenant of the Tower. Lord Rivers
then issued from the Postern gate with a body of troops and pursued
the rebels across the fields to the out-lying district of Stepney. Dispersed,
they took to their ships again.

The battles of Barnet and Tewkesbury behind him, on May 21, 1471,
Edward made a second triumphal entry into London. Coming in from
Coventry, approaching the city on its northern boundary, he paused at
Islington, where he knighted the Lord Mayor of London, the Recorder
and eleven aldermen. Then he came on in a procession such as the people
had never seen. He was preceded by blowers of trumpets and clarions,
while his own standards and banners and those captured from his enemies,
thronged the air. The most important and spectacular position in a
procession was the last, and the chief figure on this occasion was preceded
by a body of troops, six earls and sixteen barons and the Dukes of
Norfolk, Suffolk and Buckingham; but before the King himself, accompanied by the Dukes of Clarence and Gloucester 'came royally riding',
another member of the procession was borne in front of him. The head
of his father, crowned with paper, had once hung grinning and withering
above the Micklegate Bar. The head was now buried but not the memory
of it. In an open chariot, under the eyes of hostile and jeering Londoners,
Margaret of Anjou was paraded.*

* C. L. Kingsford, *English Historical Literature in the XV C.*, p. 375.

14

THE Tower was a royal residence and a place of detention for important prisoners, and one or other of its scaffolds, on Tower Hill or on the pavement outside the chapel of St. Peter ad Vincula, was the usual place of execution for criminals of high standing. Such beheadings were performed in the open air, before a crowd of spectators, and though a moving and dreadful sight, were at least free from the terrors of mystery and silence; but there were deaths which were terrifying because of the darkness in which they were shrouded. On October 23, 1399, a meeting had been called of the Lords in Parliament to determine what should be done with the deposed Richard II. First, the conclave listened while it was charged by the Archbishop of Canterbury to keep silent on its findings; then it decided by a majority vote that Richard should be removed to a place from which no mob could rescue him, and no former member of his household should have access to him. He was to be condemned to perpetual imprisonment and the place of his custody should be secret. On the night of October 28, the king was disguised in a forester's dress and hood, and under cover of darkness was taken down the river to Gravesend; from there he was conveyed to Leeds Castle in Kent, and thence to Yorkshire, to Pontefract. By the end of January, 1400, he was known to be dead.* Compared with this, the fate of Charles I was enviable, tried publicly in Westminster Hall and executed on a scaffold put up in a London street, in a radiance of immortal glory.

Edward's entry into London was made on Tuesday, May 21, 1471. That night Henry VI was put to death in the Tower. While his son Prince Edward of Lancaster lived, the Yorkists would gain no advantage from putting Henry VI to death; but from the hour of the Prince's death at Tewkesbury, his father was as good as dead also. Several chroniclers repeated that Gloucester had been responsible for King Henry's death; it is now generally accepted that there is no proof of this. Warkworth says the murder was committed that night, 'in a place apart', 'the Duke of Gloucester being then at the Tower with many others'; but whoever were there, the prime responsibility for the deed must rest with Edward IV. The octagon chamber on the first floor of the Wakefield Tower was

* Jacob, E. F., *The XV Century*, pp. 22–3.

the place in which, except for the brief interval of his re-adoption, Henry had been confined for the past six years, with a chaplain to say divine service for him twice a day, a few books and the society of such approved people as cared to visit him. Within this chamber was an oratory which could be entered from the royal apartments. It was more than probable that someone coming from these apartments in search of him should find him in this 'place apart'. The tradition of the Tower is that this is where he met his death. When his bones were exhumed in 1910 it was found that those of the skull had been 'much broken'.* The writer of *The Arrival of Edward IV*, who wrote his account within three weeks of the battle of Tewkesbury, a French translation of which was sent by Edward IV to the Burgundian court as his official communiqué, had absolved Edward, first, of the reproach of violating sanctuary, and secondly of procuring the death of Henry VI, who, the writer declared, died that night in the Tower 'of pure displeasure and melancholy'. This explanation did not cover the fact that when King Henry's body was being carried for burial at Chertsey Monastery, and was deposited on the way, once in St. Paul's and once in the abbey church at Blackfriars, on each occasion it bled on the pavement.

On June 24, 1471, a sum was paid to Hugh Brice the king's goldsmith, for 'wax, linen, spices and other ordinary expenses incurred for the burial of the said Henry of Windsor who died within the Tower of London, and for wages and rewards to divers men carrying torches from the Tower . . . to the Cathedral church of St. Paul's, London, and from thence accompanying the body to Chertsey'.† Henry VI was nature's victim as well as man's. For the last years of his life he was despised, dirty, half-witted. It comes as an awe-inspiring surprise when, in all the beauty and solemnity of the Festival of the Nine Carols, sung by candlelight in King's College Chapel on Christmas Eve, his memory is celebrated for the 'royal and religious foundations of Eton College and King's College'. If, in prison, he had foreseen his death in a place apart, and his corpse bleeding on a church pavement, he would still have composed the 'Devout Prayer of King Henry VI'; 'Oh Lord Jesus Christ, who hast created and redeemed me, and hast brought me hither where I am, Thou knowest what Thou would'st do with me; do with me according to Thy will, in mercy. Amen.'‡

Edward had now, it appeared, cleared from his path all claimants to his throne, and his Queen had produced the heir male, whom his father called 'God's precious sonde, [sending] and gift, and our most desired treasure'.§ The child was created Prince of Wales early in 1471, and to

* *Archeologica*, Vol. LXXXIV.
† Pell Records, *Issues of the Exchequer*, 1471.
‡ *Kings' College Chapel: A Short Guide*.
§ *Letters of the Kings of England*, Vol. I, ed. J. O. Halliwell.

make assurance double sure, on July 3 of that year, the King arranged for an oath of loyalty to his son to be administered to the Great Council: 'I acknowledge, take and repute you, Edward Prince of Wales, Duke of Cornwall and Earl of Chester, first begotten son of our sovereign Lord, Edward IV, to be very and undoubted heir to our said sovereign Lord . . . and promise and swear that in case it hereafter happen to you . . . to overlive our said sovereign Lord, I shall then take and accept you for true, very and rightwise King of England, and faith and truth to you shall bear and in all things truly and faithfully behave me towards you and your heirs as a true and faithful subject oweth to behave him to his sovereign Lord and rightwise King of England'.* The terms of the oath admitted the validity of the child's claim to suceed his father and vowed to support it. Among the signatures stood those of—G. Clarence, R. Gloucestre, H. Bukinghame.

But Jasper Tudor who had been ready to join forces with Margaret of Anjou if she could have reached him, now decided that it was safer for his nephew, the fourteen year old Henry Tudor, to be across the sea. His mother, the Lady Margaret Beaufort, had, for the last twelve years, been married to Henry Stafford, the late Duke of Buckingham's younger brother. She seems to have seen very little of her enigmatical young son, but she always maintained a keen interest in his welfare and his prospects, and it was said that it was she who now encouraged Jasper Tudor to take him abroad. In the summer of 1471, the uncle took his nephew to the court of the Duke of Brittany.

The Queen meanwhile established a chantry chapel in Westminster Abbey. Her son had been safely delivered and her husband had returned to her across the sea. She dedicated the chapel to Saint Erasmus, one of the Fourteen Holy Helpers, who had under his special protection, seafarers and children. Some twenty years later, Fortune's wheel had turned again with dreadful effect and the chapel of St. Erasmus was demolished to clear a site for the Chapel of King Henry VII.

Royal children were very early provided with a separate household and residence of their own, but the eight months old Prince was still in his mother's care. A large staff of attendants waited on him. Ten years afterwards, two of them were still being pensioned with imports of wine— Elizabeth Darcy, 'lady mistress of the King's nursery, for her good services to the King and his consort the Queen and his son the Prince, a grant for life of a tun of wine yearly in the Port of London', and Avice Wells, widow, 'nurse to the King's first born son, Edward Prince of Wales, a grant for life of one tun or two pipes of wine yearly at Christmas in the Port of Bristol'. Besides female nurses, the Prince had a male attendant. The King appointed Thomas Vaughan, a personal servant of his own, to be the Prince of Wales' chamberlain. Vaughan filled this post to the

* Rymer, *Foedera XI*, p. 714.

end of their joint lives but when he first took it up, his duties included those of a nurse; he carried the little Prince in his arms at public functions.

Warwick had died himself in his struggles to regain his ascendancy but he had managed first to put out of the way two of the Woodvilles, Lord Rivers and his youngest son. The remainder of the family now returned to influence, power and pleasure. They were thoroughly congenial to Edward and as they were not, with one exception, of any personal capacity, and owed their good living entirely to his favour, Edward could count on their loyalty with confidence. Whether faithful to her or not, he was still enamoured of the Queen; he had made her pregnant again by August. Her elder son by her first marriage, Thomas Grey, had inherited the title his father had not lived to take, that of Lord Ferrers of Groby, and in the year of his return Edward created him Earl of Huntingdon. He, and his younger brother Richard, and the Queen's brother Sir Edward Woodville were known as the companions of the King in his cheerful debauchery. Her brother Lionel, however, was in orders and in the way of ecclesiastical promotion. Mancini says of the former three, 'They were certainly detested by the nobles because they, who were ignoble and newly-made men, were advanced beyond those who far excelled them in breeding and wisdom'.* This general accusation leaves out the member of the family who could, if chance had allowed, have been really formidable. Antony Woodville Lord Scales, on his father's death had become Lord Rivers. Cool, supercilious and sly, he was as determined as his relatives to enjoy wealth and power, but he combined these desires with a graceful, pensive exterior; how misleading this was Mancini showed when he called him 'a kind, serious, just man'. Edward relied on his capability and trustworthiness in one highly important particular: Rivers was presently to be entrusted with the post of Governor of the Prince of Wales and head of his household; but while giving him credit for the qualities he had, the King had not much personal liking for a character so essentially different from his own and those of his chosen friends, although the coolness and reserve which was shared by the brother and sister had made part of the naiad-like charm which Edward had found irresistible in the latter.

While Warwick was still in power and had the post of Captain of Calais, Edward had appointed Rivers Lieutenant. Then he himself had been obliged to fly the country. When Rivers had played his part in dispersing the rebels led by Faulconbridge, he announced that he meant to go on a crusade against the Saracens. This term was used to cover all Mohammedans. The Turks had been left in possession of Jerusalem since the capture of Acre in 1291, and were masters of Constantinople which they had sacked in 1453; but any enterprise directed against them, such as helping the Venetians to repel them from the Venetian spheres

* Mancini, *op. cit.*

of influence was called a crusade. The realm was not altogether in quiet and John Paston wrote on July 5, 1471: 'The King is not best pleased with him for that he desireth to depart, in so much that the King hath said of him, that whenever he hath most to do, then the Lord Scales will soonest ask leave to depart, and weeneth that it is most because of cowardice.' Paston said that he thanked his mother for nothing in that she had persuaded Lord Scales to give him his protection; Paston had no opinion of Scales' influence with the King: 'He may do least with the Great Master'. As it turned out, Rivers decided not to go against the Saracens, but Edward, either having believed that he was about to go, or thinking better of appointing him to a post that required so much practical ability, cancelled his appointment and bestowed it on William Lord Hastings, his chamberlain and dearest friend, of whose fitness there could be no doubt. Rivers was very angry, and her brother's disappointment increased the Queen's enmity to Hastings to a dangerous pitch. It was said that she was hostile to him because he was a promoter of Edward's pleasures with other women. It was not her policy to show anger to her husband or to make scenes in an attempt to interfere with his amusements, but this very restraint towards the King may have intensified her venom towards the man who was, she considered, a party to injuring her. Rivers himself was not helpless; he had the King's ear, and he managed to carry his revenge so far as to create a dangerous though short-lived suspicion in Edward's mind as to Hastings' loyalty. Edward had once been too generously careless when he had been given grounds for suspecting Warwick, and since his return he had been altogether more cautious. The body of armed retainers which Hastings maintained may have given Rivers grounds for his attack; whatever the grounds were, he threw himself into the work; among the papers of his secretary Dymmock there were afterwards found four copies of an informer's deposition against Hastings. During the brief time that Hastings knew he was under the King's suspicion, he met, on Tower Wharf, a pursuivant of his own, whose name was also Hastings, and stopped for the relief of his mind in friendly talk with him. More said that Hastings was 'easy to beguile, as he who of good heart and courage fore-studied no perils. A loving man and passing well beloved; very faithful and trusty enough; trusting too much'. At this meeting, Hastings, standing under the very walls of the Tower, told his pursuivant, as a less ingenuous and open-hearted man of his rank would scarcely have done, of the danger which the malignity of the Queen and her relatives had brought him into, and of his keen anxiety for his own safety. As he spoke, he was within a few paces of the moat which separated the wharf from the curtain wall of the Tower, overlooked by the royal lodgings which his ill-wisher the Queen occupied with so much elegance and splendour. To the left of the Tower ran Thames Street, on the level of the shore.

Mancini said that there were three principal streets in the city: Thames Street, where the cranes stood and the warehouses for wines, honey, pitch, flax, tow, ropes, thread and minerals. Above this and parallel with it ran Candlewick Street, where cloth of all kinds was sold, and above this again, on higher ground, was Cheapside where the shops stood that sold precious wares, gold and silver cups, jewellery, silks, carpets and tapestries. The area between the Tower and Westminster was noisy and humming with activity; but part of Thames Street ran through the Vintry Ward; Stow said that here were large, old, stone houses. Among them, Rivers had his town house; it stood conveniently near to the Queen's town house, Ormonde's Inn. For Hastings, the neighbourhood was charged with menace.

Whatever grounds for suspicion had been put into the King's head, Edward soon dismissed them, and Hastings was restored to his usual close intimacy and favour, but it was clear that the episode had given him a severe fright. Mancini said: 'Edward was of a gentle nature and cheerful aspect; nevertheless should he assume an angry countenance, he could appear very terrible to the beholders'.* A change had been noticed in the King after his return; he had become altogether more formidable.

* Mancini, *op. cit.*

15

THE year of the return was however, marked with joyful ceremonies. In September he and the Queen made a pilgrimage to Canterbury. The cathedral shone with some of the most brilliant and beautiful stained glass in Europe, but the shrine of St. Thomas à Becket was more brilliant still; covered with plates of gold and studded with precious stones placed there as offerings, till the shrine had become 'like starlight, hid with jewels'. In front of it, the knees of pilgrims had worn a slight but perceptible hollow in the marble floor. The occasion was made one of general thanksgiving. Sir John Paston wrote: 'The King and Queen and much other people are ridden and gone to Canterbury; never so much people was seen in pilgrimage heretofore at once, as men say'.*

The conclusion of the year 1471 was especially festal. An account by Blue Mantle Pursuivant† says: '1471. Christmas Day, the King our Sovereign Lord Edward IV after the conquest, was crowned‡ at Westminster and the Queen also. He kept his estate in the Whitehall the same day'. In other words, the King in the large presence chamber, the Whitehall, sat on a chair on a dais under a canopy, for all who liked to see him. Being seen, to great advantage, was an important function of sovereignty which Edward was well fitted to carry out.

The Queen had worn her crown on Christmas Day but when they went in procession to the Abbey on Twelfth Day, January 6, the King was crowned, 'the Queen not crowned because she was great with child'.§ At her coronation mass her mother had relieved her of some of the weight of the crown by holding it on her head; at her coronation banquet she herself had taken it off while she ate; now in the sixth month of pregnancy the weight of solid gold and jewels was too much for her to support as she walked in procession. On April 19, the child was born, another girl, the Princess Margaret. The following month 'Dr. Dominic Serego, physician to the King and his consort Elizabeth Queen of England', was paid £150. He should have received £120 from a tax on sweet wines

* Paston, *Letters*, Vol. III, ed. Gairdner, 1900, no. 676.
† Kingsford, C. L., *Historical Literature of the XVth Century*, p. 379.
‡ i.e., wore his crown.
§ Kingsford, *op. cit.*, p. 379.

imported from Venice, but the carrack that was bringing them in had been captured by French pirates. He was now paid the £120 owed to him by the grant and £30 'for regard and salary'.* In spite of his having misled the King by his prophecy that the first royal child would be a boy, Serego must have had sufficient purely medical skill to retain the King's and the Queen's confidence.

Edward had not lost his hearty, easy-going approach but the power of taking surprisingly rapid action, which he had shown in the field at Mortimer's Cross and Tewkesbury he was now developing in the political sphere. With Warwick and Montagu dead, the only important member of the Neville family on the scene was their surviving brother, George Neville, Archbishop of York. His relations with the King had been chequered: Edward had deprived him of the Great Seal, and he had taken Edward into captivity when Warwick had ignited the rebellion of 1469; but it had seemed that in spite of the high treason of his brothers, he was safely restored to the King's favour. There was however a connection between him and the not entirely extinguished Lancastrian cause. One of his sisters, Catherine, was married to William Lord Hastings, but another, Margaret, was the Earl of Oxford's wife. Oxford, a Lancastrian supporter, encouraged by Louis XI to stir up the embers of trouble for the Yorkist King, was conducting raids on the English territory outside Calais. Edward would seem to have had information of the Archbishop's complicity with Oxford, and even to have had some suspicion that Clarence might be involved with them.† He made no public accusation but on April 25, 1472, when the Archbishop was actually expecting the King to visit him at his house in Hertfordshire, The Moor, for a hunting party, he was suddenly placed under arrest and taken across the Channel to the fortress of Hammes in the marches of Calais, where he was kept imprisoned for the next two years. When he was released to return to England in 1474, his health and spirits were so broken that he died two years later. Edward meantime sent down the Comptroller of the Royal Household, Sir William Parr, and the Prince of Wales' Chamberlain, Thomas Vaughan, to the Moor, to confiscate the Archbishop's immense personal treasure, which Warkworth says, had been amassed 'through his great covetousness'. The jewels and plate the King put aside for the Prince of Wales, but he performed one act which had not only a material value but a symbolic significance. The Archbishop's mitre, said Warkworth, was set 'with many and rich stones'. Edward had it broken up and the jewels re-set as a crown for himself.

The public emphasis on the royalty of the House of York continued in splendour. When the oath of allegiance to Prince Edward had been taken in the previous July, the child had already been styled Prince of Wales,

* Calendar of the Patent Rolls, May 8, 1472.
† Ross, Edward IV, pp. 191, 192.

but the ceremony of investiture was not performed till May 1472. The magnificent scene, created for the baby of nine months old, was enhanced by music. On May 16, Thomas Vaughan was given £20 to pay out 'from the Lord King, to his heralds and minstrels, on the day of the creation of my Lord Prince'.*

In May 1472 the Duchess of Bedford died. Fascinating but not of good repute, she had had alternatively a successful and harassing existence. She had managed, with a high degree of adroitness, her daughter's secret marriage and its secret consummation. She had kept a vigilant eye on her daughter's well-being, supporting the crown in her hands so that Elizabeth should not suffer from its weight at her coronation mass. She had watched the rising prosperity of her other children, of whom Antony Woodville seemed, after his sister, the one most to have repaid her care. She and her brood had long been recognized as being on the make, but it was her impudent and horrible rapacity over the goods of Sir Thomas Cook that had indelibly stamped her reputation. She had not come off scatheless; her husband and her youngest son had had their heads cut off, and an attempt had been made to indict her on the highly dangerous charge of witchcraft. There were few people to speak well of her but as a mother she had done her best, according to her lights, and on one occasion at least she must have been of the greatest use; when Elizabeth fled into sanctuary on the night of October 1, 1470, her mother went with her, no doubt from motives of self-protection, but she was therefore present at the childbirth in that scene of misery and privation in the sanctuary hold, and must have had on her hands the care of three grand-daughters, Elizabeth aged five, Mary, four and Cecily, one. It was fortunate for her that she lived to see her daughter restored to the position of Queen of England and the baby who had been born in sanctuary, created Prince of Wales; it was fortunate for her also that she died at the best time.

The second part of Edward's reign was largely free from rebellion and strife, except in the north where his young brother Richard, now twenty years old, lived a dedicated life as England's vigilant protector against the Scots. The King himself devoted his great practical intelligence to building up the wealth, and therefore the power, of the crown. It has been said that Edward was the first monarch to apply to the organization of the crown lands the methods by which competent landowners administered their private estates. The King was the greatest landowner in his realm, and his domains had been increased by the estates of attainted Lancastrians. An efficient, thorough-going system of surveyors, receivers and auditors was instituted, under a set of educated, experienced and able men, who retrieved the income of the royal domains from the waste and ruin of the years of Henry VI. This picture of the King and his

* Pell Records, *Issues of the Exchequer*, May 16, 1472.

doings is given by the authority known as the Second Continuator of the Croyland Chronicler, now accepted as Dr. John Russell, Bishop of Lincoln, in whose diocese the Abbey of Croyland lay.* From his experience as a doctor of canon law, a royal councillor, Edward IV's Keeper of the Privy Seal and Richard III's Lord Chancellor, his relation of affairs from 1471–1483 is of unique value. Besides a businesslike attitude to the management of his territorial possessions, Edward had an instinct and an enthusiasm for commerce. He traded in wool, cloth, pewter vessels and blocks of tin; he also imported, 'exchanging goods for goods' as the Continuator of the Chronicle of Croyland said, 'with the Italians and the Greeks, through his factors'. Among the wares he imported were woad, alum, wax, writing paper and wine. His relations with the City of London were excellent, and the city being the most important trading centre in the kingdom, it is interesting to see that in the *Great Chronicle*, supposed to be Fabyan's work, when he notes who were aldermen of the City of London in a particular year, they were mercers, grocers, drapers, haberdashers, goldsmiths, salters, fishmongers. The crown owned a few ships, and Edward began the expansion of the royal navy by buying more. The first of these was the *Antony* which he bought from her master, the ship which had brought him back to England. He was a magnificent builder; the greatest of his buildings were for pleasure and glory: the great hall of Eltham Palace begun in 1475, St. George's Chapel at Windsor begun in 1478; of his purely domestic works, those at Fotheringhay and Westminster were in the nature of alterations for comfort, but his addition to Nottingham Castle must have been one of the most beautiful of all the domestic works in fifteenth-century gothic, which, in complete contrast to the Norman architecture of massive walls and slit-windows, was one of 'reduced bulk and surface for the benefit of luminosity', 'the philosophy of light'. This was a central polygonal tower, with, Leland said, 'marvellous fair windows and chambers'. An idea of it may be gained from pictures of the polygonal chapel on London Bridge, with its lofty windows on two storeys, but the lower of these was on water-level. Nottingham Castle stands aloft on a great mound, and the airiness, transparency and light of the central tower must have been amazing.

Edward has been accused, justly, of avarice, but a humanizing element in his greed was that he so much enjoyed spending money. Austerity and simplicity were tasteless to him. 'The sun in splendour' and 'The rose en-soleil' were not only his devices: they were vivid expressions of his personality. The Continuator of the Croyland Chronicle said that for collecting rich objects—gold and silver vessels, tapestries and precious ornaments—he was unequalled by his predecessors. Beauty and value were united in his possessions. His taste was for the beautiful thing, and the beautiful thing cost a great deal of money. Before his re-conquest

* Ross, *op. cit.*, Appendix I, p. 430.

86

he had borrowed £200 from Cardinal Bourchier, giving as a pledge two sacred books and a gold drinking cup. These he redeemed in 1472. The books were 'covered with gold and jacinths'. The flame-coloured jewels on a background of gold must have given the book-covers the richness of a sunset. When the gold cup was in his hands again, Edward saw how it might be improved. He ordered Brice the goldsmith to set a large ruby in the knop, the ball that united the base of the chalice with the stem.*

Everything of richness and splendour that he could command was mustered in September 1472, to entertain a guest to whom he owed an immense debt of gratitude—Louis of Bruges, Lord of Gruthuyse, who had welcomed him and protected him and his following, supporting him until it was safe for Charles of Burgundy to receive him, his generous rescuer and friend.

Gruthuyse arrived at Windsor at the end of September. Hastings already knew the guest, for he had been with the King's party when they took refuge in Sluys, 'the most distressed company of creatures that ever was seen', as Commines said. Now, as Edward's Lord Chamberlain he welcomed their benefactor in the King's name. On the far side of the Castle quadrangle the King and Queen were awaiting him in a suite of rooms hung with arras of cloth of gold. He dined with Lord Hastings and after dinner the latter conducted him to a family evening in the Queen's Chamber of Pleasance, where she and her ladies were playing, some of them at carpet bowls, some at ninepins, with 'closheys' of ivory. There was dancing, and in one of the dances the King, in his great height, fairness and splendid dress danced with his six year old daughter, the Princess Elizabeth.

Next morning, after mass and breakfast the King greeted his guest in the quadrangle and 'my Lord Prince' was present also, 'borne by his chamberlain Mr. Vaughan'. From Vaughan's arms, the Prince 'bade the foresaid Lord Gruthuyse welcome'. The day was spent hunting in Windsor Great Park; Gruthuyse rode the King's horse and the King gave him a magnificent crossbow with silk strings in a velvet case, the arrows to which were gilt-headed. They ate their dinner at a lodge in the park, and towards evening the King brought him back to the Castle through the gardens, showing him the Vineyard of Pleasure where vines were trained on trellises. That night the Queen gave a great banquet for him in her own apartments; again there was dancing and the little Princess danced with her uncle by marriage, the eighteen year old Duke of Buckingham. At about nine o'clock the King and the Queen attended by her ladies and gentlewomen, brought him to a suite of three rooms which had been prepared for him. (It seems strange that he had not been shown into them on his first arrival; the narrative of Blue Mantle Pursuivant which is in two parts, places the doings of September after

* Pell Records, *Issues of the Exchequer*, 1472, p. 498.

those of October, and it may be that passages inside the two sections have become transposed.) The rooms were hung with white silk and each floor was carpeted. In the first room was the guest's bed, with sheets of Rennes linen and a counterpane of cloth of gold furred with ermine; the canopy was 'shining cloth of gold', the curtains of white sarcenet. The Queen herself had seen to the bedding; 'his bed-sheets and pillows were of the Queen's own ordering'. The next room also contained a bed, draped all in white, and a couch piled with down cushions, 'hanged above like a tent, knit like a net'. The third room was a bathroom; it had two baths in it, covered with tents of white cloth. The King and Queen then withdrew, leaving the visitor with Hastings who helped him to undress; they took their baths together, and when they had sat in them as long as they liked, they were brought green ginger, syrups, comfits and ypocras, a light, sweet wine.*

The chief honour to be paid to Gruthuyse was his creation as Earl of Winchester. This took place at Westminster on the Feast of St. Edward, October 13. On this day the King 'kept his estate in his Palace of West-Minster, then he came into the Parliament chamber wearing his cap of maintenance and his parliament robes'. Edward IV was frequently described as wearing these garments, on ceremonial occasions, and it is very interesting to see him in them in the miniature at the head of Waurin's *Anciennes et Nouvelles Cronicques d'Angleterre*, which shows the author kneeling to present his work to the King who sits in a canopied chair on a dais, wearing the velvet cap of maintenance with a very broad ermine border, and a robe stamped with gold fleurs de lys with a deep ermine collar.

In the Parliament chamber the Commons said they wanted specially to commend 'the womanly behaviour of our Sovereign Lady the Queen, the King being beyond the sea. Also the great joy and surety to this his land, the birth of my Lord the Prince.'

The investiture of the Earl of Winchester was to take place in the Chapel of St. Stephen, and Gruthuyse was taken into the Chapel of Our Lady of the Piewe, where he was helped 'to vest himself as an earl'. Then the King entered, robed and crowned, his train borne by the Duke of Clarence. The two royal brothers must have made a splendid appearance, even against the brilliant scene of St. Stephen's Chapel. When the stately ceremony was done, the party went back to the Whitehall of Westminster Palace where they were joined by the Queen, crowned, and 'my Lord Prince in his robes of estate', whom Mr. Vaughan carried, walking immediately behind the King. They all proceeded to the Abbey and so up to the shrine of St. Edward the Confessor, where they made their offering.

The next occasion noted in that year which took place in the Chapel

* C. L. Kingsford, *English Historical Literature in the XVth Century*, pp. 385–7.

88

of the Confessor was an entombment. On December 11, the eight months old Princess Margaret died. In the semicircle of royal tombs with their recumbent gilded effigies, a very small grey marble sarcophagus* was placed, at the head of Edward III and the feet of Richard II. A brass plate, since wrenched away by thieves, was engraved with the name and age of the Princess and a Latin epitaph, saying: 'Nobility and beauty, grace and tender youth, are all hidden here in this chest of death.'† The lines did not add that death in infancy was not the worst fate that could befall the child of a king.

* *Gentleman's Magazine*, January, 1831.
† *Lives of the Princesses of England*, M. A. E. Green.

16

THE strain and stress of maintaining York over Lancaster was largely over for Edward IV by 1472; what overshadowed his splendid existence was the split in the family of York itself. For the next six years a feud was in existence between his brothers Clarence and Gloucester, and between Clarence and himself. Clarence, already dowered with wide estates and very wealthy, and with a shocking record of treachery to his king, set himself up as a savagely greedy attacker of rewards bestowed on his loyal and steadfast younger brother. Clarence would never forget that during his alliance with Warwick and Margaret of Anjou, it had been settled that if Prince Edward of Lancaster and Anne Neville had no heirs, he himself should succeed to the English crown. An act of Parliament had confirmed his so-called rights. Since Prince Edward had died childless, Clarence, oblivious of the claims of his own family, the house of York, which implied the right to the crown of his elder brother, appeared to consider that he, Clarence, ought now to be recognised as King of England. He did not assert the claim in public, but it was known, or at least strongly suspected that he harboured it, and it seemed to colour all his dealings. If Clarence had been less of a fool, the pretension would have been very dangerous; as it was, it created a situation that many rulers would have ended in summary fashion; but Edward had not only a great deal of family affection: he had also the self-confidence that made him feel able to deal with and control any personal situation. His tolerance was in the end deceptive. Nine times out of ten, it is not dangerous to annoy a good-tempered animal. The tenth time it will be dangerous, if the animal is a lion.

The greatest heiresses in the land were Warwick's daughters, Isabella Duchess of Clarence and Anne, widow of Prince Edward of Lancaster. As the latter's husband had been killed in action against Edward IV, Clarence assumed that all her domains would be forfeit, and would fall to his share as well as his wife's inheritance. The two shares together would make him master of a vast territory, but even so, not wide enough for a man who ought to be King of England. Richard of Gloucester was twenty and unmarried. He had a bastard son and daughter by different mothers: John of Gloucester and Catherine Plantagenet, and it was natural and right that he should now marry. He and Anne Neville had known each other as children; at the banquet for the enthronization of Archbishop Neville, they had sat at the same table. Anne, now sixteen years of age, was frail; she died of consumption at twenty-nine, but the writer of the Rows Roll, celebrating the family of the Earl of Warwick, says that she was 'seemly, amiable and beauteous, according to the interpretation of her name: full gracious'. Richard, a young man of reserve and courage, intense, highly strung and of very strong personality, was a husband who naturally gained an influence over the girl who married him. The story of a passionate romance between them rests on nothing, but the little evidence there is of their relationship suggests that it was a happy one.

As it has been pointed out, the over-riding motive for the match was its high material advantage to both of them. Anne Neville's inheritance made her the most eligible bride in England for the Duke of Gloucester, and the Duke of Gloucester was the only husband strong enough to protect her property from her rapacious brother-in-law. Even Gloucester found this a formidable task.

When Tewkesbury had been fought, Margaret of Anjou and Anne Neville were found in the Priory of Little Malvern and brought to Edward at Coventry. After the dreadful exhibition of her in Edward's triumphal entry into London, Margaret was lodged in the Tower. What happened to Anne is recounted only by the Croyland Continuator, who says that Clarence, to hide her from his brother, persuaded her to disguise herself as a cook-maid in a London house, that Gloucester discovered her there and removed her to St. Martin le Grand, the most important sanctuary in London after that of Westminster.

It was soon known that Gloucester meant to make this marriage and that it was a matter of dispute in the royal family. In February 1472, the King and Queen and the two Dukes were at the Queen's palace at Sheen; the royal party went to confession and on February 17 Sir John Paston wrote: 'Yesterday the King and Queen and my Lords of Clarence and Gloucester went to Sheen, to pardon, men say, not all in charity; what will fall, men cannot say. The King entreateth with my Lord of Clarence for my Lord of Gloucester and, as it is said, he answereth, that he may well have my lady his sister-in-law, but they shall part no livelode'. Gloucester did not wait to marry for adjudication on the inheritance; he and Anne Neville were married at Westminster on some date in February or March, 1472. He did not even wait for the papal dispensation necessary for the marriage of cousins. As the marriage therefore was not strictly legal according to canon law, the settlement covered this in the complicated matter of the inheritance; it stated that if he were to be divorced from his wife, the lands should remain his, given that he attempted to re-marry her, and did not marry anybody else. This has sometimes been unjustly twisted into an accusation that Richard provided for the getting rid of his wife even in the moment of marrying her.

The dispute went on; the Croyland Continuator gives a reminder of something apt to be overlooked: of how extremely able the Yorkist brothers were, even Clarence, when they applied themselves to a mental problem. He says: 'Such violent dissensions arose between the brothers and so many arguments were, with the greatest acuteness, put forward on either side, in the King's presence, who sat in judgment in the Council Chamber, that all present, and the lawyers even, were quite surprised that these princes should find arguments in such abundance to support their respective causes.' The brothers' talents were so great, he says, if only they could have lived in agreement they would have formed a triple cord almost impossible to break.

On March 18, Clarence was promised perpetual possession of the forfeited lands of Courtenay, Earl of Devon. Gloucester was to have the Lordships of Middleham and Sherrif Hutton in Yorkshire and Penrith in Westmorland. He also received the estates forfeited by John de Vere, Earl of Oxford, in the eastern counties, fifty manors in all. Clarence was granted the earldoms of Salisbury and Warwick, Warwick's manor in Essex and his town house, the Erber, a fourteenth-century stone building off Carter Lane and near London Stone. Gloucester, on the restoration, had been appointed Great Chamberlain. This office he now consented to give up, that it might be bestowed on the snarling Clarence. A point of great importance arose on the matter of the largest part of the Warwick lands: the Midland estates that the widowed Countess of Warwick had inherited from her father Richard Beauchamp, Earl of Warwick, and her mother, Isabel Despenser. The Countess was their legal owner, and from the sanctuary of Beaulieu Abbey she wrote to the King, and to everyone else whom she thought might help to see justice done to her, entreating that her legal ownership should not be set aside in favour of her daughters and their husbands. Her pleas went unheeded, and the Council decided that these rich lands should be divided between the Dukes of Clarence and Gloucester, as if the Countess of Warwick 'were now naturally dead'. This was the earliest of the ruthless appropriations of land in which Edward IV saw no harm. Gloucester tried to behave kindly to his unhappy mother-in-law; when he and his wife went north to Middleham Castle, which, as the Earl of Warwick had done before them, they made their favourite home, he got the King's permission for the Countess to leave Beaulieu and come up to live at Middleham with them. Clarence was angry that permission should have been given. He suspected that Edward might mean to restore the Countess's estates to her, and that she would then confer all of them on Gloucester.

Much of Clarence's enmity was open, and destructive of family comfort; but it is suspected that in 1473 he took, in secret, another of his steps towards high treason. The Earl of Oxford was the last Lancastrian noble attempting to rekindle the energies of resistance, and as such he was cautiously supported by Louis XI. The Earl had made an attempt, in May 1473, to land on the Essex coast and assemble support. He was driven off by the Earl of Essex and he then, in September, seized St. Michael's Mount, the small, rock-based fortress separated at high tide from the south coast of Cornwall. The King's forces went down to the mainland opposite the Mount and prevented supplies from reaching it. Edward IV called on Sir John Arundell, the Sheriff of Cornwall, to attack the Mount and dislodge Oxford and his garrison. The sally was repulsed and Sir John was left for dead on the shore; a 'wise woman' had once prophesied that 'he should be slain in the sands'.* In December the King sent an expedition to reduce the rebels; Oxford capitulated a month later and was granted his life but sent to imprisonment in Hammes Castle, outside Calais. The episode was a small one; its importance lay in the fact that Oxford had been acting with the knowledge if not the aid of Louis XI, and that he had given the French king a list of men in England who could be relied on to support a rising. The list contained the names and seals of twenty-four knights and esquires: and one duke.†

* *National Trust Guide to Trerice, Cornwall*, p. 4.
† Ross, *op. cit.*, p. 192.

17

BUT whatever Clarence might attempt, the influence of the Woodvilles was stronger than ever. The inhabitants of the Welsh marches were not setting up a Lancastrian opposition but they were in a wildly lawless state; robbery and murder were rife and it was thought essential to have a council permanently established in one of the marcher castles, to restore order and maintain it.

Ludlow Castle was a natural choice. On the borders of Shropshire and Herefordshire, ringed with a wall that was entered by seven gates, the town of Ludlow had a strategic importance; it had also a thriving commercial life, and its burgesses owed many of their privileges to the patronage of the House of York. The castle stood above the town; Edward IV's father had inherited it from his uncle Edmund Mortimer, and Edward and his brothers had spent much of their childhood in it. When the Duke of York was defeated at Ludford in 1459, the Lancastrians not only pillaged the castle but destroyed some of its fabric. Edward had had the damage repaired and the castle was now a large, stately but commodious dwelling. Its building had begun in 1085 and, in 1473, it showed the fashions of four centuries. The keep was Norman, so was the circular chapel; the main gateway was fourteenth century, as were the Mortimer Tower and the Pendover Tower; to other buildings, castellated roofs and gothic windows gave an air of modernity and comfort. There were great apartments, presence-chambers decorated with carved stonework, and small, convenient rooms. Sanitation had been thoroughly provided; one tower had a privy on each floor, with a stone seat and a lancet window. The great hall stood high above the river Teme; its windows were relatively narrow, but the innersides were so sloping, that inside the hall the window apertures were large. Beyond the castle, the river Corve ran into the river Teme. Water-meadows, hills and hanging woods surrounded it with exquisite beauty.

In 1473, the three year old Prince of Wales was already playing a part in public life. At the Feast of St George in April the previous year, he had been elected to the Order of the Garter. The next year he had appeared at state functions with his parents, carried by his chamberlain Mr. Vaughan. Edward now decided that the residence of the infant Prince in Ludlow Castle would invest the Council with a charismatic importance. Early in 1473, the Council had been formed and arrangements made for the Prince's large retinue and household. John Alcock, Bishop of Rochester, later to be Bishop of Worcester, was appointed President of the Council. In an era when distinguished politicians were rewarded with church appointments, Dr. Alcock had had a characteristic career of churchmanship and politics. He had been Dean of St. Stephens, Master of the Rolls, Dean of St. Paul's and Privy Councillor. But besides the appointment of President of the Council, he was also given that of tutor to the Prince. Alcock was extremely interested in teaching. He founded a free Grammar School in Hull; he was the Visitor of Peterhouse and endowed the college, but his chief memorial is the foundation of Jesus College, Cambridge. Whether he himself actually taught the child of three is not recorded, but he must have supervised those who did. The Prince was intelligent and by the time he was twelve he was advanced in his studies and had a precocious enjoyment of them. Dr. Alcock's tutoring had been a success.

The Prince's chamberlain Thomas Vaughan remained with him, but otherwise the officers of his household were overpoweringly composed of his mother's family. Her brother Lionel was chaplain; he would scarcely have been able to hold this office for more than five years, except as a titular one, for he was Dean of Exeter in 1478, Chancellor of Oxford University in 1479 and Bishop of Salisbury in 1482. However, the appointment gave him the opportunity of gaining influence over the most important of his young relatives in the latter's formative years. Sir Edward Woodville and Sir Richard Woodville were councillors; the Queen's younger son by her former marriage, Lord Richard Grey, was Comptroller of the Household. Richard Haute, her cousin, also spoken of as comptroller, must have held a position under him; her brother-in-law by her first marriage, Lord Lyle, was the Prince's Master of the Horse.* The most important post of all was reserved for her brother; Antony Lord Rivers was made the Prince's Governor.

The King must have had complete confidence in the trustworthiness of everyone whom he stationed about his son. At the same time he himself drew up, or caused to be drawn up, a set of regulations governing the child's day. Among the directions for his hours of attending mass, of working and playing, of looking on at various sports which he must presently learn, of mealtimes and having stories read to him aloud, and of cheerful amusement in the evening before he went to bed, two of them show how all-powerful the Governor's control was to be: 'That he shall arise every morning at a convenient time, and till he be made ready, none but Earl Rivers, his chamberlain and chaplain to enter his chamber, and one other chaplain to sing matins and then go to his chapel or chamber to hear mass'; and 'that no man sit at his board but as Earl Rivers shall

* Scofield, *op. cit.*, Vol. II, p. 56.

95

allow; and that there be read before him noble stories, as behoveth a Prince to understand'. Finally, 'that he be in his chamber and for all night, and the traverse to be drawn by eight of the clock'. After this curtain had been drawn across the alcove that contained the child's bed, everyone was to be turned out of the bed-chamber except 'the attendance'.* No women servants are mentioned; the work usually done by a child's nurse was done by Vaughan; there must have been women available to do the cooking and laundering a nursery requires, but neither they nor anyone else outside the Prince's family had a chance of making an intimate relationship with the little boy and gaining an influence over him that might be exploited later on. The supervision was in very capable hands. Affection, duty and above all, self-interest bound Rivers completely to a thorough and conscientious discharge of the duties of his task. His wife, Elizabeth, Lady Scales, whom he had married in 1461, died in the year of his appointment to the Prince of Wales. There were no children of the marriage, whose importance to him was the acquisition of her lands in Norfolk, Suffolk and Hertford, of which Middleton in Norfolk seems to have been his favourite seat. He was not childless, however. He begot a daughter on Gwentlian the daughter of William Stradling. This child, Margaret, was ultimately married to Sir Robert Poynz of Iron Acton in Gloucestershire, one of Edward IV's esquires of the body. In 1481, the receipts of the office of Constable of the King's Castle of St. Briavels in the Forest of Deane were divided between Antony, Earl Rivers, Robert Poynz Esquire and Thomas Beynam Esquire. It may therefore be supposed that the girl, though she did not achieve the high-flying matrimonial success of her Woodville uncles and aunts, made a reasonably good marriage with one of her father's friends; but the area, either of Rivers' marriage or of his romance, seems to have made no mark in contemporary records. He was free to devote himself to the task which was of the greatest importance to his family's future. However, the Queen had so packed the Prince's household with her relatives—as Hall said: 'that drift by the Queen seemed to be devised, whereby her blood might of right, in tender youth, be so planted in the Prince's favour that afterwards it should hardly be eradicated out of the same', that it was safe for Rivers to leave Ludlow when he was inclined; other members of the Woodville family would both take care of the Prince and isolate him from undesirable contacts.

In July 1473, the first year of the Prince's establishment at Ludlow, Rivers determined to take the pilgrimage to St. James of Compostella. He shipped from Southampton. While he was in the Spanish Sea, out of sight of land, with a good wind and fair weather, he asked if anyone could lend him a good book, and another of the Pilgrims, Monsieur de Bretaylles, lent him a French translation by Jean de Tenonville of a Latin work,

* J. O. Halliwell, *Letters of the Kings of England*, Vol. I, pp. 136–44.

The Sayings of the Philosophers, which Rivers had not seen. He admired it so much that he thought of translating it, but had no leisure then, because the 'takers of a jubilee and pardon' have their time fully mapped out for them, and 'also, for the great acquaintance which I formed there of worshipful folks with whom it was fitting I should keep good and honest company'. However, when he returned to England, 'as it listed the King's Grace to command me to give mine attendance upon my Lord the Prince, and that I was in his service, when I had leisure I looked upon the said book and at last concluded in myself to translate it into the English tongue'. This was the translation, with Rivers' preface attached, which Caxton set up at Westminster, the first book to be printed in England.

The Prince had been established in Ludlow the previous February. The King and Queen took him there. The Milanese Ambassador at the French court heard that the King of England had taken his son to Wales 'and styled him Prince . . . and left him in the country'. But the Queen remained with her child. On April 12, 1473, John Paston wrote: 'Men say the Queen and the Prince shall come out of Wales and keep this Easter with the King at Leicester, and some say, neither of them shall come there.'

It was very hard on the Queen that she should be obliged to part with her three year old son. The plan had seemed to the King a good one and she had acquiesced in it if she had not agreed with it. Beside the longing for the child's presence there was anxiety which no staff of devoted relatives could entirely do away. This was shown in one of the provisions made by the King that a physician and a surgeon should be always at hand, in case of illness, to care for 'God's precious sonde [sending] and gift, our most desired treasure'.* She had now another cause of care; she was five months pregnant and while the King went from Ludlow on a progress to Coventry, Kenilworth, Leicester, Nottingham and Fotheringhay, instead of going back to London, she arranged to lie in at Shrewsbury, about thirty miles north of Ludlow. This town was another which had benefited from the House of York. Edward had incorporated the Fraternity of Drapers of Shropshire and so, it was said, secured the prosperity of the town and the county for the next three centuries.

The castle of Shrewsbury bore no comparison with that of Ludlow. Its walls mounted drum towers of the kind introduced by Edward I; built on a knoll, its further side overlooked open country; on the nearer side, its walls came down into a street. The building was in a bad state of repair; in the reign of Henry VI, the outer walls of the dungeons had collapsed into the moat, and it was no longer used as a royal residence. Royal lodgings were taken up at the Abbey. Religious houses often had infirmaries, and the Queen chose to be confined in the infirmary of the convent of Dominican Friars. This stood near the edge of the Severn,

* J. O. Halliwell, *op. cit.*

at the bottom of Water Lane.* It had been founded in the thirteenth century, but the Queen could command and bring with her every comfort and convenience that had been invented since. On August 17, 1473, she was brought to bed there. The child was a boy; he was christened Richard after his grandfather, and was known at first as Prince Richard of Shrewsbury. When he was one year old, he was created Duke of York. The Queen was obliged at last to leave the neighbourhood of Ludlow and return to London; but unlike most princes, the little Duke of York was never given a separate palace, even one in the neighbourhood of his parents. His mother kept him always with her until she was finally parted from him.

On November 10, 1473, Earl Rivers was officially appointed Governor and Ruler of the Prince of Wales.

The establishment of the Prince of Wales at Ludlow probably meant that the Queen, if not the King, paid more visits to Shropshire and the West Midlands than have been recorded. A festival held in honour of the Prince of Wales at Coventry in 1474 may have been attended by the Prince and his mother. Its promoters were anxious to show the Queen's lineage in a highly favourable light. With this end in view, there were brought forward the Three Kings of Cologne, who were none other than the Magi, so called because Charlemagne was said to have discovered their bones in Italy and had them re-buried in Cologne. As the family of Elizabeth Woodville claimed descent from Charlemagne, the transition was easy from Charlemagne to the Wise Men, and one of the Three Kings hailed the Queen as his descendant, a brilliant *coup de theatre* indeed, if she were there in person.

In spite of such a gesture, there was no sign that the unpopularity of the Queen's relatives diminished, nor that their influence waned. With the protection of a husband as robust and powerful as Edward IV, who was always ready to further her wishes when they did not interfere with his own, Elizabeth Woodville had no reason to fear any evil consequences of her designs; she was concerned only in bringing the designs to bear. It was a shortsightedness for which she was to pay very dearly. In 1465, the year of her coronation, she had been dowered with some of the lands which had been a part of the duchy of Buckingham, and she had obliged the eleven year old duke to marry her sister Catherine. When Mancini wrote his report on the state of English affairs in 1483, it was still current that the Duke of Buckingham detested the Queen because she had forced him to marry her sister. Henry Stafford, second Duke of Buckingham, was descended from Edward III's fifth son, Thomas of Woodstock, Duke of Gloucester; by birth he was the most important member of the peerage after the royal dukes themselves. At eleven years old he had known that this marriage was a *mésalliance* and he had never lost his sense of

* Owen and Blakeway, *History of Shrewsbury*, 1825.

injury. It is not recorded how he felt about the other child, his wife, or whether he became personally reconciled to her; but men were accustomed to getting children on women they did not love, or even like; the important matter was the fathering of an heir. Even so, Buckingham's first son was not born till 1478, when he himself was twenty-four. Then, the King stood godfather and gave the baby a splendid gold cup, worth £42 15s. He gave Buckingham the Garter in 1474, but the young duke did not take the part either in politics or society to which his birth entitled him; he stood in the background; some people must have known very well what he was like, but this knowledge did not seem to have made its way to the royal circle.

In this year, the Queen worked hard and with success on behalf of her elder son by her first marriage. Thomas Grey was made Marquess of Dorset in 1475, a creation of great unpopularity as marquisates were very rarely bestowed and gave their bearers a position of superiority over every member of the peerage below the rank of duke; but this was not the cause of the worst displeasure. In 1466, the Queen had tried to get him married to Ann, daughter and heiress of John Holland, Duke of Exeter, and his wife who was Edward IV's sister. She had paid the Duchess of Exeter 4,000 marks in consideration of the arrangement, but the money was a dead loss, as the girl died before the marriage could be brought about; but in 1475, Dorset's industrious mother had found him another rich match: this was the step-daughter of William Lord Hastings, the heiress of the Bonville and Harrington families. It was a business transaction, with which the mutual animosity of the Queen and Hastings had nothing to do. A son, Thomas, was born in 1477; and it was in connection with this child that the Queen's rapacity reached an unexampled pitch. The Duke of Exeter had been attainted as a Lancastrian and the Duchess had been granted a divorce and had married her lover, Sir Thomas St. Leger. Their child, Anne, was adjudged to be heiress to the whole of the Exeter estates, entirely overlooking the claims of the Duke of Exeter's family, and when the marriage was arranged of the children, Thomas Grey and Anne St. Leger, not only was the whole Exeter property conferred on Thomas Grey by Act of Parliament; it was also enacted that out of this property, enough should be set aside to produce an income of 500 marks for the Queen's second son, Richard Grey, the infant Thomas's uncle. This astounding impudence makes it easy to understand why Ralph Neville, Earl of Westmorland, the nephew of the Duke of Exeter, was a firm supporter of Richard III.*

But an era of existence was dawning which was to bring with it something more important than money and lands, or kings and queens. William Caxton came to London in 1476, and Dr. Esteney, the Abbot of

* Pugh, T. B., *The Magnates, Knights and Gentry, in XV Century England*, ed. S. B. Chrimes.

Westminster, allowed him to set up his press in one of the now demolished Abbey buildings outside the West Door. Books issued from this press bore the words 'Emprinted by me, William Caxton, at Westminster', or 'Emprinted by me, William Caxton, in the Abbey of Westminster, by London'. But at least two books of great interest in the English scene were printed by him before he left Burgundy, in his press at Bruges which was managed by Colard Mansion. He had already printed here the *Recuyell of the Histories of Troy*, dedicated to the Duchess of Burgundy and it was natural to seek the patronage of her brother the King of England. Caxton said he had translated from the French a collection of stories about Jason, which he now called *The Whole Life of Jason*. This work was a suitable choice, for Duke Philip of Burgundy had founded the Order of the Golden Fleece, of which King Edward was a member; but though Caxton regarded himself as under 'the protection and sufference' of Edward, his 'most dread natural liege Lord'; he was not presuming to offer him this translation; he did not doubt that the King possessed the work already in the original French, 'which he well understandeth'; but with the encouragement of his 'liege-lady and most excellent Princess, the Queen', he ventured to dedicate it to 'the most fair and my most redoubted young Lord, my Lord Prince of Wales, our to-coming Lord', the now five-year-old Prince Edward, to help him to learn to read English.

The other book, much more interesting, as a picture of the times, was, again, a translation from the French: *The Game and Play of Chess*, written, Caxton said, by a Doctor of Divinity 'who hath made a book of the chess moralized . . . full of wholesome wisdom and requisite to every degree'. The book not only sets out to teach the game, and give its history; it gives also a picture of contemporary society of which all the ranks are seen in terms of chessmen; and which describes, first, the offices of Kings, Queens, Bishops and Knights, and then of Pawns who represent, labourers, farmers, smiths and other metalworkers, notaries, advocates, scriveners, drapers, cloth-makers, merchants, money-changers, physicians, leeches, spicers, apothecaries, taverners, hostellers, victuallers, city guards, toll-keepers, messengers, couriers, ribalds and players at dice. This part of the book is a guide to conduct for all ranks, to help them 'to govern themselves as they ought to do'. Caxton had the publishing field to himself and felt able to take a severer attitude to the reader than his sound commercial instinct would allow him to adopt in the cut-throat competition of today. The work is 'for the knowledge and understanding of such as be ignorant'. Some such undertaking is called for, since, as he says, 'The number of fools is infinite.' The second edition of this wholesome work was the first illustrated book to be printed in England. Caxton's notes for the guidance of the artist who made the drawings for the woodcuts are very interesting. It is not unreasonable to see, in his directions for the drawing of the Queen, one aspect of the public image of Elizabeth

Woodville: 'Thus ought the Queen to be made: she ought to be a fair lady, sitting in a chair and crowned with a crown on her head and clad with a cloth of gold and a mantle above, furred with ermine, and she should sit on the left side of the King for the amplections and embracings of her husband.'*

The most surprising detail of the book, with its high-minded emphasis on public virtues is the dedication to the Duke of Clarence: 'Forasmuch as I have understood and known that you are inclined unto the common-weal of our said sovereign lord, his nobles, lords and common people of his noble realm of England, and that ye saw gladly the inhabitants of the same informed in good, virtuous, profitable and honest manners'. This was a picture of Clarence which many people who knew the Duke would scarcely have recognized; but when it was written, Caxton was not yet living in London, and if he had been, the royalty and splendour of the King's brother, seen at a distance, might well have made a figure in which no protégé would see a fault. Clarence, being beyond comparison the favourite brother of the Duchess of Burgundy, the Croyland Continuator said: 'The Duchess, Lady Margaret, whose affections were fixed on her brother Clarence beyond any of the rest of her kindred'—it was natural so far for Caxton to see him, larger than life, through a golden haze.

Edward IV had taken pains to see that the Prince of Wales' education should be thorough, and he himself is said to have been the first English king to form a large and valuable library. He had a wonderful collection of illuminated manuscripts, some of which were copies commissioned by him of ones he had seen in the library of Gruthuyse. These volumes, some measuring a foot by eighteen inches, containing three to four hundred vellum pages, have miniatures illustrating the text, while the pages are bordered with flowers, curving sprays of leaves, birds, and small ornaments scattered like stars, forming a dense, rich background to the royal arms, the insignia of the Garter, and the Rose-en-Soleil, the five petalled white rose surrounded by gilt rays. He possessed some service books in Latin, but the secular works, histories, historical romances, tales of chivalry and chronicles, were, many of them, in French; books with a strong story-interest seem to have been the King's favourite. His books were not merely put on shelves; they were supplied with markers and carried about with him. The Wardrobe Accounts for 1480 note payments: 'To Alice Claver, for the making of XVI laces and XVI tassels for the garnishing of divers of the King's books, and to Robert Boillett for black papers and nails for closing and fastening of divers coffins of fir wherein the King's books were conveyed and carried from the King's Great Wardrobe in London unto Eltham'.†

* Amos, *Typographical Antiquities*, Vol. I.
† *Wardrobe Accounts of Edward IV*, ed. Sir Harris Nicolas, 1830.

The Wardrobe, a large, fourteenth-century stone house stood, Stow said, in Carter Lane, 'beside St. Paul's Churchyard'. It stored not only the King's clothes and bedding, and provided work-rooms for tailors and sempstresses; it had also something of the functions of an office. Stow said: 'The secret letters and writings touching the estates of the realm were wont to be enrolled in the King's Wardrobe and not in the Chancery.' It may also have been the scene of the trying on of clothes. Elizabeth Woodville had at one time used a room there; in 1480, a man was paid for '3¼ pounds of iron wire to hang the tapestry against the great bay-window in the Queen's old chamber in the Wardrobe', and 'for crotchetts and tapet hooks for the hanging of the same tapestry', and 'for his workmanship in hanging the same'. There were payments, too, for 'ten burdens of rushes spent in the same wardrobe at divers times when the King's highness and good grace came thither'. Also payments to 'William White, tallow chandler, for ten dozen and nine pounds of candles for to light when the King's highness and good grace on a night come into his Great Wardrobe and at other times'.*

---

* *Wardrobe Accounts of Edward IV*, ed. Sir Harris Nicolas, 1830.

18

THE perpetual problem of English foreign policy concerned the balance of power between France and Burgundy, Louis XI ceaselessly scheming to engulf the duchy in French territory, the Burgundians ceaselessly struggling to maintain their independence. It was very much to England's advantage that the latter should prevail. By 1474, Edward IV had decided that he ought to check Louis XI's hostile attempts against England; these had been shown by the French King's support of every attack on Edward's supremacy; he had aided Margaret of Anjou, Warwick, Oxford, Clarence; Edward felt that statesmanship required him to teach Louis XI a lesson, and he believed that the chance to reassert the English claims to France and to give English knights and their retainers a chance to pillage the rich cities which they felt belonged to England by right, would be extremely popular. In this he judged correctly, but the success of the invasion depended entirely on the help he would gain from the Burgundian alliance; without this, effective attack on France would be impossible. This alliance he was supposed to have; but Charles the Bold, instead of concentrating on his duchy's defence against France, had become a victim of *folie de grandeur*, and was attempting to extend his domains east and west. In 1474, Edward heard that he was besieging the Rhine town of Neuss. Edward decided to send Rivers on a diplomatic mission to his brother-in-law, to persuade Charles to withdraw from this course, and concentrate his energies on the campaign in which Edward intended to engage. Rivers, perhaps not sorry to leave the seclusion of Ludlow for a time and distinguish himself in courts, set out on this mission, in which, owing to the hot-headedness of Charles, he met with no success. The position he had temporarily left behind him in Wales however was a very strong one.* The authority was officially that of a council but in effect it was a large regional authority wielded by the Woodville family, of whom he was the undisputed head. The building up of the Woodville power is ominously reflected in a joke played for the King's amusement by his *diseur* Woodhouse. The summer of 1475 was, Warkworth says, 'a great, hot summer'. Men and women died of heat-stroke in the fields, and this made the jest more biting. *The Great*

* Ross, *op. cit.*, p. 335.

Chronicle says: that Woodhouse was in great favour with the King for his 'mannerly railing' in which he could be relied on not to go too far. 'Upon a day of the hot, dry summer', he came into the King's chamber, 'clad in a short coat cut by the points'. The hose, or tights, were joined to the doublet by tagged laces, the points, threaded through eye-let holes. In the Wardrobe Accounts for 1480, John Pointmaker is paid for pointing forty dozen points of silk, pointed with aiglets of laton, for every dozen points, seven pence. Woodhouse's coat was, therefore, cut up to the hips, 'and a pair of boots on his legs as long as they might be tied to the points of his hose, and in his right hand a long marsh pike'. When the King gave him his cue by asking what he meant by this extraordinary appearance, Woodhouse exclaimed: 'Upon my faith, sir, I have passed through many countries of your realm, and in places that I have passed, the Rivers be so high that I could hardly scape through them but I was fain to search the depths with this long staff. The King knew that he meant by it the great rule which the Lord Rivers and his blood bare at that time within his realm and made thereof a disport.' Edward was jovial, easy-tempered and confident that where people's fortunes depended on his good pleasure, he could control the different parties and oblige them to maintain an appearance of good humour. He had endowed the Woodvilles lavishly, he did not mind a joke at their expense; but the Chronicler added: 'This was an ill prognostication, as ye shall shortly hear.'*

Edward's plan for the invasion of France went on, in spite of the uncertain nature of Burgundian support. His determination to attack Louis XI was perhaps an instance of the nature which, when provoked beyond a certain point, would round on an assailant with unexpected speed and weight. 'The King's Great Matter' as the projected invasion was called, demanded the collection of money on a very great scale; taxes were voted by Parliament and forced gifts, termed Benevolences, were exacted from private persons; the great lords of the realm were commanded to provide so many archers and mounted spearmen. On a summons issued by the King the Dukes of Clarence, Gloucester, Norfolk, Suffolk and Buckingham, are set down for so many men; the heraldic device of each duke is beautifully drawn opposite his name.† Gloucester is to provide 120 mounted lancers, and 1,000 archers. The King's artillery train of guns and their gun carriages was formidable; it included 'a chariot with a great iron gun, a chariot with the great brazen gun, a chariot with a great bombard of iron, a chariot with a bombardell called "the Edward".' There were 'a crane and two gins to ship and unship, cart and uncart the great guns'; and of ammunition, 'hundreds of shot of stone, barrels of gunpowder, sulphur, brimstone, saltpetre'. There were also thousands

* *The Great Chronicle of London*, ed. A. H. Thomas and I. D. Thornley, 1938.
† Illustrated in Cheetham, *op. cit.*, p. 84.

of bows and arrows and 'great hooks of iron for pulling down draw-bridges'; there were assaulting ladders, a floating bridge that took apart in separate pieces, a leather boat that was packed in three parts; then there were shovels, spades, pick-axes, crow-bars, hammers, pincers, horse-shoes and horse-shoe nails.* The transport of the horses was a major operation in itself; beside the mounts for the spearmen, each knight had two horses of his own, or three. As well as his embarkation prepara-tions, the King had of course to arrange the affairs he left behind him. The Prince of Wales, aged five, was to be the titular Keeper of the Realm. He was brought up from Ludlow on May 12, and received by his mother into the royal household. The Queen was to be allowed £2,200 a year for household expenses while the King was away, and as much again 'because that my Lord Prince is assigned by the King to be in household'.† On Whit Sunday the child was knighted by his father at Westminster. The administration the King left in the hands of Cardinal Bourchier, Archbishop of Canterbury and Bishop Alcock the Prince's tutor. On his way to embark, Edward stopped at Sandwich. Here he made his will. In this, dated June 20, 'at our town of Sandwich', he named the Queen first in the list of his executors. She was again pregnant and the will made alternative provisions for the child, as to whether it proved boy or girl.

The enormous army and its equipment had struck dread into Louis XI before it left the English shore; and as a war for the re-conquest of France could, in the end, have brought nothing but long-drawn-out suffering and loss to both nations, it was a piece of the greatest good fortune that it came to an end before it had begun, and without the shedding of a drop of blood. Louis XI was ready to offer peace on the most generous terms; but the cause of Edward's readiness to accept them was the complete failure of the Duke of Burgundy to implement his share of the alliance. Charles told Edward that with so fine an expeditionary force, the English king could sweep through France to the gates of Rheims and capture Normandy. When he had accomplished this, Charles would bring his army to join the English army. Meanwhile the Burgundian troops were pillaging Lorraine. In recording these events, Commines observed that God had troubled the Duke's understanding.

The treaty between the Kings of France and England was agreed upon at Ameins, where Louis XI feasted and wined the English soldiers to such an extent that they could not have fought even if they had been commanded to. The terms of the treaty were, that there should be a truce between the two kings for seven years, free trade between the two countries, that Louis XI should pay Edward seventy-five thousand gold crowns down and afterwards an annual payment of fifty thousand crowns;

* Scofield, *op. cit.*, Vol. II, p. 119.
† Scofield, *op. cit.*, Vol. II, p. 125.

that the English King's daughter, or, in case of mischance to her, his second daughter, should be married to the Dauphin; that the French should dower her with an annual sixty thousand crowns; finally that Margaret of Anjou should be ransomed by the French King for sixty thousand crowns. These terms seem to have been so favourable to the English, it is difficult, at first sight, to see what the French gained from them, except the trade concessions; but first of all, the treaty got the English out of France; the payment of ransom for Margaret of Anjou meant that Louis XI was able to take over from her any rights of succession she had to her parents' domains, and finally, no treaty was binding on Louis XI once it had proved inconvenient. Meantime the treaty itself was signed on a bridge over the Somme at Pecquigny and after much feasting and enjoyment, and an offer from Louis XI to Edward to make him free of beautiful French ladies and to provide a French confessor to absolve him afterwards, the English host withdrew to begin the lengthy process of re-shipment to the coast of Kent.

Edward from his own point of view had gained a great success. He was a talented military commander of high personal courage, but unlike most soldiers of his distinction, he was not fond of fighting. He was extremely interested in commerce and he had secured valuable commercial advantages; his way of life required a great deal of money, and he had gained such a hoard of French gold, with promises of more, as, with his other sources of income, enabled him to 'live of his own' for the rest of his life. The people who were discontented with the outcome were the English commanders and their men, who had looked forward to an orgy of fighting and plunder, and the leaders who felt that the English name for bravery and conquest had been blighted by this tame conclusion. Among these was the Duke of Gloucester, an intrepid soldier and a young man of driving purpose rather than impartial views. Too loyal to his brother to refuse his signature to the treaty, it was noticed all the same that he was absent from the banquets and entertainments with which it was celebrated. He was no doubt one of the English who were stung by the French calling the money paid to Edward a pension, while the English themselves persisted in referring to it as a tribute.

On his return to England, Edward received a triumphal welcome. If there were murmurs of dissatisfaction, the King did not care about them. The return of the disappointed English soldiers who began to prey on their countrymen since they had not been allowed to prey on the French, gave some trouble for a time; but it was soon realized that on his return the King had become a more formidable ruler; he showed himself alert to receive reports of lawlessness and very severe in punishing them. He also set himself with increased activity to augment the wealth of the crown. The Croyland Continuator says that in this pursuit, 'he examined the Chancery Rolls to find those who had taken possession of estates without paying legal dues . . . These, and more than can be conceived of by a man who is inexperienced in such matters, were his methods of making up a purse.' He began now to luxuriate in the pleasures of wealth he had the means and the leisure to enjoy.

The Queen was highly elated by the betrothal of the Princess Elizabeth to the Dauphin. She showed more excitement at the prospect of her daughter's being Queen of France than she had shown at becoming Queen of England herself; that event she had borne, publicly at least, with a cautious and frigid dignity. The Princess was now called the Dolphinesse or Madame la Dauphine; as she was five years older than the Dauphin the Queen was resigned to a considerable waiting before the bridegroom could be considered marriageable. Though she herself would have been ready to force on a marriage between children, as in the case of the Duke of Buckingham and her sister Catherine, it was clear that the King of France would not, in this case, entertain the idea. Edward made some attempt to get the annual payment of the dowry of 60,000 crowns begun now that the troth-plight was sealed, but it was explained to him that in France, no one dreamed of paying down a dowry before the marriage had been consummated.

The Queen, however disappointed at this postponement of her ambitions, was now occupied with her personal concerns. In November, her child was born; it was another daughter, who was christened Anne. The tale of beautiful little girls now numbered five.

Edward had returned to England in September, but since the Prince of Wales was with his mother, Lord Rivers had felt free to continue his absence. He made a pilgrimage to southern Italy, and then he visited the Duke of Burgundy, whose warlike activities had now taken the direction of laying siege to the Swiss town of Morat. He invited Rivers to join him in this enterprise; Rivers declined and Charles spoke of him scornfully.

Rivers then took his way south again. Outside Rome, in July 1476, he was waylaid by thieves and his baggage train was robbed of his jewels and plate. On hearing this, the Queen in her sisterly concern, sent him a letter of exchange for 4,000 ducats. Meantime, he heard that his valuables were being exposed for sale in Venice. He went there after them, and when he had made his grievance known to the Authorities, the Senate ordered that the treasures should be restored to him freely, out of respect to the English King.*

* Paston, *Letters*, Vol. V, p. 258.

19

IN 1476, the Duke of York, aged three, was invested with the Garter. His brother had received it at the age of two. How much of the elaborate ceremony was enacted in the children's presence, is not recorded, but there is some reason to think that the infant princes wore Garter robes. The Prince of Wales wore 'his robes of estate' when he was carried in Vaughan's arms, and since he had these, he may well have had miniature Garter robes for his investiture. Edward IV's Wardrobe Accounts note the making of Garter robes for the Duke of York: 'a mantle of blue velvet lined with white damask', when he was seven, an age when he would require larger ones if the previous set had been made four years previously. The present Garter blue, a deep sapphire, was adopted in 1688; before, the velvet had been sky-blue. The official Book of the Order was originally termed: *Liber Ceruleus*.

Since he practised a personal sovereignty, Edward's affairs were always absorbing, but though he was never without concern over commercial, domestic and foreign affairs, he had no outstanding cause of anxiety in these spheres; this came from within his own family.

In October 1476, Isabella Duchess of Clarence was brought to bed of a son. Her first child, stillborn, had been buried at sea outside Calais harbour; her daughter, Margaret, born in 1473, and her son, Edward, born in 1475, had survived. For the birth of the coming child, she chose, like her sister-in-law the Queen, the infirmary of a monastic establishment. Clarence had estates in Gloucestershire and seems very often to have lived there; on this occasion the Duchess lay in at 'the new infirmary' of Tewkesbury Abbey. She was very ill, but her husband took her back to Warwick Castle in November. Here on December 22 she died; in January the baby died too.

In this January there died also Charles the Bold; his son had predeceased him; his daughter Mary was therefore hereditary Duchess of Burgundy and the richest heiress in Europe. Clarence saw, in the possibility of a marriage with her, something to assuage the gnawing sense of injury and spite which came from his not being King of England. His sister Margaret, the Dowager Duchess, was eager for this promotion of her favourite brother, and Clarence on the face of it was not entirely unsuitable: he was the King of England's brother, he was very rich; but matters never got so far as an official proposal. Edward forbade the match. He had once before forbidden a marriage to Clarence, but then Clarence and Warwick had defied him and the marriage with Isabella Neville had taken place. No one could defy Edward now, and he had sound reasons for his decision. Charles the Bold had always maintained that he had a claim to the English crown, as his mother Isabella of Portugal was a grand-daughter of John of Gaunt. This claim, such as it was, would descend to his daughter, and since it was known that Clarence had for many years nourished the belief that he ought to be King of England, the two claims, united, and backed by the wealth of Burgundy, might create a really formidable threat to Edward and his dynasty.

The rebuff and disappointment had already caused Clarence acute anger and suffering, and then something happened which drove him into frenzy. The Queen saw in the present situation another opportunity to advance her own family; she urged Edward to put forward the suit of Antony Rivers to the Duchess of Burgundy.

Rivers had had many connections with the Duchy; he had fought in the tournament against the Burgundian challenger that had been arranged as one of the celebrations of his sister's coronation, he had accompanied Edward in his flight there in 1470, he had been on several diplomatic missions to Charles the Bold; but a knowledge of the terrain did not qualify him to be the husband of the Duchess; as Commines observed: 'he but a petty earl and she the greatest heiress of her time'. Edward was a seasoned diplomatist who must have known as well as anyone the preposterous nature of this suggestion, but his actions were sometimes those of an indolent man who doesn't want trouble at home. If the proposal were put forward by him he would have done all that it lay in his power to do; the inevitable result could not be laid at his door. The result was not long in doubt. As Hall said: 'The Queen wished it, but the Burgundian Council were very deaf to so unmeet a proposal'. Plancher says* 'The English Queen was beside herself at the scorn with which the Burgundian court treated the suggestion'.

According to the Croyland Continuator, Edward, so far from wishing Rivers to succeed, did all he could to further the claims of Maximilian, son of the Holy Roman Emperor and Duke of Austria, whom Mary did in fact marry in 1478; but the mere fact that the King should have put forward the suit of the Queen's brother while forbidding his, was too much for Clarence's weak head. In April 1477, he rushed into a criminal outrage against an elderly woman, Ankarette Twynhoe, who had been in attendance on the Duchess of Clarence, but who was also a dependant of the Queen,† which appears to be the explanation of his insane

* *Histoire Générale et Particulière de Bourgogne*, IV, p. 482.
† Article on George Plantagenet, Duke of Clarence, D.N.B., Vol. XLV.

vindictiveness. Acting on a maniacal impulse, whatever its origin, Clarence sent eighty of his men to Ankarette Twynhoe's house at Cayford, in Somerset, who, charging her with having caused the Duchess's death by giving her a drink of poisoned ale, brought her forcibly from Somerset up to Warwick, her daughter and son-in-law following helplessly in her wake. Since the crime of which she was accused was said to have been committed at Warwick, it was right that she should be tried at Warwick; but Clarence had not procured a warrant; he acted as if he had the power of arbitrary arrest, which no one could exercise except the King. At Warwick he had Mrs. Twynhoe robbed of her jewels and money and imprisoned for the night, to be brought before the justices sitting with a grand jury in the Guildhall at nine o'clock the next morning. Meanwhile he ordered the daughter and her husband out of Warwick; they were obliged to find lodging eight miles distant at Stratford on Avon. The grand jury returned a verdict of guilty and Clarence ordered Mrs. Twynhoe to be hanged immediately. The victim was put to death within three hours of her being brought into the Guildhall; even so, some of the jury found time to beg her forgiveness; they confessed that they had not thought her guilty, but they had pronounced that she was because they feared the great might and vengeance of the Duke of Clarence.

Clarence, meanwhile, intended to show that the Queen and her party were, through Ankarette Twynhoe, responsible for the poisoning of his wife. He came to court very rarely, and when he did, he ostentatiously refused anything to eat or drink.

Edward, for the time being, took no official notice of this shocking crime, but he struck rapidly and hard in another direction. It was forbidden to set up the horoscopes of the royal family without the King's permission, and an astronomer, Dr. John Stacey of Merton College, was accused of casting those of the King and the Prince of Wales. Under torture he named Thomas Blake and Thomas Burdett as his accomplices. Blake was the chaplain of Merton, and this was unfortunate for the college; the sinister detail was the position of Burdett: he was a member of Clarence's household. With the help of Stacey and Blake, it was said, he had engaged in this unlawful traffic 'to know when the King and the Prince should die', and had 'declared to certain ones, the King and the Prince would die within a certain time'. Besides this, in March and May of that year, Burdett had spread the old tale that the King was bastard-born and put abroad 'bills, writings, rhymes and ballads . . . to incite the King's subjects to rebellion'. The judges on circuit held the King's commission of 'oyer and terminer', to hear and decide, but the King could appoint persons to assist them on the bench. The exceptional seriousness with which Edward viewed this trial was shown in the number of people he appointed to hear it—six justices, four earls, twelve barons, and as a make-weight, the Marquess of Dorset, a member of the party violently hostile to Burdett's patron. All three prisoners were found guilty of treason. Blake was saved by the intervention of the Bishop of Norwich; the other two were hanged the following day, May 20, one month and five days after the death of Ankarette Twynhoe. Whoever the prisoners had been, once they were convicted on this charge, unless they were reprieved, death would be their inevitable fate; but the imposing body of commissioners appointed to try the case of his own follower, should have warned Clarence that the King's temper was now dangerous; but Clarence was beyond the reach of warnings. While the King was away at Windsor, Clarence burst into a meeting of the Council sitting at Westminster, bringing with him a Franciscan preacher, Dr. John Goddard, whose very presence was an affront, since it was he who, at the re-adeption of 1470, had made the public announcement at Paul's Cross that Henry VI was the lawful king. The astonished and indignant councillors, interrupted in their work, had to listen while Goddard, at Clarence's orders, read aloud to them the declarations of innocence which Burdett and Stacey had made at the scaffold. At the news of this invasion of his Great Council, Edward's patience finally gave way. He returned to Westminster and ordered Clarence to appear before him in the Palace of Westminster. He summoned also the Lord Mayor and aldermen of the City of London, and in their presence he accused Clarence of having behaved as though he had the powers of a king, and, further, of having threatened judges and juries. He then commanded that Clarence should be removed to the Tower. The Duke was taken away and lodged in the Bowyer Tower. This, like the Beauchamp Tower, the Wakefield Tower, the Garden Tower, was, inside, much like the house of an ordinary citizen, well-windowed and, if the fireplaces were kept supplied with fuel, warm. The prisoner's plight depended on who he was and what he had done, whether he were 'straitly kept' or merely detained, allowed the attendance of his own servants and the bringing in of supplies. Clarence's position was scarcely one of physical hardship; it was, of intolerable exacerbation. The sinister feature of the Bowyer Tower was not its accommodation, but where it stood, on the wall between the Brick Tower and the Flint Tower: the massive and enormous White Tower rose between it and the royal apartments. No one from the windows of the latter could catch sight of the King's brother.

Prophesying by the stars was a subject highly interesting to monarchs. The art was available to anyone, however humble, but a king had so much to lose, and his fortunes, in spite of every exercise of insight and precaution, seemed so often to be at the mercy of chance, to those who believed it could be done, the temptation to read the future was irresistible. Edward was at least interested, if not a confirmed believer in divination. A poem, 'The Song of the Lady Bessy', written in the reign of Henry VII

III

by Humphrey Brereton,* a follower of Lord Stanley, relates the secret arrangement for the marriage of the Princess Elizabeth with Lord Stanley's step-son, Henry Tudor. It cannot be accepted as fact, but some of its detail is very interesting; the Princess's hair 'shone as golden wire', and in a nocturnal interview between her and Lord Stanley, 'Charcoals in chimney there were cast, Candles on sticks were burning high', and the family picture of Edward IV which is put into the Princess's mouth may well be founded on fact. She says that she can read and write easily because the King sent for the best scrivener in London to teach her and her sister the Princess Cecily. She then relates this story: One day her father was standing, deep in thought, a book of astrology in his hand. He was surrounded by lords, none of whom ventured to speak to him because there were tears in his eyes. The little girl was the only creature who dared to approach him. The King picked her up, caressed her and sat her, high up, on a window ledge. Weeping, he gave her the book, telling her to keep it and show it to nobody:

> 'There shall never son of my body be gotten
> That shall be crowned after me,
> But you shall be Queen and wear the Crown
> So doth express the prophesy.'

Needless to say, no one would have dared to put in print such a statement as this; anyone who had been found responsible for it would have shared the fate of Stacey and Burdett; but the impression is convincing of Edward's fondness for his small daughter and of his interest in prophecy. Henry VII's historian, Polydore Vergil, was the first to record that one of the King's grievances against Clarence was a saying that 'after King Edward, one should reign, whose first letter of his name should be G'. The ominous confusion of George and Gloucester strikes a thrilling chord in the hearer's imagination, but the credibility of all prophecies is injured when the prophecy is not disclosed till after the event, and there was enough of ascertainable fact to enrage the King against the Duke of Clarence. The Duke had been taken to the Bowyer Tower in May, 1477; for the next nine months Edward was turning over in his mind what was to be done with him, his fair, eloquent, persuasive younger brother. The author of *The Mirror for Magistrates*, when he conjures up a procession of public figures whose tragic fates are meant to convey a lesson, makes Clarence accuse Warwick of having drawn him into treason:

> He stole my heart that erst unsteady was,
> For I was witless, wanton, fond and young,
> Whole bent to pleasure, brittle as the glass—†

* 'The Most Pleasant Song of the Lady Bessy', Humphrey Brereton, Percy Society, *Early English Poetry*, Vol. 20.
† *Mirror for Magistrates*, ed. J. Higgins, 1815.

The lines were not published till 1559, but they convey the same impression as the contemporary drawings of Clarence in the Rows Roll, smiling and debonair, in one of which he is dangling from his arm a collar of suns and roses.

The Queen's last child had been born in 1475. She was pregnant again, and once more she decided to lie in at the Dominican infirmary at Shrewsbury. She must have found herself comfortable and in good hands on the previous occasion, but she can hardly have found better accommodation there than she found at Westminster; the choice of the Shrewsbury infirmary must have been made with a view to seeing the Prince of Wales at Ludlow, perhaps of being visited by him at Shrewsbury. The child born here was another boy. With only two sons among a flock, even of beautiful, daughters, his appearance must have been very welcome to his parents. He was christened George, not, it must be supposed, after his uncle of that name who was now lying in the Tower, but after the patron saint of the most noble Order of the Garter. The little boy was given the title of his birthplace as his brother Richard had been, and was known at first as Prince George of Shrewsbury.

The King considered several matches for the Prince of Wales; the infanta of Aragon and Castile, the sister of Maximilian of Austria, the daughter of the very wealthy Galeazzo Maria, Duke of Milan, the heiress of Duke Francis of Brittany. He was guided not only by the political value of an alliance, but by how much money the bride's dowry would bring. The Milanese ambassador had warned his Duke: 'the chief difficulty will be the great quantity of money the King of England will want . . . [he] being one who tends to accumulate treasure'. When Mary of Burgundy had married Maximilian of Austria and their son Philip was born, Edward proposed the Princess Anne as a match. Maximilian asked for a dowry of 200,000 crowns with her. Edward, knowing the Burgundians were at that point in sore need of the English alliance, wanted to pay no dowry at all as the price of it. None of the matches he planned for his daughters or for the Prince of Wales came to anything, but he arranged one for the Duke of York which he was able to see celebrated.

In 1476, John Mowbray, Duke of Norfolk, Earl of Nottingham, Earl of Warenne, had died, leaving as his immediate heir his four-year-old daughter Anne; this child, the last of the Mowbray line, inherited, besides the very large Mowbray estates, the titles of her family. She was hereditary Duchess of Norfolk, and even hereditary Grand Marshal of England. Edward thought that with such a rich inheritance she was fit to marry the Duke of York, and he began negotiations with the child's grandmother, the Dowager Duchess of Norfolk, she who had been married in her old age to John Woodville, and divorced from him by the axe seven years since. The marriage settlement was to confer all the Mowbray properties on the bridegroom for his lifetime, even if his wife predeceased him. Two distant heirs of the Mowbray family were disinherited by this —one, William Lord Berkeley was not altogether injured as he owed the King a very large sum of money and was excused from repayment under the settlement; but the other, John Lord Howard, whose claims were also swept aside, not only owed the King nothing: his account books stated that the King had never paid him for the plate bought to use at the Queen's coronation. He had been throughout a loyal subject and a generous friend to Edward, and this treatment of him was a fatal blunder. It had far-reaching consequences.

In June 1476, the little Prince was given one of the late Duke of Norfolk's titles; he was made Earl of Nottingham and in February 1477, the Dukedom of Norfolk was recreated for him; he became Duke of Norfolk and Earl of Warenne. During this year, it would seem that the Prince of Wales and the Duke of York cannot have been separated all the time. Caxton, at some date after February 1477, published his translation from the French of the tale of Godfrey of Boulogne, one of the Nine Worthies. He dedicated it to: 'My Lord Prince and my Lord Richard, Duke of York and Duke of Norfolk . . . at their leisure and pleasure to see and hear read this simple book, by which they may be encouraged to deserve laud and honour and that their name and renown may increase and remain perpetual, and after this life, short and transitory, we may all attain and come to the everlasting life in heaven, where is joy and rest without end'. The dedication, in the perspective of future events, strikes a chilling note; but it also assumes that the Princes are together; it even evokes the picture of their listening together to a story's being read aloud. Caxton was working within a stone's throw of the Palace of Westminster, and if the Prince of Wales had been the whole time at Ludlow, and the Duke of York never with his brother, the fact must have been public property, in which case, surely, the dedication would have been differently phrased. There is some slight suggestion that there may have been a family party of the Queen and her two sons at Shrewsbury in 1478. The Duke of Gloucester, like the King his brother, loved music and was attended by a famous consort of minstrels; these, when their master did not immediately need their services, travelled about, playing at the houses of other great lords. The accounts of the bailiffs of Shrewsbury convey an idea of considerable merry-making between their town and Ludlow: 'To William Harper, Minstrel to the Lord Prince, 3/4. Wine given to Master Haute, Comptroller to the Lord Prince, 3/8. Wine given to William Young, knight, and other gentlemen of the Lord Prince, 6/-. Wine given to a minstrel of the Duke of Gloucester, called the Taborer, 3/4. Reward to six minstrels of our Lord the King, 20/-'.

Before 1477 was out, Caxton had produced the first work to be printed on his Westminster Press; this was Rivers' translation, *The Dictes or Sayings of the Philosophers*. Caxton dated the edition, November 18, 1477.

1 Micklegate Bar, York – the gateway through which the king traditionally entered the city
A. F. Kersting

2 Westminster Palace, view from the river showing St. Stephen's chapel on the extreme right, by Hollar
Victoria and Albert Museum

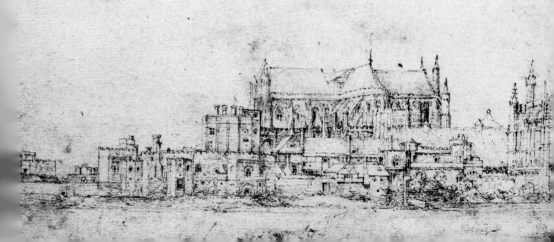

3 Angel censing, Westminster Abbey. In the spandrels of the triforium arch of the South Transept there are figures of two censing angels. Authorities regard them as the finest examples of large-scale thirteenth century sculpture in the Abbey

Courtesy of the Gordon Fraser Gallery

4 St George's Chapel, Windsor: Frieze of angels with sunbursts – the symbol of Edward IV – in their crowns and in the stonework below

Reproduced by permission of the Dean and Canons of Windsor

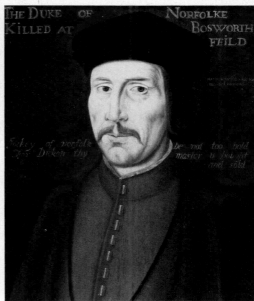

5 Edward IV, portrait by an unknown artist but attributed to the Netherlands School, and based on a portrait datable before 1472

6 John Howard, 1st Duke of Norfolk. This portrait, by an unknown artist, was probably painted in the sixteenth century, and inscribed with the message given to Howard before Bosworth: 'Jockey of Norfolk be not too bold, For Dickon thy master is bought and sold'

7 Anthony Woodville, Earl Rivers, presenting the *Dictes and Saying of the Philosophers* to his brother-in-law, Edward IV. Elizabeth Woodville sits to the far right with Edward Prince of Wales in front

8 The Tower of London, from an engraving by Stanislaus Hollar, showing the royal apartments in foreground, and Forebuilding at left of front facade of the White Tower

Crown copyright, by permission of the Controller H.M.'s Stationery Office

9 Ludlow Castle

Reproduced by courtesy of National Monuments Record

10 Miniature from *Quinte Curse Ruffe des fais du Grand Alexandre*, translated by Vasco de Luceña. The translator is portrayed presenting his book to Edward IV

11 Richard III, portrait by an unknown artist. This is a sixteenth century version of the standard portrait of the King, probably taken from life, but now lost. Another, earlier, version is in the Royal Collection

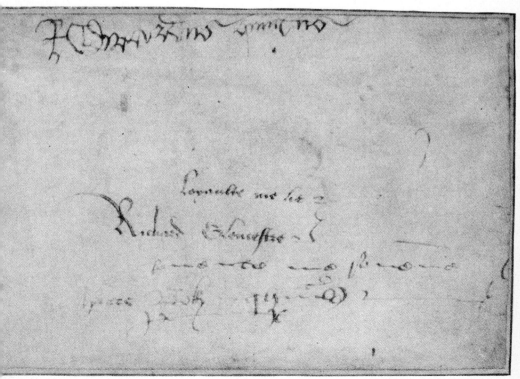

12 The piece of parchment bearing at the top the signature *Edwardus Quintus*, with below Richard's motto, *Loyaulté me lie*, and his signature; and at the bottom *Souvente me souvene* and 'Harre Bokingham', the motto and signature of Buckingham. This was probably written at St Albans, on 3 May, when the young King halted overnight with Richard and Buckingham on their journey to London

Nicholas Servian FIIP, Woodmansterne Ltd

13 Stained-glass window in North Transept of Canterbury Cathedral, about 1482

Prince Richard Duke of York   Edward Prince of Wales   Queen Elizabeth Woodvill

14 Windows in Little Malvern Priory Church: (*left*) Edward Prince of Wales; (*right*) Princesses Elizabeth, Cecily, Catherine and Anne

Roy Smith

15 Christchurch, Misericord, Richard III in jewelled crown

Edwin Smith

16 The skull in the coffin of Anne Mowbray, showing the hair in a state of extraordinary preservation. The body was discovered during building work in Stepney in December 1964, and reburied in Westminster Abbey

Keystone Press Agency

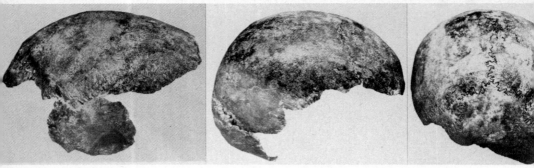

17 Skulls of Edward V and Richard Duke of York (from *Archaeologia LXXXIV*, Society of Antiquaries)

18 Urn containing bones in Westminster Abbey which Charles II caused to be reburied there, believing them to be the remains of the royal children

The Dean and Chapter of Westminster

19 Westminster Abbey, Henry VII's Chapel: glass in east window of East Apsidal Chapel, showing the devices of the crown and hawthorn bush

Reproduced by courtesy of National Monuments Record

The opening of the preface which Rivers supplied, says that whereas every human creature is ordained by God 'to be subject and thrall unto the storms of Fortune, of which', he says, 'I, Antoine Wydeville, Earl Rivers, Lord Scales etc. have largely and in many different manners had my part', and since God in His great goodness has now relieved him of them, he feels obliged, so far as his incapacity will allow, to spend his 'recovered life, in performing works pleasing to God, in satisfactions of his past iniquities and faults'. It was in furtherance of this design that he undertook the pilgrimage to St. James of Compostella, which, with a fair voyage, pleasant company aboard and agreeable social gatherings when he got there, does not seem to have been too irksome a religious duty. But Rivers' *forte* was the combination of a philosophical pensiveness with a keen enjoyment of material benefits. At the time of his death, it was discovered that he was wearing a hair-shirt under his splendid clothing. The timing of Caxton's edition of this work marks the transition of the era of manuscripts to that of printed books. Six weeks after the appearance for sale of the printed volume with its type that looks like beautiful script, a manuscript copy of the work was presented to Edward IV with some lines attached:

> This book, late translate, here in sight,
> By Antony, Earl, that virtuous knight,

the King is entreated to read, for it is a precious jewel for the whole land. What excels The Sayings of the Philosophers in interest, is the miniature at the head of this manuscript.* It shows Edward IV seated with Elizabeth Woodville beside him, the Prince of Wales standing at her knee. Rivers kneels on one knee before the King, presenting him with a massive tome in a cover of apple-green. That the King and Queen are wearing crowns and holding sceptres gives the picture a symbolical rather than a realistic air, but the face of Edward IV bears a strong likeness to other drawings of him, and the picture of Elizabeth Woodville has the rich gold hair and the very heavy eyelids which seem to have been put in as unmistakable features in other attempts at taking her likeness. Portraits of the Prince of Wales are so rare that this one has a particular value. He was seven years old in 1477, and he looks about this age. The drawing of his face has a distinct resemblance to the drawing of his mother's, except that he has not her weighted and drooping eyelids. His hair is very fair. The facial likenesses may not be exact but the clothes must be copied from real life. The King wears a jewelled crown with crossed hoops rising from a circle of alternate crosses pattées and fleurs de lys, which rests on his ermine-trimmed cap of maintenance. He is wearing a violet robe and mantle very heavily trimmed with ermine. The Queen wears a similar crown, a little smaller than the King's, but without the

* Lambeth MS 265.

ermine, and the jewelled metal resting immediately on her head gives the impression of that hard weight she found so difficult to support. She wears a robe and mantle like the King's. The Prince of Wales had in this year a wardrobe of rich clothes made for him by George Lovekin, Tailor and Yeoman of the Wardrobe, doublets and matching long gowns of purple satin, green satin, purple velvet and black velvet, with several velvet bonnets;* but in the miniature he, like his parents, is wearing robes of estate: a blue robe down to his feet with ermine round the hem, and a scarlet mantle, ermine collared, ermine bordered, ermine lined; he wears a small coronet, above the ermine edge of his cap of maintenance. The figure of Rivers is in armour, with a surcoat whose devices include the King's Sun in Splendour. This is the only known portrait of him. He is bareheaded, his straight brown hair is cut in a fringe across his forehead and hangs to the nape of his neck. He has a long, clean-shaven face with good features; that their cast is somewhat sly is owing either to the fact that the miniaturist was not reliable as a taker of likenesses, or that he was.

Whether the presence of the Prince of Wales in this miniature meant that he was in London with his parents in 1477 or not, he and his uncle Rivers were in the capital in January 1478. Parliament was to meet on January 19, but the 15th was the day of the Duke of York's marriage to Anne Mowbray. Rivers, though often on his Norfolk estates, was based on Ludlow Castle, and was obliged to depend on others for his business affairs in Norfolk and London. One letter, undated, written from his manor of Middleton to the King's master-mason, Daniell, whose services he was able to employ, gives instructions for work which he could not stay to over-see: He orders that his dais should be half a foot higher than was originally planned, and that a turret should be erected on the roof fourteen feet high 'from the lead'. He says: 'You will have room before the coming in at the gate in the new wall, where you think it may be best seen, for a scutcheon of the arms of Woodville and Scales and a Garter about it. Write me as often as you can how you do, and Jesu speed you.'†

By January 11, Rivers had not made up his mind whether to be in London for the 19th or not. He wrote from his Norfolk estates on that date to 'Mr. Molyneux, Chancellor to my Lord of York' and to his own attorney, Andrew Dymmock: 'Master Chancellor and Dymmock, I pray you remember where is best that I be lodged this parliament time. I pray you send me of your tidings and whether ye think it best by such advice as ye can get, that I be at London for the first day of the Parliament or not. And speak to Jorge and see that my parliament robes be made. Written at Walsingham the XI day of January with the hand of your

* Scofield, *op. cit.*, Vol. II, p. 56.
† Gairdner, J., *History of the Life and Reign of Richard III*, Appendix II.

friend, A. Rivers.'* As he was not in London and able to test public opinion for himself, it was natural that Rivers should ask advice of two people on the spot who were competent to give it, as to his appearing at the opening of this parliament. The houses had been summoned to pass an Act of Attainder against the Duke of Clarence.

* ibid.

20

THE wedding ceremonies of the four year old Duke of York and the six year old Anne Mowbray began the day before the actual marriage. On January 14, a voyde, or serving of light refreshments, was held in the King's Chamber in Westminster Palace. As it had been decided by or for Lord Rivers that he should be present in London by this time, he was of course given a conspicuous part to play on the occasion. It was he who led the bride into the chamber among the assembled guests.

On the following day, January 15, the child was brought in a procession through the apartments of Westminster Palace, from the Queen's Chamber, through the King's Great Chamber, through the White Hall and so to the door of St. Stephen's Chapel. On her right hand was the King's nephew, the Earl of Lincoln; on her left, Earl Rivers.

The Chapel, a scene of gold and silver, painted angels and jewel-like coloured glass, was now adorned with sky-blue hangings, patterned with gold fleurs de lys; under a canopy of cloth of gold, the royal party awaited the entrance of the bride: the King and Queen, the Prince of Wales, the old Duchess of York, the Duke of York himself and his sisters, the Princesses Elizabeth, Mary and Cecily. The beauty of Edward and his Queen and of their gold-haired children assembled under the canopy of cloth of gold, must have been a radiant sight. The bride's escort halted her at the chapel door; of the three clergymen officiating, one made the ritual statement that a marriage within the prohibited degrees: the Dowager Duchesses of York and Norfolk were sisters: could not proceed without a special licence from the Pope. A second clergyman produced the papal bull showing that the marriage might go forward. The little Duke of York was led to his place by the Queen. Then the Bishop of Norwich, who was to perform the ceremony, asked who would give the bride to the Church and to him? The King stepped forward. Towering over the small girl, Edward said that he gave her.

The populace crowded about the entrance to the chapel and great quantities of gold coins were thrown among them out of gold basins by 'the high and mighty Prince the Duke of Gloucester'. Spices and wine were handed about among the guests, 'as pertaineth to matrimonial feasts'. From the chapel the party then ascended to the Painted Chamber where a stately banquet was spread. This time the bride, now not Duchess of Norfolk only but Duchess of York, was led, on her right hand by the Duke of Gloucester, on her left by the Duke of Buckingham.*

Five days later on January 20, a great tournament was held at Westminster in honour of the marriage. The lists must have been erected in some space very near to the Abbey, for this event, like others, was said to have taken place 'in the Sanctuary'. A long list of knights had assembled compete, and when each knight rode into the tilting ground, his three other horses were led in after him. The first to ride in was 'the Lord Marquess of Dorset, armed in great triumph'. His choice of an attendant was ominous in the light of after events: 'The Duke of Buckingham bare his helm'. The contestants included three more of the Queen's relatives—Lord Richard Grey and Sir Richard Haute appeared, but the cynosure was Earl Rivers. Over his armour he wore the habit of a White Hermit and his horse carried the simulacrum of a hermitage, covered with black velvet with eight glass windows in it, above it the cross of St. Antony, the Earl's namesake, with a bell ringing over it and a rosary hanging down, but all this, the chronicler said, was 'pleasaunce'. When he emerged from the hermitage, his servants 'pulled from him' the hermit's habit, and he was revealed in full armour, his horse 'trapped in tawny satin and gold'.

Three prizes were to be awarded. The little Duchess of York was to present them, aided by the Princess Elizabeth. As Madame la Dauphine it was fitting that the latter should bear a part in this magnificent spectacle, and the company of a twelve year old sister-in-law would help and encourage the six year old 'Princess of the Feast'. The prizes were gold badges; the one to be awarded by the Princess Elizabeth was in the shape of an E and was set with a large diamond; the other two were in the forms of A and M, the initials of the Duchess of York, set with a ruby and an emerald respectively. Sir Thomas Lynes gained the A, Lord Robert Clifford the M, Sir Richard Haute the E. The officials explained to the little girls who had won the jewels, and when the victors were brought before them, the knights received their awards from the childish hands.

Earl Rivers sent twenty marks to be distributed among the Heralds and King of Arms.†

The previous day, Parliament had assembled. The Duke of Clarence was now brought from the Tower to the bar of the House of Lords, and the King, facing his brother, pronounced the grounds of his attainder. He reminded the hearers of his record of magnanimity to traitors, but this treason of the Duke of Clarence, he said, was 'more malicious, more unnatural, more loathly' than all the rest. He recalled his past forgiveness of Clarence's treachery, the generosity with which he had given him

* Sandford, Francis, *Genealogical History of the Kings of England*, 1677.
† Black, W. H., *Illustrations of Ancient State and Chivalry*, 1840.

'gifts, and grants of goods and possessions'; utterly lacking in gratitude and loyalty, Clarence had set about destroying the King and his family, 'by might to be gotten as well outward as inward', a reference to what Clarence had said he would do in England, once he were Duke of Burgundy. He had sent his servants about the country to sow sedition, giving them money to make venison-feasts for assemblies, where they persuaded the people that his follower Burdett had been wrongfully put to death, that the King used necromancy to destroy his subjects, that the King himself was illegitimate 'from the incontinency of his mother', that he had seized what was his, Clarence's right to the crown, that the Duke had induced several of the King's subjects to swear fealty to himself, that he had ordered his retainers to be ready in harness at an hour's warning, that he had threatened judges and jurors, that he had attempted to get a strange child brought into Warwick Castle to pass for his son, while his own son should be sent secretly to Ireland to act as a magnet for rebellion. (The Duke was Lord Lieutenant of Ireland and Clarence was an Irish title.) With these accusations piled one on top of another, the King asked for a Bill of Attainder to be passed against his brother. When the bill should have been passed and become an Act, it would be Clarence's death warrant. The scene was considered by those who heard it awe-inspiring and unique. It was astonishing to hear the King himself in the role of accuser, and the Croyland Continuator was shocked by the fact that the witnesses whom the King produced to confirm his charges, behaved less like witnesses than prosecuting counsel: 'these two offices not being exactly suited to the same person in the same cause'. That the King spoke in person showed how deeply he was stirred. It was perhaps natural in these circumstances that no one ventured to speak in the Duke's defence, but this was commented on, none the less. In all the assembly, Clarence had no supporter who would plead for him even in deprecating terms. The confrontation of the furious king and his slippery, brilliant, hopeless brother, caught and pinned down at last, struck the beholders dumb. Where defenders might have been expected to speak, the awful silence remained unbroken.

Clarence then made his own defence. It was merely a denial of everything that had been alleged against him; and it concluded with a demand of utter desperation—that he should be allowed to prove his innocence by wager of battle.

The tournament celebrating the Duke of York's wedding had been held a few days before; troops of knights had entered the lists followed by three coursers apiece, Lord Rivers had graced the occasion in fancy dress, and jewelled tokens had been bestowed on the winners, but though all this had taken place a few hundred yards from where Parliament was now sitting, it was a world away from the harsh realities of treason, imprisonment and death. Parliament declared that they were satisfied of the truth of the King's accusations and the Duke of Buckingham, the most highly born member of the peerage, was appointed Steward of England, that he might pronounce sentence of death. On February 8 this sentence was uttered.

Clarence was now in the Bowyer Tower under sentence of death, but his brother had not yet signed the death warrant. This, the last step, was going to prove the most difficult to achieve by those who were working for it, but who were they?

21

SUFFICIENT grounds for a conviction of high treason, for which the penalty was death, had been publicly brought against Clarence, but treason—conspiracy, rebellion, assumption of the royal prerogatives— these were the King's affair. It was not plain, from the grounds of the attainder, why the Queen should use her influence with the King to get the sentence carried out. Anything which threatened the King's security was of course a threat to the Woodvilles, but the rumour was shortly current and widely believed that the Queen and her family were insistent with the King that Clarence should be put to death and Mancini recorded as an accepted fact that, later, they were frightened of the Duke of Gloucester because they had been responsible for the death of his brother.*

Philippe de Commines has been described as the first of the modern historians—the earliest of the writers who gave detailed studies of the personalities of the men who moved events. He is now considered to have been too severe in his estimate of Edward IV; his charges of lechery, gluttony, ostentation and avarice can hardly be rebutted, but he did not give the King sufficient credit for his statesmanship. Commines was never in England, though he saw Edward in Burgundy and in France. He gives the picture of him at the signing of the Treaty of Pecquigny. The King of England, tall, very handsome, beginning to grow fat, came walking along the causeway in cloth of gold, a black velvet cap on his head decorated with a large fleur de lys of precious stones. He took this off and bowed magnificently, to within six inches of the ground. The French King spoke to him with affectionate courtesy. The English King replied, 'in quite good French'. Commines had the historian's talent for acquiring information, and though his details may be occasionally inaccurate, as is natural in a work written in a country other than the one whose history he relates, he had sources of intelligence, whatever they may have been, which produced extremely interesting material. The story of Edward IV's not having been in a position legally to marry Elizabeth Woodville became so important an element in the situation after his death, and was so generally credited, it is strange that the earliest authority for it should be Commines, who relates it in his *Mémoires*, written between 1489 and 1491. He says that Edward

* Mancini, *op. cit.*

had been troth-plight to the widowed Lady Eleanor Butler, daughter of the great Talbot, Earl of Shrewsbury, the hero of the last phase of the French war. The troth-plight was supposed to be as binding as the marriage, unless it were dissolved by mutual consent, and was sometimes used or abused by the man as a means of persuading the woman to go to bed with him before the marriage ceremony. This troth-plight had, it appeared, been sworn before Robert Stillington, a cleric who became Bishop of Bath and Wells in 1465 and Lord Chancellor in 1467. After a long illness he resigned or was dismissed from this office in 1475. He then retired to his diocese; and Gloucestershire which marches with Somerset was the county where Clarence's favourite seats were placed. His wife and her sister as the daughters of Warwick were co-heiresses of the Lordship of Tewkesbury; Isabella had been confined in the infirmary of Tewkesbury Abbey, and later the Duke and Duchess were entombed in the Abbey itself. Their grave lay behind the high altar and above them in the roof of the choir was a decoration that commemorated the great Yorkist victory. In the centre of the vault was a stone carving like a wheel, and alternating with the eight spokes, eight suns-in-spendour had been introduced with their starry rays, a circlet of gleaming gold.

An aquaintance, an alliance even, was natural between the royal duke, the greatest landowner in the west, and the Bishop of Bath and Wells. Stillington was not any longer one of the clerical statesman who sat on the King's Great Council; Somerset was remote from London, and the charm of the Duke of Clarence might well tempt a disappointed man of not very distinguished mind or strong personality to make himself immensely important by confiding to the Duke a secret whose implications were deadly to Clarence's envied brother.

As the whole matter had been kept dark, and the Lady Eleanor Butler was many years dead, it was not possible to find out whether or not the troth-plight had been relinquished by mutual consent. As it stood, the story meant that the King's marriage was void and the children of it illegitimate. It was said that Elizabeth Woodville had once used her influence with Lord Worcester when he was Lieutenant of Ireland, to have the Earl of Desmond put to death because the Earl had suggested that her husband might divorce her and marry a wife more suited to the position of Queen of England; it needed no imagination to see how she and her family would behave once they heard that Clarence had put about this story. How they heard it was not disclosed, but Clarence, 'brittle as the glass', had not the brains to keep such a secret, and anyone who gained the information, could sell it to the Queen or one of her relatives for a rich reward. The immediate reaction of the Woodville party was to importune the King to carry out the death sentence on which he himself had already decided; it was the only sure way to stop Clarence's mouth.

It is sometimes said that since this story was afloat, it was scarcely possible that Richard of Gloucester should not have heard it; he may, of course, have regarded it as part of the flotsam and jetsam of rumour that gathers about kings, until chance reminded him that it was there to use; at all events, it was the general opinion, recorded by Mancini, that he believed the Woodvilles had played their part in bringing about his brother's death.

Not only was the most urgent reason for carrying out the sentence not made public; mystery conceals the final truth about the method of the execution. The one accepted fact is that it was performed in the Tower on February 18, 1478. The shame of his brother's treason and the aweful-ness of putting him to death, even the fear of a demonstration on his behalf, may have decided the King not to have him beheaded on Tower Green, in view of as many of the populace as chose to come. Of the contemporary mentions of his death, most of them say that he was drowned in a butt of Malmesey wine, one that he was drowned in a bath. The most brilliant speech in *Richard the Third* is the one Shakespeare gives to Clarence, describing the prophetic dream he has had the night before his murder:

> Oh Lord! Methought what pain it was to drown!

The restrictions of the stage demanded that the first murderer should stab him, dragging the body off and saying that if the victim be not quite dead, he will drown him 'in the Malmesy butt within'. This was stating the popular belief in theatrical terms.

The most interesting statement about the death occurs in a note by another hand added to Fabyan's second work, *The Great Chronicle of London*. The date given is a month out, though Fabyan has given it correctly on the same page, and there is a serious mis-statement about the death of the Duchess of Clarence, but the rest of the passage brings us as close as we are likely to get to the actual scene. It appears to be taken from a book belonging to someone called Spencer, though a note to the 1938 edition of *The Great Chronicle* says: 'Spencer as a collector or possessor of books is unknown'. It runs: 'The Duke of Clarence was by Parliament attaint of treason and on the 21st of March offered his own mass-penny in the Tower of London, and about twelve o'clock of noon, made his end in a rondelet of Malvesey, and after he was carried to Tewkesbury and there buried by his wife, which died a little before him, of poison etc. so sayeth the Spencer book'. The passage, if believed, shows that the execution was not a sudden, unexpected onslaught but that Clarence attended mass in preparation for his death. There is another memorandum, casting a ray of light from a different angle. The Calendar of Patent Rolls (1476–85) notes a grant of the incomes from some of Clarence's manors for six years, to Earl Rivers, 'in consideration of the injuries perpetrated on him and his parents by George, late Duke of Clarence, and because the said Duke on the day of his death and before, intended that he should be recompensed'. Did Clarence have a 'lightening before death', in which he repented that, with Warwick, he had been responsible for beheading Antony Woodville's father and brother, and accusing his mother of witchcraft? Or did he accept the suggestion of benefiting the present Earl Rivers, with glittering irony and scorn? Whatever the origin of the arrangement, the outcome was not in doubt; for the next six years, Earl Rivers stood to gain a hundred pounds a year; while by 1480, the Marquess of Dorset had been given the wardships of a dozen of Clarence's manors and lordships, from which he was to draw the revenues until the late Duke's son should come of age.* The Croyland Continuator, whose knowledge and judgment makes him in the last resort the most valuable of all the commentators, says merely: 'After a few days, the execution, whatever its nature may have been, took place'. He added, 'The King, as I really believe, inwardly repented very often of this act.'

The Yorkist Plantagenets had by nature a strong family affection, and this had been strengthened because in their youth they had shared and triumphantly survived, hardship and danger. No one could have been surprised if, after Clarence had deserted the King for Warwick, with the declared intention of seizing the crown, Edward had doomed him to a traitor's death. A man of harsher temperament would not have given Clarence another chance to betray him; but Edward had forgiven his brother until the mounting tale of the latter's disloyalties was such that any other man would have been condemned to death for them. Clarence's treason was particularly odious because he was the King's brother who, as such, had been treated with lavish generosity. Was this to be a reason for not visiting him with the penalty he had earned?

It is difficult to believe that in the circumstances and the temper of the times, Edward was unjustified, or even ill-judged in what he did. And yet:

> It hath the primal eldest curse upon it,
> A brother's murder.

The putting to death of one of the immediate family was a dreadful step, requiring a summoning-up of intense resolution. But in unnatural deeds, the shock of the first one is the worst. To repeat what has been done already is easier.

* Ross, op. cit., p. 381.

22

CLARENCE was put to death on February 18, 1478. The next month, Bishop Stillington was imprisoned in the Tower. The charge against Clarence that was most injurious to the Queen had not been made public; the charge against Stillington was not made public either. For three months he was held prisoner; by the middle of June the King had apparently sifted the matter and the Calendar of Patent Rolls says that on June 20, the Bishop 'was pardoned for words uttered against the King and his state'; the declaration was accepted that 'Robert, Bishop of Bath and Wells, has been faithful to the King and done nothing contrary to his oath of fealty, as he has shown before the King and certain Lords'. In other words, whether the story were false or true, Stillington had entirely dissociated himself from it. Since the imprisonment must have acted as a most severe warning, he would not be likely to tell it again. He continued to be employed by the Crown on certain commissions, but he was not a leading statesman any longer.

In this year Edward set in hand the building of a chapel only surpassed by the contemporary masterpiece of Kings' College Chapel at Cambridge. The chapel at Windsor Castle had been built by Henry III, and refitted by Edward III as a chapel for the Order of the Garter, with stalls for the members over which each knight's sword and helmet was displayed. The building was in decay by the 1470's and Edward IV set about building another chapel of St. George, whose east-end wall should be the triple-arched west front of Henry III's building. In the centre arch remains an exquisite relic of Henry III's aesthetic patronage: a pair of doors painted in scarlet gesso and covered with iron scroll-work, gilded, the whorls breaking into leaf. Edward IV began his new structure in 1478 and, fifty years later, it was finished by Henry VIII. The first part undertaken by Edward was the north aisle beside the choir. In this he caused to be erected a tomb for himself, behind a screen 'of steel, polished and gilt, representing two gates betwixt two tall towers, all of curious, transparent workmanship, after the gothic manner'.* The loveliest of the chapel's ornaments is the garland of angels, running all round the choir, nave and transepts at clerestory level: carved in stone, only their heads,

* Sandford, *Genealogical History of the Kings of England*.

feathered wings and hands are visible; they are linked by holding an endless, ribbon-like scroll of music. Below the ledge over which they lean is a frieze of crowns, sunbursts and roses. Their eerily radiant faces smile beneath coronets set with sunbursts and jewels. In 1479, Edward ordered from William Morton the London vestment maker, seven copes of white silk damask, embroidered with angels playing various musical instruments.*

1479 was a year of great plague. As the death of the three year old Prince George occurred in it, it is thought he may have died of the sickness; he was buried in the chapel his father was building. The rest of the King's family remained healthy and in August the Queen bore her sixth daughter, the Princess Catherine. At the end of the year, Holinshed says: 'King Edward began his Christmas at Woking, and at five days' end, removed to Greenwich, where he kept out the other part of his Christmas with great royalty'.

Shakespeare made the Earl of Westmorland say to King Henry V that it was 'a saying very old and true: If that you will France win, Then with Scotland first begin', so fully was it understood that no English king could afford to leave the Border unguarded while he went abroad, and that France could tip the scale against England by supporting the hostile Scots. Richard of Gloucester and the Earl of Northumberland had held the north against threats of full-scale invasion, but border-forays were endemic; how grimly these bore on the population may be guessed from the remains of stone keeps still standing in the fields of the border counties, the 'barstle hooses' or 'bastille houses' into which men brought their families, horses and cattle when word came round that the terrible moss-troopers were out. Edward tried to gain a firm alliance with James III, but it was difficult to treat with him. 'King James,' said Holinshed, 'was known to be a man so wedded to his own opinion, that he could not abide them that would speak contrary to his fancy'; this led him to shun his able councillors and give himself up to the guidance of incompetent flatterers. In 1473, Edward had attempted to seal an alliance by the betrothal of James' seven months old son, the Duke of Rothesay, to the most beautiful of his own children, the four year old Princess Cecily. The English King pleased the Scots by paying yearly instalments of the Princess's dowry, and in 1478, they agreed to a marriage between King James' sister, the Princess Margaret, and King Edward's brother-in-law, Earl Rivers. This was to take place at Nottingham the following year. The children's marriage must remain in abeyance for some years, and though he had assented to it, King James seemed in no haste to conclude his sister's.

Louis XI was working ceaselessly at his life's aim: the absorption of the duchy of Burgundy into the territory of France. One of his chief

* Scofield, *op. cit.*, Vol. II, p. 434.

obstacles was the possibility of substantial English help being given to Burgundy, and to avert this he instigated the Scots to a series of truce-breaking raids and forays across the border. In the summer of 1480, the Dowager Duchess of Burgundy came to England to try to secure Edward's full-scale commitment to Burgundy. This Edward refused to give; he did not want to lose the 50,000 crowns he drew annually from the French King; but neither did he altogether repudiate his sister's plea. The Dowager Duchess's visit to England had alarmed Louis XI, and Edward's equivocal behaviour kept him in a state of anxiety.

The Duchess was treated by her family with affectionate ceremony. She was escorted from Calais to London by a fleet under the command of Sir Edward Woodville and attended by a retinue newly dressed in purple and blue velvet. Edward lodged her in the Cold Harbour, a large house in Thames Street, near the Tower. It was a stone building of five gables and four storeys of mullioned, latticed windows, rising sheer out of the water like her mother's house, Baynard's Castle, further down the shore. In the centre of the river front, a flight of stone stairs under an archway led up to the interior of the house.

Apart from its diplomatic mission, the Duchess's visit was of considerable significance. When, in later years, she gave her support to the 'feigned boy', Perkin Warbeck, who called himself Prince Richard, Duke of York, it was said that she had coached the imposter in his part, and this has been denied, notably by Horace Walpole in his 'Historic Doubts', on the ground that the Duchess never saw her nephew, since she had left England before he was born. This visit, which Walpole overlooked, was paid when the Duke of York was seven, and as he, unlike his elder brother, was not banished to a distance but lived with his mother, it is not only likely that his aunt should have seen him, but almost impossible that she should not.

In November 1480 the Queen bore her last child, the Princess Bridget. This infant, like her sister before her, was born at Eltham Palace. She was christened in the palace chapel by the Bishop of Chichester; the Lady Margaret Beaufort, Countess of Richmond, still so called though she was now married to Lord Henry Stafford, younger brother of the Duke of Buckingham, carried the baby to the font; the Marquess of Dorset assisted her. The Princess's godmothers were her grandmother, the Dowager Duchess of York, and her sister, the Princess Elizabeth, her godfather the Bishop of Winchester. The god-parents 'gave great gifts to the Princess', and these were carried in front of her in the procession which took her back to her mother's chamber. 'One hundred torches were borne by knights, esquires and other honest persons', and after the christening, 'were lit all the aforesaid torches', in the murk of St. Martin's Day. The Lord Hastings, the King's Chamberlain and the Lord Stanley, Steward of the King's House, were in charge of the proceedings, but the most important gentleman present was the seven year old Prince Richard of York. In the absence of his brother the Prince of Wales the rôle of chief nobleman at his sister's christening fell to him.*

The intercourse of the sisters-in-law, the Queen and the Dowager Duchess of Burgundy had no doubt been strictly controlled by etiquette, diplomacy and the good manners that are the result of intensive social training; otherwise there were sources enough of disquiet to make it uneven. The grave of Clarence yawned like a pit, and there had been the repudiation of Lord Rivers as a suitor to the young Duchess of Burgundy.

In this year, Caxton printed another of Lord Rivers' works translated from the French: a series of thoughts 'on the four last things undoubtedly coming: Death, Judgment, Hell and Heaven'. Caxton said in the preface that Lord Rivers wanted this work 'to go abroad among the people, for he desireth with a great zeal and spiritual love . . . that we shall abhor and utterly forsake the abominable and damnable sins which commonly be used nowadays, as, pride, perjury, terrible swearing, theft, murder and many other'. The catalogue breaks off discreetly; if lechery and gluttony had been particularized, it might have seemed to glance too nearly at the King. To do Lord Rivers justice, the urge he felt to improve the world at large was at least implemented by some financial sacrifice of his own. At the end of the same preface Caxton says that Lord Rivers 'hath procured and gotten of our holy Father the Pope, a great and large indulgence and grace unto the Chapel of our Lady of the Piewe, by St. Stephen of Westminster, for the relief and help of Christian souls passed out of this transitory world'. Stow relates that this shrine, with its richly jewelled statue of the Virgin was burnt out, because the man who should have seen to the extinguishing of its candles and lamps had left the task to a schoolboy, and that Lord Rivers had restored it at his own expense. In his will, Rivers named the chapel as his first choice of a burying-place, a wish not to be granted. Meanwhile, the date had gone by when he should have been married to the Princess Margaret of Scotland.

But affairs on the Border were growing beyond the power of diplomacy to control. The raiding, pillaging and burning went on. In 1480 Edward sent a demand to James III that hostilities should cease, that Berwick which Margaret of Anjou had ceded to the Scots, should be returned to the English crown, and that the young Duke of Rothesay should be sent into England as a pledge that his father meant to carry out the engagement to the Princess Cecily. He threatened war if these demands were not met immediately. In May he appointed Gloucester Lieutenant General and commissions of array were sent in Yorkshire, Cumberland

* Records of Garter King of Arms, quoted in *The Gentleman's Magazine*, January 1831.

and Northumberland for the defence of the Border. Meanwhile the Scots reply to the English King's ultimatum was a raid led by the Earl of Angus twenty miles over the Border into England, ending with the burning of Bamburgh. Gloucester and Northumberland carried a counter-raid into the south west of Scotland, burning and destroying as far as Dumfries. Edward's determination to make full scale war against Scotland meant that he was prevented from providing help to Burgundy; and though the complete annexation of Burgundy to France would have serious consequences for England, to avoid entering hostilities on the duchy's behalf would safeguard the annual payment of fifty thousand gold crowns from the French King and leave intact the betrothal of the Princess Elizabeth to the Dauphin. The English King and Queen were very eager for this marriage; John Lord Howard was sent to France to enquire from Louis XI when the English Princess should be sent to him. Louis XI replied that as soon as his pressing business with Burgundy allowed him any leisure, he would send for the Princess himself, with a train of such magnificence as befitted her.

23

EDWARD continued his preparations for the Scots invasion. He ordered several cannon to be shipped back from Calais for use in the north and he appointed John Lord Howard to the command of the fleet. In May 1481, he took the Prince of Wales with him to Sandwich for a naval inspection.*

This child was now ten and a half. It was policy to speak with great praise of a Prince of Wales, but the little boy seems to have been attractive and interesting. The Croyland Continuator refers to King Edward's 'most sweet and beautiful children', and coming of a handsome father, enamoured of their beautiful mother, there were eugenic reasons for their loveliness. Mancini said of Prince Edward: 'He had such dignity in his whole person, and in his face such charm that the beholders were never tired of looking at him'. This suggests the effect of careful training on a child of natural gifts. The court poet of Brescia, Petrus Carmelianus, who was in London to make his way, dedicated a Latin poem, 'Easter Verses', to the Prince in April 1482: 'The youth of the nation, the boys and old men, rejoice in you, and all the stars delight in your face. You, most beautiful Prince, are the glory of the noble kingdom. You will rule the realm in happiness after your father, and the fates will give you for long the royal authority.' The tragic emptiness of the prophecy does not devalue the personal description.

In the nine years during which he had lived mostly at Ludlow, Bishop Alcock had taught him not only to know but to enjoy. Mancini spoke of 'his special knowledge of literature which enabled him to discourse elegantly, to understand fully and to declaim most excellently from any work, whether it were in verse or prose, that came into his hands', unless, Mancini adds, 'it were from among the most abstruse authors'.

The academic teaching of a receptive pupil had been excellent and the psychological training no less effective. The Prince had an unquestioning trust in his uncle Lord Rivers and no one gains the complete confidence of a clever child without in some way deserving it. Rivers was absolutely loyal to the Prince's parents, the great, splendid father and the mother who was grander than any other lady, and with the beauty of an enchantress.

* Ross, *op. cit.*, p. 280.

Everything that Lord Rivers taught him about his duties as a Prince was accepted as the King's mandate. Made conscious at an early age that his person was of very great importance, but that his behaviour must be schooled in a way that was not enjoined on any other boy, the difficult path which as a small child he had had to tread, had been made easier for him because his uncle was not only affectionate but even-tempered and gentle in manner. He was also very clever and could gain the Prince's admiration by writing books. The Prince had had printed books dedicated to him by Caxton. He must have possessed copies of them, or Caxton's earnest, affectionate prefaces would have been thrown away. He also possessed some of the illustrated manuscripts, of which his father had such a fine collection. Two at least were Books of Hours. These were manuals of the prayers appointed to be said at seven set times during the day, and the Flemish artists made of them absorbing picture books; they illustrated them with events of the New Testament, or of the lives of saints, or of famous living personages, of feasts or tournaments or battles or seafaring. The pictures were often surrounded by wide borders of gold or red or blue, on which were painted in exquisite detail in their natural colours, roses, wild roses, pinks, lilies, columbines, pansies, speedwell, pimpernels, daisies, wild strawberries, with sometimes snails, ladybirds, butterflies and moths. The scenes themselves were of vivid interest, imagined in fifteenth-century surroundings; the verisimilitude of the picture of St. Elizabeth of Hungary giving food and clothes to beggars in the Book of Hours produced in Ghent for the Prince in 1480, makes the more impressive the presence of an angel floating in mid-air on outspread wings, holding two crowns above her head.

The infant mortality of the time, though very high, spared all but three of the King's ten children, but on November 19, 1481, his little daughter-in-law, Anna Duchess of York, died just before her tenth birthday. Richard Cely, writing to his brother on November 26, says: 'As for tidings, I can none but my young Lady of York is dead'.* She died in the Queen's palace of Greenwich and was buried in Westminster Abbey, in the chapel which the Queen had dedicated to St. Erasmus. Her tomb was one of those displaced when the chapel was demolished to make way for the Chapel of Henry VII. The lead coffin was removed to Stepney. In this countrified region, east of the Tower, the Bishop of London owned landed property, a house known as Bishopshall and two forests. He may have afforded what was perhaps meant to be a temporary sanctuary. At all events the coffin was re-buried and forgotten. In 1964 it was discovered while foundations were being dug for a building site. The inscription on it identified the bones inside. The hair was wonderfully preserved, and in spite of the eyeless sockets, the fallen nose and the upper teeth projecting over the space from where the lower jaw had

* *The Cely Papers*, ed. H. E. Malden, 1900.

132

dropped away, the forehead of the skull from which the hair had been swept back, still gave the idea of a little girl. Whether the eight year old Duke of York were moved by the solemnity of the event, whether he were sorry to lose a companion, by his father the material aspect of the death was treated as highly important. The marriage settlement had provided that the Mowbray lands conferred upon the Duke of York were to remain his property for life even if his wife predeceased him without children. Edward now thought it safer to have the settlement turned into an Act of Parliament. John Lord Howard had already acquiesced in the confiscation of his inheritance; Lord Berkeley now re-affirmed his share of the agreement, but with what turned out to be an ominous proviso—that the lands were to return to him if both the Duke and his father the King died without male heirs. Two years saw the restitution of them to Lord Berkeley.

In March 1482, a death occurred of much greater significance. The young Duchess of Burgundy died as the result of a fall from horseback. She left two small children, a boy and a girl. Louis XI at once claimed that the Duchy and its territories reverted to the French crown and he began a negotiation which was to affect Edward IV very keenly. The latter however was absorbed in negotiations nearer home. In April, a scheme appeared to offer which would secure him against the perpetual menace of Scots hostility. James III's younger brother the Duke of Albany, lurking in France, was, as Clarence had been, avid for his brother's throne. Edward offered him English help to gain it, if Albany would promise to cancel all treaties made with France and agree to the terms Edward had already tried to impose on James III. In June, Edward and Gloucester had a meeting with Albany at Fotheringhay and the following month the offensive against James III began. Gloucester commanded in chief. In August he re-took the town of Berwick. The castle held out and for the time being he did not stay to reduce it, but pressed on to Edinburgh, which he entered in triumph but magnanimously forbore to sack.

While Gloucester was extending the English sphere of influence in the north, the Queen was vigilantly protecting her own rights at home. Sir William Stonor, an Oxfordshire knight, was a follower and friend of the King, but she heard that he had been exceeding his privileges and hunting on land that belonged to her, 'in contempt of us, thus uncourteously to hunt and slay our deer, to our great marvel and displeasure'. She informed him that 'we intend to sue such remedy therein as shall accord with my Lord's laws'. She wrote from Greenwich, and the King was elsewhere, for she went on: 'Whereas we furthermore understand that ye purpose, under colour of my Lord's commission in that behalf granted unto you, as ye say, to take the rule of our game and deer within our said forest and chase, we will that ye show unto us or to our Council your said commission, if any such ye have.' Meanwhile, he was to stop hunting on the Queen's land, 'as ye will answer at your peril'.* Considering the vast amount of property she had amassed over the last sixteen years, it was strange that she should so vindictively resent the slightest infringement of her rights by one of her husband's friends.

The next news from Scotland was that Albany, now face to face with his brother, had decided to withdraw and accept the very substantial concessions offered to him. Gloucester, seeing that Albany was of no further use, and alive to the very heavy expense of keeping his army in the field, decided to withdraw his troops from Edinburgh. On his way south he besieged and captured Berwick Castle. The fortress and the citadel were now in English hands once more, a considerable gain, though the Croyland Continuator said that what with the expenses of the campaign and the cost of maintaining the stronghold, it really was not worth the money. But the expedition had at least made the Scots anxious for peace; James III re-opened negotiations; he declared himself eager for the marriage alliance of the Duke of Rothesay and the Princess Cecily; he even renewed the overtures for that of Lord Rivers with the Princess Margaret.

By October however, Edward seemed determined to refuse all approaches. He finally broke off the betrothal of Princess Cecily, demanding the return of that part of her dowry which he had already paid. Lord Rivers' betrothal went by the board at the same time.

At some time after October 1482 and before April 1483, however, Lord Rivers achieved a second marriage. The lady was Mary, daughter and heiress of Sir Henry FitzLewis of Hornden, Essex. Her mother had been Elizabeth Beaufort, daughter of the second Duke of Somerset. The match made no stir; there were no children of it, and, more strangely, it did not commit the newly wedded pair to living under the same roof. By the spring of 1483, Lord Rivers had resumed his duties with the Prince of Wales at Ludlow.

Edward was preparing for a crushing onslaught on the Scots early in 1483, but before Christmas of 1482, Louis XI had concluded a treaty with Burgundy which dealt the King of England a shattering blow. The widower Maximilian had tried in vain to enlist English support against the relentless acquisitiveness of Louis XI, but the councils of Flanders and Brabant saw their security and their commercial prosperity in terms of an alliance with the French power rather than a struggle against it. They agreed that Burgundy and Artois should acknowledge French authority. The compact was sealed by the betrothal of their infant Princess, Margaret, to the Dauphin.

This insolent and unexpected demarche by Louis XI, annihilating without one word of warning or apology the betrothal contract between

* Stonor *Letters and Papers,* 1290–1483, ed. C. L. Kingsford, Vol. II, p. 150.

the Dauphin and Princess Elizabeth was a severe wound to the English King's *amour propre* as well as to his statesmanship; his health was beginning to fail, and it was said that he never recovered from it. The French *volte-face* had also serious political consequences. The Treaty of Arras was signed in December 1482. The next payment of the French pension to Edward was due at Michaelmas, September 29; but by the end of September, 1482, Louis XI had already calculated that he should not need the English alliance any more and the gold crowns expected at Michaelmas were never sent, nor any further instalment of them. More injurious, Calais, the greatly prized English stronghold, was now at risk, because Artois, the district in which it lay, would be in French possession. Edward's preparations for war were pushed ahead; it was not announced whether they were for use against France or Scotland.

In spite of a maelstrom of cares, Edward IV kept Christmas splendidly at Eltham. Holinshed says that two thousand persons were feasted in the palace daily; but though lavish, the King was not spendthrift. Early in his reign he had caused to be compiled the Liber Niger, a book of orders and regulations for the conduct of his immense household, and in 1478, this had been revised to set right 'certain enormities and misguidings'. Under the new rules, food left over from the King's table and the Queen's table was to be distributed daily to people waiting for it at the palace gates, but 'neither messes of meat nor bottles of wine nor pots of ale or other victual' were to pass the gates 'without a special commandment of the steward, treasurer or comptroller'.*

The King was a very hearty trencherman; his large frame required keeping up and he combined a healthy appetite with the tastes of an epicure. Mancini had heard that he had such a passion for his food, he sometimes adopted the Roman practice of making himself vomit when he was replete, so that he could begin another banquet immediately. His becoming fat was generally put down to his eating and drinking so much. At the same time, he had always had a confidence in the medical profession. One of the earliest books known to have belonged to him was a collection of medical tracts bound in one volume, inscribed as the property of Edward, Earl of March; and a part of his household regulations provided that the King's doctor of physic was to consult daily with the steward, the chamberlain and the master-cook, 'to devise by counsel what meats or drinks is best-according to the King's diet'. This care and attention was no doubt merely the precaution of a sensible man; it was in no case the vigilance of an invalid or a hypochondriac. An immense faculty for enjoyment helped greatly to make Edward popular, as he liked to promote the enjoyment of others, and it is reflected in the luxuriousness of his appointments and his dress. The Wardrobe Accounts of Edward IV for 1480 show the King's idea of a comfortable bed: 'a great, large

* Scofield, *op, cit.*, Vol. II, p. 217.

featherbed with the bolster thereunto stuffed with down'; hangings of tapestry with crowns and roses in blue and crimson, a canopy of blue and white velvet with valance and counterpane of the same, another entry records eighteen yards of white woollen, to make six pairs of blankets. The King's clothes were famous for their richness and their mode. The Croyland Continuator speaks of his appearance in his court at the Christmas before his death, 'clad in a great variety of most costly garments, of quite a different cut from those which had hitherto been seen in our Kingdom'. The Wardrobe Accounts mention lengths of stuff: white damask with flowers of divers colours, white velvet tissue cloth of gold, white velvet with black spots. Of long gowns, the King had one of blue cloth of gold lined with green satin, one of white damask furred with fine sables, a loose gown of purple cloth of gold furred with ermine. To the high and mighty Prince Edward, then aged twelve, by the Grace of God Prince of Wales, Duke of Cornwall, Earl of Chester, was issued five yards of white cloth of gold tissue for a gown. The Queen and the Princess Elizabeth were given fifteen yards of green tissue cloth of gold. Nor were the Queen's relatives forgotten. The Marquess Dorset and Earl Rivers were given each three yards of white tissue cloth of gold, for one short gown.

As the Croyland Continuator evoked the vision of Edward IV and his seven remaining children, at court, it was another instance of the Prince of Wales being in London with his parents. The Continuator speaks of 'those most sweet and beautiful children, the issue of his marriage with Queen Elizabeth'. They were 'Edward Prince of Wales and Richard Duke of York' 'who had not yet attained puberty', and 'their five daughters, most beauteous maidens'. Golden-haired in their garments of glittering tissue, a fairy-like band about their parents:

> Too like the lightning, which doth cease to be
> Ere one can say:- it lightens.

24

OF Edward IV's last days, two other memorials remain, in stained glass. Dr Alcock, the Prince of Wales' tutor, had been Bishop of Worcester since 1476. From his close connection with the royal family, he might have wished to put up portraits of them in the Priory Church of Great Malvern, whose glass is famous and where the Magnificat window, containing portraits of his own family, was afterwards put up by Henry VII. This however Dr. Alcock would not have been able to do; Great Malvern Priory is a cell of Westminster Abbey, over which the Bishop of the diocese has no jurisdiction; Little Malvern Priory on the other hand, was under his control, and here he put up his celebration of Edward IV. The tower and the choir are all of the church that remain standing but fortunately the latter includes the east window, of which Dr. Alcock filled five lights with a series of portraits in coloured glass: of Richard Duke of York, Edward Prince of Wales, King Edward IV, his Queen, and four Princesses, Elizabeth, Cecily, Anne and Catherine, all in one light, looking over each other's shoulders. There remain only the figures of the Prince of Wales, the four Princesses and the headless one of the Queen. The one of the Prince of Wales, invested as it is with a high degree of scarcity value, shows a clear-featured child with gold hair under a gold circlet, in a blue robe under a crimson mantle with an ermine cape, kneeling before a table on which a heavy book is lying: a natural pose in which to take the young Prince in a portrait commissioned by his admiring tutor. That the figure of the Queen, famous for her beauty, should now be headless, is disappointing, but there remains an elegant pair of clasped hands, emerging from tight crimson sleeves with ermine cuffs; over the crimson robe is a sapphire blue mantle with an ermine border. The Princesses, crowded together in the fifth light are an interesting group of natural-looking girls. The Princess Elizabeth is foremost, wearing a head-dress of the kind which covered the ears with a jewelled net and mounted a U-shaped erection on top of it; a large jewelled ornament hangs on her forehead. The Princess Cecily wears one shaped like a flower-pot, poised slanting to the back of the head. The headgear of the other sisters is indistinct, but these two are so familiar from pictures of the period they give an air of domestic realism which does not appear when the subjects are wearing crowns or coronets. Damaged as it is, the window is extremely interesting; with its bold drawing and rich colours, it gives an impression of vivid homeliness.

This is not an attribute of the great window in the north transept of Canterbury Cathedral. This, with its wonderful range of royal portraits, is said to have been put up about 1482*, and to have been the work of the King's glazier, William Neve. (It contains the figure of the Princess Mary, who died in 1482, aged fifteen, but not of the King's youngest child, the Princess Bridget, born in 1480.) The King and Queen kneel opposite each other; behind the King, in line, are the two Princes, behind the Queen, the file of the Princesses. All the figures are clothed in violet velvet, ermine and cloth of gold. The Princes wear arched crowns; the Princesses, their gold hair streaming down their backs, have gold coronets like wreaths of flowers. The boys' faces are insipid, the girls', pinched and sour. The difference between the crudely drawn faces of the children and the superb pictures of their parents, is owing to the fact that only the two latter are part of the original work. The other heads were restored after the smashing of the glass by Richard Culmer, the Puritan Vicar of Chartham in 1643.† By inexpressible good fortune, Culmer was led to spare the figures of the King and Queen. Though they are *portraits d'apparat*, they have not grandeur only but arresting conviction and naturalness; in particular that of Elizabeth Woodville with the massive gold crown accentuating the delicacy of the head, the look of discretion and coldness, the fluid grace, comes on the gazer with the force of a revelation.

Edward IV's reliance on medical aid and his affectionate care of his brother appear in the Issues of the Exchequer for February 1483. While Gloucester was still with the army in the north, the King sent his physician and surgeon, William Hobbs, 'to attend upon the Duke of Gloucester in the King's service against the Scots, with eight surgeons of his retinue'. The King paid their wages for the coming month, and he paid his apothecary John Clerk thirteen pounds, sixteen shillings and ninepence halfpenny 'for syrups, alexandrines, (antidotes) bottles of electuaries and other necessaries . . . for the use of the said Duke in his service against the Scots'. For his own luxurious well-being, ten pounds was paid to Lewis of Naples 'for rose and divers other waters presented by him to the King'.

But doctors cannot do much when the patient works consistently against his own health. In March 1483, Edward's once-magnificent constitution was beginning to fail. Powerful and athletic men, once their struggles are over and they can take their ease, sometimes put on weight; in Edward's case this had been increased by habitually eating too much, and it was considered that a riotous indulgence in sexual pleasures had

* Rackham, Bernard, *The Windows in Canterbury Cathedral.*
† ibid.

138

undermined his strength. The Queen and the Duke of Gloucester, at opposite poles on most matters had sound reason for enmity against the people who encouraged the King's licentiousness. By March 25, the King was known to be seriously ill, but there is some reason to think that his state had alarmed the Queen three weeks earlier, that she had seen for the first time in a married life of eighteen years, that his health and vigour showed signs of breaking up. On March 8, Lord Rivers wrote from Ludlow to his attorney Dymmock in London, telling him to send to Ludlow the copy of the patent appointing himself Governor of the Prince of Wales. This had been revised and re-issued the previous month. Its provisions for the Prince's regime had been left largely unchanged, except that the hour for his going to bed had been advanced to nine o'clock; but the document gave Rivers the right to direct the Prince's household, of which every man was to be furnished with horse and armour, to receive and pay out the Prince's revenues, and to remove the Prince from place to place at his discretion. He also instructed Dymmock to send him the patent by which Edward IV had given him powers to raise troops in the Welsh marches. As it has been said: 'In the event of any mishap to the King, these were powers sufficient to put political initiative into the hands of the Earl'.* Another highly significant passage in the letter concerns Rivers' nephew Dorset. Rivers was Deputy Constable of the Tower, a post which cannot have demanded much attention to duty since he was so often away from London, but an office which, if it were held by a man on the spot, could be used to considerable purpose. Rivers told Dymmock that he had decided to transfer his office to Dorset. Dymmock was to arrange the matter with the Constable of the Tower, John Lord Dudley. In ordering that the transfer should be effected, Rivers makes no single reference to the King.

Dorset was on familiar, affectionate terms with the King, Hastings was the King's dearest friend; the Queen, haughty and inimical, was the member of the circle who, although obliged in the last resort to defer to the King, had up till now had the strongest influence over him. The mutual envy and jealousy of the Woodvilles and Hastings were a standing cause of inflammation, but Edward had not greatly minded it; his powerful personality and his charm had made him able to control the dissident elements of his court. His brother Gloucester, whose hard-working existence was spent out of the court's orbit, had always disliked the King's marriage, and time had not reconciled him to it; time had only exposed the injurious influence of the Woodvilles on the great head of the House of York, in encouraging his hedonism and his inclination to rate riches above honour; nevertheless he admired and loved his elder brother, and was prepared to continue in an uneasy situation which

* E. W. Ives, *Andrew Dymmock and the papers of Antony Earl Rivers*, March 1483. *Bulletin of the Institute of Historical Research*, xli, 1968.

was made tolerable by the distance between London and Yorkshire.

It so happened that another member of the King's circle, whose position was a humble one, was to play an important part in coming events. Jane Shore, the daughter of a goldsmith, was the wife of a rich mercer of Lombard Street. Thomas More, great lawyer as he was, and a man whose personal virtue was beyond suspicion, was charmingly sympathetic in his account of her. She had been married too young, he said, and when the King's allurements of fine clothes, luxurious living and a privileged social position were held out to her, there was no founded affection to tie her to her husband. Her figure, More said, was perfection, unless you would have liked her to be a very little taller, and though at the time he wrote, her face was withered and skull-like, anyone looking at it could imagine how fair it had once been; but her beauty was not her chief fascination; that lay in her sweet nature and her amusing gaiety. What made her altogether extraordinary in court circles was that she would do a good turn if she could, but not demand to be paid for it. The King remained enchanted with her. In More's words: 'Many he had but her he loved'. The Lord Chamberlain Hastings, he said, 'was sore enamoured of her', but while the King lived, 'he forebore her, either for reverence, or for a certain friendly faithfulness'. She was, clearly, one of the women, lovely and light-hearted, who make a sexual relation an earthly paradise, without care or pain; but the alignment of her lovers was to produce appalling consequences. Edward was becoming a worn-out, elderly man and he was very fond of the young and flourishing Dorset. Jane Shore, with the expertise of a courtisane, may have been clever enough to manage an amour with both of them without offending the King. The situation became lethal when she afterwards took on Hastings. For the time being, however, these people and their friends and adherents on either side, went on as they were accustomed, rubbing shoulders with their enemies and keeping a sharp look-out for themselves. The Queen may have had an uneasy premonition and conveyed it to her brother, but none of them had foreseen that the King would be dead within three weeks of his forty-first birthday.

His illness was increasing, and a premature report of his death reaching York, a funeral mass was held for him in the minster; but within two days of his actual death, the King summoned a solemn meeting in his bedchamber at Westminster Palace. The nature of his illness has been variously described, from apoplexy to malaria to appendicitis; but as he was able to make a highly important speech on his death-bed, this seems to preclude the idea of a stroke, and as there is no record of his suffering frightful pain, this seems to put appendicitis out of the question. That, as Mancini heard, he had caught a chill while fishing, sounds a probable explanation, and Dr. John Rae,* thought the clinical picture

* *Deaths of the English Kings.* 1913.

140

was consistent with pneumonia because 'the King laid him down on his right side', as if the left lung were hurting him. This disease, without, at first, any violent symptoms of fever, weakness or pain, would have seemed an illness from which, as the Croyland Continuator said, a humbler person 'might have been cured without very much difficulty'.

The King's mind was not in a state to give any help to his body. He had been for four months profoundly disturbed and humiliated by Louis XI's having repudiated the Treaty of Pecquigny; and at home he had allowed a very dangerous situation to develop because he had been confident of his power to control it. Not only had he endowed the Queen's family to the indignation and disgust of his nobles: he had placed the Prince of Wales entirely in the hands of the Queen's relations, and dislike of the Woodvilles might ultimately overcome loyalty to the Prince. There was no danger so long as the King was alive; once he were dead, danger would immediately threaten. Edward realized that he was dying, that the saving control he had exercised would die with him, and he attempted to put up some barrier for security, the only one within his power.

More, describing the scene from the account he had received from an eye-witness,* says that the King sent for Lord Hastings and the Marquess Dorset 'with divers others of both parties' and when they had all assembled, 'the King, lifting himself up and underset with pillows', begged them with desperate earnestness to settle their differences and be reconciled to each other, for the sake of his children. His sons were so young that if they were not protected by faithful, disinterested and united councillors, the rising flood of perils would overwhelm and destroy them. If, in the uneasy hours the King looked back, across twenty-two years, to the savage untimely deaths of his father York, his brother Rutland, Prince Edward of Lancaster, King Henry VI, the blood-stained spectres that had been laid by two decades of stable successful rule, must have risen again around his bed. The gist of his final appeal was phrased by More: 'For the love that you have ever borne to me, for the love that I have ever borne to you, for the love that our Lord bears to us all, from this time forth, all griefs forgotten, each of you love other . . . and therewithal, the King, no longer enduring to sit up, laid him down on his right side, his face towards them. And none was there present that could refrain from weeping'. Hastings and Dorset clasped each other's hands and promised to fulfil his dying wish.

The scene of reconciliation was one in which the Queen's co-operation would have been as vitally important as anyone's; it was strange that on this momentous occasion she was not there. There would seem to have been some distrust on Edward's part. Whereas in the will he had made before sailing for France in 1475, her name had stood first in the

* More, Thomas, *History of King Richard III*.

list of his executors, in his later will, it was said, she was not named an executor at all.

On April 9, Edward IV died, and on April 11 the twelve year old Edward V was proclaimed king. The dead king, embalmed, robed, with a cap of maintenance on his head, lay in state in St. Stephen's Chapel for eight days. On April 17, the corpse was removed to Westminster Abbey in a great procession of bishops, lords and knights. In front of the bier walked John Lord Howard, carrying the king's banner of the royal arms and the sun-in-splendour. Next day, the procession set out for Windsor; on the coffin was a life-sized figure of the King, robed and crowned, holding sceptre and orb. In two days the magnificent cortege arrived at St. George's Chapel. Here the coffin was watched all night by 'a great company' and the next day it was laid in the tomb Edward had prepared for himself. The final masses were sung, and over the tomb was hung the King's gilt coat of mail with its crimson velvet surcoat, on which the royal arms were embroidered in gold, pearls and rubies, and his painted taffeta banner. These ceremonies were concluded on April 20.

25

EDWARD IV's final will has disappeared, but contemporary commentators said that in it the King nominated his brother Richard Duke of Gloucester as Lord Protector of the realm, guardian of the young King and of the late King's family. From the hour of Edward's death, the Queen justified her husband's distrust; she and her brothers and her two elder sons set out to disregard his will. Richard of Gloucester was at Middleham and neither she, Bishop Woodville, Sir Edward Woodville, the Marquess Dorset or Lord Richard Grey, sent any announcement to him of King Edward's death. Instead, they sent to Lord Rivers at Ludlow with the news, telling him to bring the young King to London as soon as possible. The letter reached Rivers on April 14. On April 16, the young King wrote to the Mayor of Lynn, announcing his accession and saying that he intended to be at 'our city of London, in all convenient haste, by God's grace to be crowned at Westminster'. Lynn was a small town on the Norfolk coast, far to the north east of the road from Ludlow to London; its burghers were in no way qualified to receive so important a letter; but their town was in the neighbourhood of Lord Rivers' manor of Middleton where he had had his dais made higher and the scutcheon of the Woodville arms, circled with the Garter, erected on a wall where it might best be seen; as his neighbours and supporters, the burghers of Lynn were favoured with this valuable despatch, as soon, if not sooner, than the news of King Edward's death had been conveyed to his brother the Duke of Gloucester.

In Westminster the late King's council were sitting until they should be dissolved, according to custom, at the coronation of his successor. The Queen had demanded the regency but her demand had not been met. The Woodville faction was slightly in the ascendant; the bishops were at first inclined towards them, and with the Marquess Dorset and Lord Richard Grey they commanded a slender majority. The council carried out matters of outstanding business, and Dorset who appears to have assumed powers that no one challenged, brought up the matter of French pirates who were waging an intensive war in the Channel. He got the Council to agree that his uncle, Sir Edward Woodville, who had naval experience, should be put in command of the fleet. He then reaped the benefit of his uncle Rivers' having inducted him into the office of Deputy Constable of the Tower. This rich storehouse of the King's armaments and treasure was open to him. How much of the treasure he took out is disputed, but he pillaged a great quantity; some of it he made over to Sir Edward Woodville who stowed it aboard; the rest he brought into Westminster Palace and divided between his mother and himself.

In all these doings, neither he nor the Queen, nor anyone appointed by them, had informed the Duke of Gloucester of King Edward's death. This was done by Lord Hastings, who, having given the awe-inspiring news, informed Gloucester that the King's will had left him Lord Protector of the realm and guardian of the royal family. Spurred on by what he had seen at close quarters of the Council under Dorset's management, he urged Richard to come south at once, with a large force, so that, as Mancini reported, he might take, 'before they were aware', the people who were setting aside the late King's will.

Dorset and the Queen had achieved two important points in gaining control of the fleet and the treasure; they now hazarded the most important throw of all. The office of a Protector lasted only till the new king was crowned; after that, it needed to be renewed by Parliament. Once 'the rich crown of King Edward the Confessor' was put on the head of a twelve year old boy, the authority of the formidable Duke of Gloucester would vanish like smoke. It might indeed be renewed by Parliament, but the mere act of consecration carried an influence so arcane and powerful, that once the boy was crowned king, his mother, his uncles and his half-brothers would receive an augmentation of their power which might enable them to carry all before them. The vital matter was to get the child crowned as soon as possible.

Dorset convened another council meeting, in the presence of the Queen, as if she were in fact regent, and proposed that the date for the coronation should be May 4, some three weeks ahead. The Council who could see by now the implications of all this, began to demur; the Croyland Continuator, who, as Bishop Russell of Lincoln, was, it is assumed, actually present at the council meetings, says that they had now firmly decided that the guardianship of the young King 'ought to be utterly forbidden to his uncles and brothers by the mother's side'. They were therefore in no mood to accept Dorset's view that the size of the retinue which was to bring the King to London should be left entirely to the King's decision, in other words to that of Lord Rivers. Many members of the Council saw this as really dangerous: the Lord Protector had been swept on one side, and Lord Rivers was to bring the King into London with an army. Hastings exclaimed passionately that if the escort were not definitely limited, he would retire to Calais, of which he was still governor. Elizabeth Woodville did not need to be reminded that it was from this massive base that Warwick had launched his rebellion against her husband. She agreed, however reluctantly, that Lord Rivers should be told to limit the escort to two thousand men.

Another question of great moment, arising while the Duke of Gloucester was still absent in the north, was the exact definition of the Protector's powers. Dorset maintained that he was *primus inter pares*, the head, merely, of the governing council. Others thought that the King's will had conferred on him supreme power. While the matter was still in debate, a letter from Gloucester was received. He had already written to the Queen, sending her his condolences; his letter to the Council expressed his loyalty to the new King and his family and asked the councillors to recognize the office conferred on him by his brother's will. The letter was so forthright and so reasonable, it had a reassuring effect on the uneasy councillors, and as it was then made public to the Londoners (Kendall suggests by Hastings),* the general feeling in Gloucester's favour was very strong. Mancini said: 'It was commonly said by all that the duke deserved the government'.

Nevertheless, Dorset managed to impose on the Council the date of May 4 for the coronation. It was very seriously debated whether the point could be settled in the Protector's absence, and suggested that it should be left till his arrival. Dorset's reply was rash to the verge of lunacy: 'We are so important', he said, 'that even without the King's uncle we can make and enforce these decisions'.† And he wrote again to Rivers, saying the King must be in London not later than May 1.

Since on April 16, the King had been told to say to the Mayor of Lynn that he was coming to London in all convenient haste, why did his cavalcade not set out till April 24? Rivers had of course a very great deal to do before leaving Ludlow; the affairs of the Council had to be arranged, the great household of the Castle to be broken up, the 2,000 men whom he was permitted to bring, assembled and made ready; but as it turned out, it would have been better to leave some of these matters at sixes and sevens and hasten the departure of the young King, letting him arrive even before he was expected. This however Rivers had no thought of doing. April 23 was St. George's Day, the day for the celebration of the Order of the Garter. Rivers had been a Knight of the Order since 1466; (the King himself had been a member for eleven years, since he was two) and the ceremony was one after the Earl's own heart, combining chivalry, pageantry and personal magnificence; but he had never enjoyed such an occasion as this promised to be, the delicious first-fruit of his new importance, when his nephew, pupil, protégé and king should occupy the central role. It was not practicable in the short time before them to bring him up to Windsor, where the feast was being held, but a form of it in the great hall of Ludlow Castle was the next best thing; the

* P. M. Kendall, *Richard III*, p. 170.
† Mancini, *op. cit.*

145

ceremonial supper the previous night, the vespers in the round Norman chapel of the castle, next day the procession in which all those taking part walked before the sovereign, as it wound about the Great Hall, singing.

The next day, April 24, Rivers and the King set out for London. Two thousand armed men and a great baggage train accompanied them. In immediate attendance on Edward was Thomas Vaughan, now a knight, who had carried him in his arms as a baby, been his devoted servant ever since and was now coming to see him crowned at Westminster. Before their setting out, Mancini says, Rivers had received a letter from the Duke of Gloucester, asking what arrangements had been made for the King's journey, saying that he would wish to accompany the King in his entry into London. Rivers had replied that he expected to arrive with the King at Northampton on April 29, and Gloucester had said that he would meet them there.

While he was still at Middleham, Gloucester received a message sent from Brecon by the Duke of Buckingham. The latter seemed to have been more closely in touch with affairs at Westminster than the Protector himself. Without preamble or explanation, he offered to join Gloucester on his journey to London and to bring with him a thousand men. Gloucester sent back word by the Duke's messenger that he was coming south to meet the King, that he would be glad if Buckingham would join him, but asking him to limit his escort to three hundred men, the number that Gloucester meant to bring himself. On April 20, the day of Edward IV's commital to the tomb, Gloucester in deep mourning, followed by his three hundred men also in black, attended a funeral mass, weeping, in York Minster; then 'constraining all the nobility of these parts to take the oath of fealty to the late King's son', said the Croyland Continuator, 'he himself was the first to take the oath'. This done, with his black-clothed band, he began to ride southwards, towards Northampton. In the words of Oliver Cromwell: 'No man oftener advances higher than he who knows not where he is going'.*

The service of the time demanded fleet couriers, but the Duke of Buckingham employed one who covered the ground at an astonishing rate. When the Duke of Gloucester and his retinue arrived at Nottingham, Persivell, who had already made the journey from Middleham back to Brecon, now reappeared with the message to Gloucester that Buckingham, with three hundred men, was already travelling towards him. Gloucester sent Persivell flying back to tell his master that Gloucester would meet him at Northampton.

The young King's half-brother, Lord Richard Grey, was a member of the household at Ludlow, but he had been in London for the council meetings, and he now came on to join the King's party at Northampton.

* Quoted by Sharon Turner, *History of England*, Vol. III, 1823.

It seems possible that he had been sent to hasten Lord Rivers, for after Lord Richard Grey had joined them, the cortege, instead of putting up at Northampton, went on to Stony Stratford, fourteen miles further on the way to London. It was from Stony Stratford, eighteen years ago, that Edward V's father had ridden over to Grafton to marry his mother, early in the morning of the first of May, 'where he had first fantasied her visage.'

Having agreed to a rendezvous with the Lord Protector and then made the King evade it, it was scarcely possible for Lord Rivers to evade it himself without an open appearence of hostility. With a small following he rode back to Northampton to keep the appointment, but before he left the King's party, he charged them, it would seem, to set off at a certain hour the next morning; he would be with them if he could, but they must not wait.

When he returned to Northampton he found that the Protector had already arrived. Rivers explained that the King had gone on to Stony Stratford because Northampton would not afford lodgings for his retinue as well as the Duke of Gloucester's. This behaviour on Rivers' part, with whatever courtesy it might be explained, was gross presumption; if the scarcity of lodgings had been a fact, he should have sent avant-couriers to meet the Protector, explaining the position and asking what should be done. Coupled with the Queen's behaviour, in sending him no announcement of his brother's death, it showed Richard unmistakably the part the Woodvilles were playing; but he betrayed neither surprise nor anger. He asked Rivers to dine with him at the inn where he had put up, and in the course of the evening, the Duke of Buckingham and his troop arrived.

Buckingham of course sat down to dinner with the other two, and an evening of harmless conversation ensued, which aroused no alarm in Rivers. Three inns stood side by side; the Duke of Gloucester's dinner party was held in one; at bed-time Lord Rivers and his servants retired to their quarters in another, but his leaving the party did not break it up. Left to themselves, Gloucester and Buckingham settled down to an intent and fateful discussion. Gloucester had spent so much time in the north, and Buckingham's existence had been so quiet, this may have been the first occasion on which Gloucester had received the full impact of his personality. It was the attraction of opposites: Gloucester reserved, determined and austere, Buckingham imaginative, volatile and with feelings easily roused. The trait they had in common was a grounded detestation of the Woodvilles and their impudent machinations. In Wales though he was, Buckingham appears to have been by some means more closely in touch with the Council's doings than Richard himself. It is supposed that during this midnight conversation he told the latter anything of which Hastings had not already told him of Dorset's seizing the treasure in the Tower, of Sir Edward Woodville's appointment to the fleet, of the Woodville party's attempt to limit the Protector's powers, of their settled determination to have the King crowned on May 4, with the Protector's sanction or without.

Gloucester had, in spite of his rigid self-control, a capacity for sudden action; this was now reinforced by Buckingham's impulsiveness. In the plan to detach the young King from his mother's family, the first step was to remove Lord Rivers. In the dead of night, the Dukes, whose authority no one else's servants would gainsay, had the doors of Lord Rivers' inn locked on him. They gave the word to their men to be ready with the first light, and at dawn on April 30, they posted guards along the road from Northampton to Stony Stratford, that no one might travel there except themselves. Rivers also was very early up; while he was demanding to know the reason of his being locked in, the two Dukes appeared before him. They charged him with having attempted to remove the King from the Protector's guardianship, and told him that he was under arrest. With the forces of their combined retinues, six hundred men without those posted on the route, they rode fast to Stony Stratford. They were just in time. With two thousand men at arms about him, his half-brother and his chamberlain at his side, the King was preparing to mount his horse.

The boy, who scarcely more than a fortnight ago had received the shock of his father's death, and become aware in the behaviour of everyone who approached him, of his accession to the throne, and had, after a week of turmoil and emotional stress, endured five days' continuous travelling, was now, when he expected to see his uncle Rivers, who managed everything for him, took care of him and told him what to do, confronted by his uncle Gloucester whom he barely knew, a stern figure in black with a sable troop behind him.

The two Dukes dismounted and knelt on the ground before the young King. Gloucester then told him that he had very serious news to impart. Edward, followed closely by Lord Richard Grey and Sir Thomas Vaughan, returned to the lodging he had just left. Gloucester first offered him his sympathies on the death of his father; then he told him that the late King's associates had ruined the King's health by encouraging him in his excesses, and that they must be put out of the way in case they injured his son. Lord Richard Grey broke out into indignant speech; Buckingham harshly ordered him to be quiet. Gloucester then explained that Lord Rivers, the Marquess Dorset and Lord Richard Grey were the leaders of a conspiracy to deprive him of the office of Protector and to take away his life. He had been obliged, for his own safety, to arrest Lord Rivers at Northampton. The King said: 'What my brother Marquess has done I cannot say, but in good faith, I dare well answer for my uncle Rivers and my brother here that they be innocent of any such matters'. As for the governing of the realm, he trusted that to his lords and the Queen. Buckingham again interrupted. The ruling of the land, he said, was for men, not women. The King had been deceived.

The shock to the boy of twelve, whom nothing would shake in his confidence in his mother and his mother's family, was catastrophic, and it was followed by an even more painful stroke. Before his eyes, Lord Richard Grey and Sir Thomas Vaughan were placed under arrest. His uncle Richard then told him that his father had appointed his uncle Protector because of his services in the field and in council, and his nearness in blood. Would the young King, he asked, accept his father's ordinance? The frightened child replied with inherent dignity. He said he would be content with the government his father had arranged for him.

In the circumstances the fate of Lord Richard Grey was inevitable. He was thoroughly committed to the Woodville faction and had been a sharer in their ill-gotten gains. The forcible parting of the King from Sir Thomas Vaughan was a piece of ruthless unkindness, but it was the first of the long train of ruthless acts, each one begetting the next, which were entailed on Richard of Gloucester by his initial decision. Vaughan's very record of affectionate, devoted service meant that he would always, invariably, put first his own relationship with the King. He could never be implicitly relied on to co-operate with the Protector's measures.

The whole party now returned to Northampton. In the absence of records, it cannot be said whether the King were allowed to see his uncle Rivers again. The latter, it seems clear, was detained in one room and Lord Richard Grey in another. During dinner, Gloucester, perhaps in an attempt to mollify the distraught young King, sent Lord Rivers a dish from his own table, 'praying him to be of good cheer, all should be well enough'. Rivers sent back a message, thanking the Duke but asking that the dish might be carried to Lord Richard Grey, who, he thought, had more need of comfort, as one to whom such adversity was strange. He himself, said Rivers with a characteristic air, 'had been all his days inured thereto, and therefor could bear it the better'. Misfortune, of the severest kind, had undoubtedly overtaken him now, but it was difficult to see how he could have viewed his past career as a succession of misfortunes.

The King had now been severed from the company of the men who had most closely attended him. It was necessary that someone should be appointed to carry out the duties of Thomas Vaughan, at least. New attendants were placed about him, alien strangers whose very presence increased the child's discomfort and distress. According to More, this was the point at which his self-control gave way; he broke down and cried.

But the Duke of Gloucester had other things to think about. He had sent a report of his doings to the Council at Westminster; his immediate task was to disband the two thousand men at arms who had come up from Ludlow with the King. This force, more than three times as large as the combined retinues of himself and Buckingham, might have given considerable trouble; Mancini said that afterwards, the Welsh were indignant with themselves that they had allowed their Prince to be carried away, but at the time they instinctively obeyed the orders of a capable and experienced general. The Duke of Gloucester told them to go back to their homes and they went.

26

As the day's events had begun at dawn, there had been time for the news to reach the Queen and the Council by midnight. The reaction of the Queen and Dorset was most revealing of the part they had intended to play and of their hostile intentions towards the Protector. After one futile attempt on Dorset's part to muster support among the lords for a scheme to remove the King from the Protector's hands by force, midnight though it was, he and his mother bolted into sanctuary.

When Elizabeth Woodville had sought sanctuary in 1470, the accounts of her movements left it in some doubt as to whether she had fled into the sanctuary building outside St. Margarets, that grim stronghold, or to the comparative comfort of the house of the Abbot of Westminster. There was no doubt about her present destination. With her son Dorset, her son the nine year old Duke of York, her daughters Elizabeth, Cecily, Anne, Katherine and Bridget, of whom the eldest was seventeen and the two youngest four and three, 'the Queen crossed from the Palace at midnight and was received by Abbot Estney in the Abbot's Place'.*

Thirteen years ago, when she had fled into sanctuary by night, the Queen had suffered extreme privation, of 'such things as mean men's wives have in superfluity'. She was not going to endure this state of things again. Not only was she provided with everything for comfort and elegance in the Palace close at hand; she now had at her disposal her share of the treasure from the Tower which she had divided with Dorset. Angry and panic-stricken as she was, she had enough self-possession to order that her goods should be brought with her into sanctuary or as many of them as could be removed on the sudden. While it was still dark, there was, More had heard, 'much heaviness, rumble, haste and business, carriage and conveyance of her stuff into sanctuary, chests, coffers, packs, bundles, trusses, all on men's backs, no man unoccupied, some lading, some going, some discharging, some coming for more'. More repeats the extraordinary statement that some were 'breaking down the walls to bring in the nearest way'. Whatever this meant, enlarging a doorway or bringing a window aperture down to the ground, it showed the very large bulk of the rich thievery which, like Time, the Queen had crammed up.

* Dean Stanley, *Antiquities of Westminster Abbey.*

Meantime, the news having been brought to Hastings, he sent a messenger to Rotherham, Archbishop of York and Lord Chancellor, at his Palace, York Place, on the edge of the river. Convincing the Archbishop's servants of the extreme urgency of his commission, the messenger was brought to Rotherham's bedside. When aroused and told the news, Rotherham was aghast; the messenger said: 'My Lord sends Your Lordship word that there is no fear, for he assures you that all shall be well'. 'I assure him, quoth the Archbishop, be it as well as it will, it will never be so well as we have seen it'. The messenger departing, the Archbishop got up, dressed himself hurriedly, and roused his servants, 'with his household about him and every man weaponed, he took the Great Seal with him, and came, yet before day unto the Queen'.

In the Abbot's Place, he came upon men bringing in her possessions in all the haste described by More. The Queen herself he found given up to despair, sitting among the rushes on the floor. The morning about to break was the first of May, the anniversary of the dawn in which she had been married to the King of England. The Archbishop tried to comfort her. He had not been much reassured by Lord Hasting's message, but he repeated it, hoping she might find some reassurance in it; but the name of the man against whom she had nourished so much hatred, frightened her more than ever. She exclaimed: 'Ah, woe be to him! He is one of them that labour to destroy me and my blood!' The Archbishop, trying again to give her some sense of security, reminded her that she had the King's younger brother in her hands. He assured her that if any one—he did not say who—if anyone were crowned other than the King her son, then he and his colleagues would immediately crown the little Duke of York. Then he said, 'Here is the Great Seal, which, in likewise as that noble Prince your husband delivered it unto me, so here I deliver it unto you, to the use and behoof of your son.' In this, as Winston Churchill said, he behaved like an old fool. When he got back to York Place, 'in the dawning of the day' he looked out of his chamber window and saw 'all the Thames full of boats of the Duke of Gloucester's servants, watching that no man should go to Sanctuary, nor none should pass unsearched'. In the course of the morning, the lords assembled for a council meeting; at the prospect of facing the other councillors, the Archbishop realized how his irresponsible action would be viewed: that he had, as Lord Chancellor, given up the Great Seal to the Queen, 'to whom the custody thereof nothing pertained, without especial commandment of the King'; and he sent a messenger to the Sanctuary, who got it away from the Queen and brought it back to him. He had sent the messenger in secret, but the transaction became known, and Rotherham was presently deprived of the Chancellorship.

News of the sending away of Lord Rivers, of the Duke of Gloucester's taking charge of the King, and of the Queen's flight into sanctuary, caused crowds to assemble in the streets and a general hubbub and confusion. More said: 'There was great commotion and murmur in many places, especially in the city, the people diversely divining upon this dealing'. Hastings addressed the Council, explaining that Rivers, Grey and Vaughan had been arrested not for any reason that would put the King in danger, but to safeguard the Duke of Gloucester, whom they had planned to murder. The Duke was now bringing the King up to London for his coronation. When the party arrived, the matter should be judicially examined. This satisfied the Council. The people in the streets were presently reconciled by the show the Duke's servants made of the carts loaded with armour which formed part of the baggage train from Ludlow. They called out to the onlookers as the carts went along that these were the barrels of armour the traitors had prepared for an attack on the two Dukes. The crowd, swayed by an appeal to their visual sense, were convinced and shouted as the carts rolled along, 'that it were an alms to hang them'. More says that any man of sense could have seen through this: in the breaking up of so great a household as that of the Prince of Wales at Ludlow, it was inevitable that some armour 'must be thrown away or brought away, and the intenders of such a purpose would rather have had their armour on their backs than bound up in barrels', all of which as regards the armour actually on display, was obviously true; but it is an interesting fact that Rivers had made a large purchase of armour from Spain.* He had meant to come up from Ludlow with a force very much exceeding the 2,000 men to whom he had been limited and when these followers had been provided with arms, some cartloads were left over.

For May the first and second, the Dukes, with a great deal on their hands, remained with the King at Northampton. The journey to London was arranged to begin on May 3, that night being passed at St. Albans, the entry into the city to be made on May 4. What was to be done with the three prisoners was a matter of serious consideration. They could not be released; to bring them to London as prisoners in the train of the young King who was bound to them all by so much affection, was impossible. Gloucester ordered that they should be conveyed to Yorkshire, to separate destinations: Rivers to Sheriff Hutton, Grey to Middleham and Vaughan to Pontefract.

Dorset's thefts upon the treasure in the Tower and some anxiety about the safety of the Great Seal, caused Gloucester to send a letter in the King's name, to Cardinal Bourchier, Archbishop of Canterbury. The Cardinal Archbishop was descended from Edward III through Thomas of Woodstock, and the King's letter began: Most reverend father in God and right entirely beloved cousin. It prayed the Archbishop 'to see for the safeguard and sure-keeping of the Great Seal of this our realm unto

* Ives, *Papers of Antony Earl Rivers, op. cit.*

our coming to our city of London', and went on to desire him to assemble the lords of the council 'to provide for the surety and safeguard of our Tower of London and the treasure being in the same, in all diligence and our faithful trust is in you: given under our signet at our town of Northampton, the second day of May'.*

On the morning of May 3, the cavalcade departed for London via St. Albans. The position of Gloucester vis-à-vis his nephew would have been one of excruciating embarrassment and pain if Gloucester had considered or sympathized with the boy's feelings; but as Gairdner said: 'Richard III was the last of a line of soldiers; Henry VII was the first of a line of statesmen'. Did Edward ask what had become of his uncle, his half-brother, his chamberlain: what was to become of them? Or was there, in spite of his childishness, his bookishness, his gentleness, a strain of regal self-control, which protected his dignity and kept his reserve intact? That Gloucester and Buckingham tried to propitiate and make friends with him is suggested by two documents preserved from the evening at St. Albans. The first grant of the reign of Edward V was, or was meant to have been, the appointment of a cleric, John Geffrey, to the rectorship of the parish church of Pembrigge. The King had spoken of this man and of his own wish to reward him and the Protector, it would seem, explained the method of putting his wishes into force. The King wrote a letter to the custodian of the seal of the Earldom of March, directing him to write to the Bishop of Hereford, asking the Bishop to confer the benefice on Geffrey. The intended kindness never bore fruit. Less than a month later the Bishop of St. David's was granted a licence to appeal for the Pope's permission to hold the benefice of Pembrigge, to augment the revenues of his see. The first attempt of the King to use what had been his father's power ended in nothingness.†
At the same time, there was no reason to think that the Protector's assistance was not given in good faith, and at some point in the evening there must have been some appearance of genuine friendliness between the Dukes and the shocked, oppressed young King. A paper remains on which they had all written their signatures. The King had practised his, in a stiff, decorative hand: Edwardus Quintus. On the lower half of the sheet appears in regular, beautiful writing: Loyaulte me lie, Richard Gloucestre; beneath that again, in sprawling letters, Souvente me souvene, 'think of me often', and the name of him who owned the motto: Harre Bokinghame. ‡

The next day, Sunday May 4, the royal train reached London. The procession approached the city from the north; the Great Chronicle says that it was met at Hornsey Park by the Lord Mayor and aldermen, 'clad

* Grants from the Crown during the Reign of Edward V, ed. J. G. Nichols.
† ibid.
‡ In the Manuscript Department of the British Museum.

154

in scarlet and fifty commoners all clothed in violet, well horsed'. The Duke of Gloucester and his followers were in black, the King 'riding in blue velvet'. The fair-haired child, lately bereaved of his splendid father and called so young to inherit his great place, was received with high enthusiasm by the crowds. As he was escorted to his first lodging, the Palace of the Bishop of London, his uncle Gloucester treated him with ceremonial courtesy, bowing and presenting him to the crowds, crying out: Behold your King! The Bishop's Palace occupied the west side of St. Paul's Church-yard. The King and his train entered its doors, and the Protector's first public act summoned the bishops, the lords of the council, the Lord Mayor and the city magnates, to take the Oath of Allegiance to King Edward V.

In the Palace, the King was attended and waited on with stately reverence; but his mother was not there, nor his brother York; there was no sign of his half-brother the Marquess or of his uncle the Bishop of Salisbury. His uncle Rivers, his half-brother Richard Grey, his chamberlain, had been left far behind. There is no record of what he thought or felt.

He was told that his coronation would take place on June 24.

At the first meeting of the Council after the King's arrival in London, the Duke of Gloucester was confirmed in the office the late King's will had given him, of Protector and Defensor of the Realm; the Croyland Continuator said: 'He was invested with power to order and forbid, in every matter just like another King'. He was also given 'the oversight and tutelage of the King's most royal person'. The Council had been managed with statesmanlike magnanimity. Rotherham had been sharply rebuked for surrendering the Great Seal to Elizabeth Woodville, and deprived of the Chancellorship, but he had been allowed to keep his seat on the Council. Bishop Alcock had been of the party that brought the King up from Ludlow, and he might have been suspected of some connivance with Lord Rivers, but he also had a seat at the Council board. Rotherham had been succeeded in the Chancellorship by Bishop Russell of Lincoln, a man of great intelligence, but the most able of the bishops, and one of the cleverest men of the age, was John Morton, now Bishop of Ely. Mancini called him: 'a man of great resource and daring, trained in party intrigue since King Henry's time'. Morton had been a loyal Lancastrian; he had escaped from the Tower after the battle of Towton and fled abroad to rejoin Margaret of Anjou. He had accompanied her army to Tewkesbury and after that defeat had made his peace with Edward IV, who was too clever himself not to take the opportunity of enlisting such talents. Morton might not unreasonably have thought that he, not Russell, should have succeeded Rotherham as Chancellor, and Russell would probably have been glad enough if he had. Rows, in Historia Rerum Angliae, said that the Bishop of Lincoln was very unwilling to be advanced above the Archbishop of York, but the decision had been made in Russell's favour; and if Morton were not to be treated by the House of York according to his intellectual merits, he might call to mind that beyond the sea there yet remained an heir of the House of Lancaster.

The young King and his entourage were still housed in the Bishop of London's palace. This had been intended only as a temporary lodging and it was now discussed as to where his household should go until the coronation. The Palace of Westminster would have been an obvious choice but for one objection. At midnight on April 30, the Queen, at the news of Gloucester's interception of the King, had thrown herself violently into Sanctuary with her children and her goods. From that hour she had rejected all overtures from the Council and refused stubbornly to come out. It might be said the news of the carrying away and imprisoning of her brother and one of her sons justified her in taking refuge herself, but if she had remained in Westminster Palace, surrounded by troops of the royal servants, in all the state of a Queen Dowager, and had, on his arrival in London, demanded access to the King, no one could have kept them apart. This is what most mothers would have done, even if it had not been to their advantage; it would have been entirely to Elizabeth Woodville's advantage, and her rush into the house of the Abbot of Westminster, though she did bring with her all the property she could lay hands on, not only betrayed what her intentions had been as to flouting the late King's will, it also deprived her of all the power and dignity which should have belonged to her state, and which would have made it extremely difficult for anyone to molest her.

Once she had put herself into this state of declared war against the Protector and the Council, it was not likely that they would allow the King into her presence. The Palace was very near to the Abbot's Place, and sounds could be heard in both places at once. In Old Palace Yard, the open space between Westminster Hall, the Palace, and the Abbey, was a clock-tower put up in the time of Edward I, which struck the hour in so carrying a tone, Stow said it could be heard by the lawyers sitting in Westminster Hall, 'and the same clock, in a calm, will be heard in the City of London'. If her son had been in Westminster Palace while she remained in Sanctuary, they would both have heard the striking 'on the great bell'. Their nearness to each other would have been both agitating and dangerous.

Westminster Palace was out of the question; someone suggested the Priory of St. John of Jerusalem in Clerkenwell. In 1467, Edward IV had imposed his brother-in-law John Woodville on the brethren as their Prior, much against their wishes; he had been executed in 1469, and his successor, John Langstrother, had been executed after the battle of Tewkesbury; altogether this might have made an objection to the Priory, to the Council's way of thinking. It was apparently left to Buckingham to make the natural suggestion, that the Sovereign should take possession of the royal apartments in the Tower.

At some date between May 9 and May 19, Edward V removed there with his attendants. A document saying that Edmund Holt, keeper of the gaol at Nottingham is to be replaced by Robert Ligh, 'on the advice of our most entirely beloved uncle, the Duke of Gloucester', was signed by the King: Given under our signet at our Tower of London, the 19th day of May, the first year of our reign'.

The Marquess Dorset's post as Deputy Constable of the Tower had naturally come to an abrupt termination when, having rifled the royal treasury, he had fled into sanctuary with his mother. Whatever arrangements might have been made with the Constable, John Lord Dudley, the Constable in May 1483 was the Protector's friend and supporter, John Lord Howard. In his Household Books, is an entry under May 21, saying Howard's man Bassley had paid out, at the Tower, wages for six men for one day's labour at threepence per man a day. Bassley had paid a carpenter for making three beds, and paid for one hundred and a quarter feet of boards, for two sacks of lime and for nails for the beds.*

At first glance, these particulars, in such a context, sound alarming, but though a reason cannot be found for the Constable's wanting three bedsteads made, or for providing a hundred feet of board and two sacks of lime, neither can these preparations be made to square with any arrangements for the King. There is no indication of which part of the Tower the beds were set up in, or where the boards and lime were used, or if they were all used on the same project or on separate ones. When the wages were paid, the King had been in the Royal Apartments for two days, and preparations were in hand for his coronation the next month.

Bishop Russell had prepared a draft of the speech with which he was to open the first parliament of the new reign. He made a strong plea for unity between all the divisions of the commonwealth. Distinguished as he was, and to be speaking on this dignified occasion, he did not resist the opportunity of a jibe: 'If there be any surety or firmness in this world such as may be found out of heaven, it is rather in the isles and lands . . . than in the sea or any great Rivers'. He went on to praise the King in terms very similar to those Mancini used about him, 'the most toward and virtuous disposition of our Sovereign Lord that now is, his gentle wit and ripe understanding, far surpassing the nature of his youth'. He spoke of 'the right noble and famous Duke of Gloucester his uncle, Protector of the Realm, in whose great wisdom, puissance and fortune' the defence of the realm now rested, and to demand on behalf of the nation that the Protector's office should continue until the King came of age. As Russell composed the draft, he conjured up the image of

* *Household Books of John Duke of Norfolk and Thomas Earl of Surrey*, 1481–9, ed. Payne Collier.

the young King standing between two noble brothers: the dead King his father and his uncle the Duke of Gloucester. 'The King our Sovereign Lord', he wrote, 'may have cause largely to rejoice himself and to say . . . Uncle, I am glad to have you confirmed in this place, to be my protector in all my business. Ita fiat. Amen'.*

This draft of the Chancellor's speech made it clear that the Council were in full expectation of the crowning of Edward V, and so were the officials of the Wardrobe, for his coronation robes were being made. A very important document in the Wardrobe accounts, containing particulars of the coronation robes for Richard III and garments supplied to 'the Lord Edward, son of the late King, Edward IV', was taken by Walpole (*Historic Doubts*) as a conclusive argument against Richard III's having kept Edward V in prison, in that he was intended to walk, or did walk, in Richard's coronation procession. This document was examined by Dr. Milles, the Dean of Exeter and President of the Society of Antiquaries.† Dr. Milles proved, first, that this was not, as Walpole had assumed, a coronation roll, but a section of the ordinary Wardrobe accounts. He then explained the manner in which it had been made up. The accounts were engrossed and closed in 1484, when an Act of Bastardy had been passed against Edward IV's children. In the copying out of the items, the list of clothes prepared for Edward V could not precede the list of those for Richard III as they must then have been charged as robes for 'the King', and Edward could not be so described in any document likely to meet the eye of Richard III. It was not in Richard III's interest, either, to have the occasion stated for which his nephew's robes had been prepared. Placed after the list of Richard's robes, Edward's own entered among those 'issued by the King's high commandment', as indeed they were, by commandment of the previous King. As Dean Milles said: 'When this account was closed, no other title but Lord Edward could be given to this Prince'.

The clothes made for Edward V must have been put in hand immediately on his father's death, possibly on the instructions of the Queen, and sent down to him at Ludlow, for they included the 'blue velvet riding gown' for himself, with the doublets of black damask and the black gowns and hoods for his henchmen, in which they were all described on the King's entry at Hornsey Park. For his coronation they had made a short gown and a long gown of crimson cloth of gold, long gowns of blue velvet and purple velvet, and for the henchmen, short gowns of green cloth of gold and white cloth of gold.

Confirming his statement that these pages are a part of the Wardrobe Accounts and not a coronation roll, Milles points out that no clothes are mentioned for the Duke of York. The latter's clothes were not supplied

* *Grants from the Crown during the Reign of Edward V.*
† *Archeologia*, Vol. I.

by the Great Wardrobe, except in cases of a gown or a saddle, given as a present by the King. Another instance of this being a Wardrobe Account is the item quoted by Dr. Milles of the issue for the Princess Bridget, who was 'sick', of two long pillows of fustian, stuffed with down, with two pillowcases of holland cloth for them. This three year old child was with her mother, brother and sisters in the Abbot's Place. The Queen, clearly, was able to apply to the Wardrobe for something she needed.

It was natural that what the Woodvilles demanded and lusted for was not merely the accession and coronation of Edward V: that was assured already; they were determined to have the child on the throne as their puppet, the source of unlimited power to themselves. If all they had wanted was that he should lawfully succeed his father, as soon as the Protector had brought him to London and presented him to the cheering crowds, the Queen would have come to meet him, and her brother, Sir Edward Woodville, would have sent a message signifying his allegiance from on board one of the ships with which he was supposed to be policing the Channel against French pirates. Instead of this, the Queen barricaded herself in Sanctuary against the Protector appointed by her husband's will and Sir Edward Woodville had a large fleet anchored in the Downs whose purpose was obviously hostile to the Government. He was circumvented by the action of two tough and experienced sea-dogs, Sir Thomas Fulford and Sir Edward Brampton. They found means to let the crews know that everyone should be pardoned who deserted the rebel Sir Edward Woodville, and this accounted for a good many. Their crowning exploit, however, was to bring over to their side the captains of two Genoese carracks who were serving under Woodville's colours. The captains gave a party at which the English guards on the vessels were made completely drunk, and the Genoese sailors brought the ships back to the port of London. Sir Edward Woodville made his escape with two ships only. He had with him, however, his share of the treasure his nephew Dorset had taken from the Tower.

27

In the Royal Apartments of the Tower the King was doing some, at least, of the work of a sovereign. An administrative body under the Protector put before him for his signature the bills which were then passed under the Privy Seal or the Great Seal. On June 11, he signed letters to the Abbess of Shaftsbury, saying he appointed the novices Elizabeth Brither and Luce Bernars, to be 'our Mynchyns', nuns whose dowry was paid to the nunneries by the Crown. These were beneficiaries of whom, probably, the boy had never heard, but on the same date another paper was put before him for his signature which must have intensified pain and misery. It said that Lord Lovell, Viscount Lovell, should now hold the position of Chief Butler of England 'in as ample wise' as it had been held by Antony, Earl Rivers.*

Though he signed the bills which they had agreed upon, it is doubtful if the King were present at the full Council meetings in the Star Chamber at Westminster or at the smaller ones in the Tower, and these were not the only sittings, for the Council was dividing itself into groups. The Protector was occupying as his town house the superb dwelling in Bishops-gate Street, put up in 1466 by the wealthy merchant the late Sir John Crosby. Stow said it was 'very large and beautiful', and the loftiest private house in London. Its great hall formed one side of a courtyard; its magnificent timber roof was supported on ranges of four arches abreast, all picked out in red and gold. Here the Duke of Gloucester kept open house for all his party, and held secret, informal meetings with some of them, chief of whom was his great new ally, the Duke of Buckingham.

Gloucester had now endowed Buckingham with so much power in Wales, that it was almost palatine.† The removal of Rivers from the Council of Wales had left a vacancy in the structure of power; Gloucester filled it by the appointment of Buckingham to an enormous sphere of influence. By the middle of May he had been given powers to recruit the King's subjects for military service in Shropshire, Herefordshire, Somerset and Dorset. He was made Chief Justice and Chancellor of North and South Wales, steward of all royal demesnes and manors in

* *Grants from Edward V.*
† Jacob, *op. cit.*, p. 615.

Wales, steward of all royal castles and manors within Wales belonging to the Duchy of Lancaster and the Earldom of March. Jacob says: 'These were grants of jurisdiction and authority, not of territory', but they were so extensive and concentrated in Buckingham's hands such an extraordinary degree of control, as could not but, among other causes, arouse the jealous enmity of Hastings.

The latter had cause to feel injured. It was he who had sent Gloucester the vitally important messages on the death of Edward IV. Without them, Gloucester might have delayed the few crucial hours in which Rivers could have brought the King to London and got him crowned in the presence of two thousand armed men. After that, as Cheetham has said,* only a civil war could have unseated the Woodvilles. Hastings naturally felt that he was ungratefully treated, and that he, who had been a faithful servant and close friend of Edward IV, and to whose energetic loyalty the Protector owed his present position, was now slighted for that newcomer on the diplomatic scene, the Duke of Buckingham. It is clear, from hind-sight, that Hastings would search for some means of redressing the balance in his own favour.

The situation as regarded the Queen was becoming very tense because of her persistent refusal to deliver her children out of sanctuary or to leave it herself. Repeated overtures had been made to her, all of which she had repudiated, and by the second week in June, the Council seemed, for the time being, to have relinquished their efforts to treat with her. On June 9, Simon Stallworth wrote to Sir William Stonor, describing the position of affairs. The Marquess of Dorset was still in sanctuary with his mother, but he had been less successful than she in carrying his spoils with him. Stallworth said: 'Wheresoever can be found any goods of my Lord Marquess, it is taken'.

But Dorset had managed to get some of his share of the treasure into the Abbot's Place, and this had got the authorities of the Abbey into trouble. Stallworth said: 'The Prior of Westminster was, and yet is, in great trouble, for certain goods delivered to him by my Lord Marquess'. Then he said, 'My Lord Protector, my Lord Buckingham, with all other lords, as well temporal as spiritual were at Westminster in the Council Chamber from ten to two, but there was none that spake with the Queen'. He continued: 'There is great business about the coronation, which shall be this day fortnight, as we say: when I trust ye shall be at London and then shall ye know all the world. The King', he added, 'is in the Tower'.†

The Queen herself was largely discredited, the Marquess of Dorset entirely so, but this was not true of the little Duke of York and the five beautiful and innocent princesses. It was going to be awkward if, while the King were being crowned at Westminster, a few paces away, his

* *Life and Times of Richard III*, p. 108.
† *Stonor Letters and Papers*, 1290–1483, ed. C. L. Kingsford. Vol. II, pp. 159–160.

family were cowering, in apparent distrust and dread of the King's government.

Hastings was not subtle, neither was he cowardly. He was not afraid of the Duke of Gloucester, but he now felt that the Duke's powers should have some limitation. If these powers were automatically to cease at the King's coronation, the re-arrangement which must take place after the coronation would afford some chance for other members of the council to fill a more important role; but now it was known that at the first parliament of the reign, the council would ask that the Protector's powers should be continued till the King came of age.

Hastings had been in the forefront of the party most hostile to the Woodvilles, but he had been so dear a friend of King Edward IV that the latter when he built his own tomb in St. George's Chapel had said that he wanted Lord Hastings to be buried beside him. It was not possible for a member of the King's court to have much intercourse with a boy most of whose time was spent in Ludlow, but Hastings had had some friendly connection with the little Prince of Wales. The beautiful Book of Hours whose broad gold borders were scattered with wild flowers which had been given to the Prince bore Lord Hastings' arms.

Although the attendants who came up with him from Ludlow had all been removed and replaced by others, there had been no attempt to deny access to the King. He was the centre of a small court, visited by his well-wishers, of whom his father's great friend, Lord Hastings, was the chief. Hastings was now seeing much more of Edward than he had had opportunity to see before, and one fact could hardly have escaped so sympathetic an observer; however correct he were in his behaviour to his uncle, the boy's affection and confidence were placed on his mother and her family. If he spoke confidentially to Hastings at all, Hastings must have understood that the twelve year old child wanted to see his mother, his brother and his sisters. In the past, the enmity between the Queen and himself had been bitter, but her brother Rivers who had been particularly offensive to him was now out of the way of doing other people injury, and she herself a poor, battered creature who could do no more harm; her only importance was the affection felt for her by her son. If an alliance with her would raise him to a position of influence and trust with the young King, Hastings would be prepared to let bygones be bygones. To bring about a rapprochement with her was not altogether easy; he was one of the best-known men in London; he could go nowhere, let alone to the Queen in sanctuary, without everyone's getting to know of it. He must find a confidential messenger and Jane Shore was immediately at hand. The Queen had no doubt abominated her, as she had abominated Hastings, but she was not likely to repulse a message of hope, whoever brought it. In the little world of London, Jane Shore also was well known, but a small woman can mouse in and out more easily than an impressive man. Jane Shore herself liked to do kindnesses, and she had once been pleased to show how much she could do by her influence with King Edward IV. She was willing now to use her powers to bring about some happiness to the little King and to execute a highly discreet mission on behalf of her lover Lord Hastings.

What Hastings had in mind, or how far he had got with it, was never disclosed, but open and ingenuous as he was, he was not the stuff of which successful conspirators are made. He had presented his protégé, William Catesby, an acutely intelligent lawyer, to the Duke of Gloucester, and Gloucester, first to oblige Hastings and then because he recognized Catesby's quality, had made him Chancellor of the earldom of March and procured for him a seat on the Council. Lord Stanley, who was much sharper than Hastings, had said to him that he, personally, distrusted this state of affairs in which separate councils were held in different places. How could they be sure of what was being said behind their backs? Hastings answered buoyantly that there was no cause for fear; his man Catesby was present at all the council meetings and would keep him informed. He named the man who had gone over completely to the Duke of Gloucester.

As A. R. Myers (*History Today*, Aug. 1954), and B. P. Wolffe (*English Historical Review*, Oct. 1956) agree, it was not so much a definitely formed plot against the Protector which was discovered, as a mistrustful attitude in Hastings, evinced by the facts of his making secret approaches to the Queen and that his three intimate colleagues were characters of dubious sympathies: Rotherham who had lost the Chancellorship by making over the Great Seal to Elizabeth Woodville, Morton and Stanley who had already turned their coats and might turn them again.

The approaching date of the coronation, June 23 by Stallworth's reckoning, was to bring immediately after it the Parliament by which, if at all, the Protector's powers were to be prolonged. The decision would not be unanimous, but the Protector's party hoped that it would be carried. The discovery that there was more opposition to it than he had realized, that the opposition had its chief source in Hastings, whose entire loyalty he could no longer command because he was committed to Buckingham, that the Woodvilles whom he thought he had crushed, were being encouraged by Hastings to hope again, were, it seems, the reasons for Gloucester's determination that the opposition must be put down with drastic suddenness. In *Henry VI*, Part III, V, 5, 86, Edward IV says to Clarence, 'Where's Richard gone?' Clarence replies: 'To London all in post, and as I guess, to make a bloody supper in the Tower'. Edward IV then says: 'He's sudden, if a thing comes in his head.'

Military commanders must often take highly important decisions with great speed, and Gloucester had been trained as a soldier. This professional training reinforced a natural capacity for rapid action. On June 10 he wrote to the Corporation of York: 'We heartily pray you to come unto us to London in all the diligence ye can possible, with as many as ye can make, defensibly arrayed, there to aid and assist us against the Queen, her blood adherents and affinity, which have intended and doth daily intend to murder and utterly destroy us and our cousin the Duke of Buckingham, and the royal blood of this realm'. On the next day he wrote to Lord Neville in Westmorland, one of the heirs of the Duke of Exeter, who had been deprived of his inheritance for the benefit of the Marquess of Dorset, and still more shamefully mulcted for the sake of the latter's brother, Lord Richard Grey: 'As ever ye love me, and your own weal and security and this realm, that ye come to me with that ye may make, defensibly arrayed, in all the haste that is possible; . . . and, my Lord, do me now good service as ye have always before done, and I trust now so to remember you as shall be the making of you and yours.'

With these letters to the north a secret, ominous background, Gloucester convened a council meeting in the White Tower for June 13. The Duke of Buckingham and John Lord Howard were in the Protector's confidence; the Archbishop of York, the Bishop of Ely, Lord Stanley and Lord Hastings were not. When the party had been assembled for some time, the Protector joined them; he apologized for keeping them waiting, he had slept late. It was now only nine o'clock, but on a summer's morning, people expected the day's work to start betimes. After a little talk, the Protector suddenly asked Dr. Morton for some of the famous strawberries in the gardens of Ely Place. Morton despatched a servant for them at once. Gloucester shortly afterwards excused himself and left the council chamber. A restlessness, a sudden demand for refreshing fruit, may well have been symptoms of mental agitation. He did not come back till between ten and eleven o'clock. Then he appeared to be in a towering passion: as More said: 'all changed, with a wonderfully sour, angry countenance, frowning and fretting and gnawing on his lips.' He demanded of the amazed councillors what they deserved 'that compass and imagine the destruction of me, being so near of blood unto the King, and the Protector of his royal person?' Hastings immediately exclaimed, they deserved a traitor's punishment, whoever they might be. 'That,' exclaimed Gloucester, 'is yonder sorceress, my brother's wife and others with her'. If Hastings were already startled, his alarm was increased when the Protector threw at him the name of Jane Shore. Relying on a coup de theatre, such as had been found effective in displaying Rivers' hoard of armour to the crowds, Gloucester is said now to have pulled up his sleeve and showed a left arm, smaller than the right, and withered-looking, and declared that the Queen and Jane Shore had wasted his body by witchcraft; but as More said, 'there was no man there present but well knew that his arm had been ever such since his birth'. This coup which might have succeeded with the ignorant multitude could not have been expected, by a man of Gloucester's sense, to have hoodwinked the knowledgable councillors assembled in the White Tower.

At all events, Hastings repeated his asseveration that any traitors deserved punishment if they were proved guilty. 'What!' cried the Protector: 'thou servest me, I ween, with ifs and with ands. I tell thee they have done so, and that will I make good upon thy body, traitor!' It was now seen how he had been employed in his absence between ten and eleven. He hit the table with a resounding blow with his fist. 'At which token, one cried "Treason!" without. Therewith a door clapped, and in come there rushing men in harness, as many as the chamber might hold.' In the confusion one of them struck Lord Stanley, who fell under the table, his head pouring blood. The Protector shouted to Hastings that he arrested him, that he would not dine till Hasting's head was off. A priest was brought in to shrive him, while Morton and Rotherham were led away to prison quarters in the Tower and Stanley was sent under guard to detention in his own house.

Some repairs were under construction and on the green between the Lieutenant's Lodging and the chapel of St. Peter ad Vincula, a log of timber was lying on the grass. Hastings was made to lay his head on it, and the head 'was then stricken off'. The event took place before mid-day on June 13.* Anyone looking out of a window in the west side of the royal apartments would have had a full view of the late King's dearest friend, a headless corpse in a great pool of blood.

* B. P. Wolffe's article in the *English Historical Review*, October 1974—'When and why did Hastings lose his head?' establishes this date.

28

GLOUCESTER had said he would not dine until Hastings' head was off. Immediately after dinner he sent, More says, for 'substantial men out of the city unto the Tower'. When these arrived, he and Buckingham appeared to them in old rusty armour such as they would never, ordinarily, have deigned to put on. They explained that the sudden discovery of treason on Lord Hastings' part, which they had never imagined before ten o'clock that morning, had forced them to arm themselves with whatever came to hand, and to order Lord Hastings' immediate execution. There was now no need for fear: the realm might be at quiet. This reassurance was confirmed by a herald with a proclamation, which stated Hastings would have killed the Dukes of Gloucester and Buckingham; that he was a source of corruption, that he had been an evil counsellor to the King's father, King Edward IV, and had spent his last night on earth in bed with the notorious Jane Shore. He had been put to death 'by the most dread commandment of the King's Highness and of his honourable and faithful council. It was their hope that by his well-deserved death, all the realm should by God's grace, rest in good quiet and peace.' Some people observed that though ten o'clock had been spoken of as the time the conspiracy was discovered, the proclamation, written on parchment and carefully indited, was being proclaimed so soon after ten, there would scarcely have been time to scribble it down on paper. Gloucester could not bring home to Jane Shore the charge, either that she had bewitched him or that she had conspired with the Lord Chamberlain against him. He had to fall back on the accusation that she was a harlot, which neither she nor anyone else would attempt to deny; but as More said, 'every man laughed to hear it then, so suddenly, so highly taken'. It was within the competence of Dr. Kempe, the Bishop of London to oblige her to do penance for her way of life, and this the Protector enjoined him to command, so on a Sunday, wearing nothing but her kirtle, she was led barefoot through the streets, a taper in her hand. More's humane account of her ordeal says that first she was very pale but the gazing of the crowds made her blush, and 'she went so fair and lovely, her great shame won her much praise among those that were more amorous of her body than concerned for her soul'.

Nevertheless Gloucester showed great respect for Hastings' memory. He had King Edward IV's friend buried near him in St. George's Chapel as the King had asked that he should be, and he assured the widowed Lady Hastings that there was no question of her husband's attainder; as this meant that Lady Hastings could inherit all his possessions and the wardship, till they came of age, both of her son, and of her son-in-law, the young Earl of Shrewsbury, it was a merciful dispensation as far as she was concerned; on the other hand, to have beheaded Hastings without trial and without attainder, was a deed so drastic, it charted the way for the rest of Gloucester's brief career.

He had had much cause of affection and gratitude towards Hastings; towards the Queen he had never had cause for either. That she should now obstruct his plans by refusing to allow the Duke of York to come out of sanctuary, was not to be tolerated. It would be better if the Queen would come out herself, but if she would not, then the little Prince must be taken out of her hands. In the discussion of this matter, Cardinal Bourchier said, that if, after all persuasions had been tried, she remained obdurate, then he washed his hands of the affair. He could not sanction the removing of the child by force: it would be a violation of the privileges of sanctuary. Some of the bishops agreed with him, others sided with the majority of the temporal lords; they agreed with Buckingham, who argued that as a child could not need sanctuary, therefore he could not claim it; consequently, the Duke of York was not in sanctuary. It was hoped that the Queen would see reason and that this casuistry would not be called for.

On June 16, John Lord Howard being Constable of the Tower, his account book shows expenses for eight boats to go from the Tower to Westminster and back. They contained, among other members of the council, the Protector, the Duke of Buckingham, Cardinal Bourchier and Bishop Russell, and a body of armed soldiers. Coming up the river from the Tower to Westminster, they probably landed at the King's Stairs which led, through an archway, into Old Palace Yard, immediately in front of Westminster Hall. There was another Stairs, a little further up, immediately under Westminster Palace, but the Abbot's Place was on the further side of Old Palace Yard and the King's Stairs were almost opposite the part of the Abbey which the Abbot's Place adjoined. On disembarking, the Protector went to the Star Chamber, Buckingham waited in the middle of Westminster Hall. It was felt that the clergy would manage this mission best if they were left to themselves. They went forward to the Abbot's Place and were brought into the presence of the Queen, who had her younger son with her. More puts into her mouth very eloquent and long speeches, showing her distrust of the Protector, her extreme unwillingness to part with the child, her plea that he was just recovering from an illness and needed her care. In the course of these orations, vivid but too long and uninterrupted to sound like life, Cardinal Bourchier is made to say that the Protector and the Council have no wish to part her from either of her sons; what they want is for her to come out of her present retreat and be with the children in some place which is suitable to their position. If she refuses to do this, then he himself will withdraw from the situation. The Cardinal, with his views on the nature of sanctuary, was the Queen's safeguard. When he threatened to leave her, she feared, More says, that the child might be removed by force, and as this visitation had found her quite unprepared, she had made no arrangements to get him into hiding or provide for his safety in any way. She consented at last, weeping, More says, 'the child weeping as fast'. The long speeches composed by More, absorbing as they are, fade into air when contrasted with the actual observation of Simon Stallworth, written down for Sir William Stonor:* 'June 21, 1483 (Saturday). On Monday last was at Westminster great plenty of harnessed men; there was the deliverance of the Duke of York to my Lord Cardinal, my Lord Chancellor and many other Lords Temporal; and with him my Lord of Buckingham in the midst of Westminster Hall, my Lord Protector receiving him at the Star Chamber door, with many loving words.' Shakespeare had picked up the tradition that the Duke of York was a lively little boy, and it is borne out by the contemporary French writer, Jean Molinet, whose 'Chroniques' were published during the period between 1474 and 1504. He said of the two Princes, 'the eldest was simple and very melancholy, but the youngest was joyous and witty, nimble and ever ready for dances and games'. Stallworth's account of the little Prince's removal ends with the words: 'and so departed with my Lord Cardinal to the Tower, where he is, blessed be Jesus, merry'. It was a fine thing, after all, to be released from the confinement of the Abbots' Place and garden, to go down the river, stirring with ships, to the royal apartments of the Tower, to see his brother and to stay with him.

If Gloucester decided on the beheading of Hastings, a man with whom his ties had been close, it followed that he would not spare Rivers, Grey and Vaughan. On his authority as Lord Protector, he sent instructions for Lord Rivers and Lord Richard Grey to be removed from their respective prisons and brought to Pontefract, where Vaughan already was, and that all three should be executed at once. It is not recorded on what date Rivers was transported to Pontefract, but he made his will there on June 23.† He left large bequests of land, to be sold for the support of the hospital at Rochester, and to pay prisoners' fees and small debts for them, to help to bury the dead, 'with other works of mercy'. All his array and horse-harness he directed should be sold, 'and with the money thereof

* Stonor *Letters and Papers*.
† *Excerpta Historica*, ed. Samuel Bentley, pp. 246–48.

be bought shirts and smocks for poor folks'. His debts were to be discharged, and any loans made him to be repaid. His wife was to have all the plate that had come from her father Sir Henry Lewis, 'and other of my plate to the value of such thing as I had of his; also that she have all such plate as was given her at our marriage'. She was to have also the furniture of a bed: 'the canopy of white silk with four pairs of sheets, two pairs of fustians, a feather bed', and the hangings of the bed-chamber. All the property in his house the Moat and at 'my place in the Vintry', was to go to his father's heirs. He added a request which put both him and the Duke of Gloucester in a very favourable light: 'I beseech humbly my Lord of Gloucester, in the worship of Christ's passion, and for the merit and weal of his soul, to comfort, help and assist as supervisor (for very trust) of this testament, that my executors may, with his pleasure, fulfil this my last will'. He left no remembrance or keepsake to his sister the Queen, to whose doings he had owed his great advancement and also the meteor-like suddenness of his fall. Either at Sheriff Hutton or at Pontefract he put into verse his melancholy, resigned views of the way Fortune had treated him:

My life was lent   But I ne went
Me to one intent,   Thus to be shent,
It is nigh spent,   But she it meant,
Welcome, Fortune!   Such is her won—*

He had never thought to be ruined like this: when he lent himself to the conspiracy to flout the late King's will: but Fortune had always meant that he should, such was her way. He did not see himself as the conspirator who had played for high stakes, whose life was forfeit because he had lost, but as the victim, gracefully philosophical, of Fortune's Wheel.

He had wished to be buried in the Chapel of our Lady of the Piewe in St. Stephen's Chapel but he saw that no-one would now regard his wishes in this matter. His nephew had arrived at the place where they were both going to lose their lives, and he added in his will: 'My will is, now, to be buried before an image of our blessed Lady Mary, with my Lord Richard in Pontefract'.

Lord Richard Grey had been brought to Middleham on May 3, and the expenses incurred for him were submitted to Richard III by Geoffrey Franke his receiver and payment was authorized for them in September 1483. They included 'Lord Richard's costs, from Middleham to Pontefract, 22s and 4d'; 'for the expenses of the Lord Richard's servants and their horses at Middleham 26s and 6d', and on June 25, 'for the Lord Richard's burial, 46s and 8d'.† All three were beheaded one after the

* Rows, *Historia Regum Angliae*, ed. T. Hearne.
† *Gentleman's Magazine*, October 1844.

other. The solemnity and horror of an execution by beheading is apt to create the feeling, apropos the victim's misdeeds, that the overplus of guilt belongs to the executioners; but in the temper of the times, Gloucester may well have been justified in thinking that to get rid of Lord Rivers, at least, was a state necessity. According to Polydore Vergil, when he had been asked by some of the councillors why he had had Rivers arrested before the meeting with the King, Gloucester had replied: 'Antony Rivers of late attempted to hinder me, that I should not, according to my duty, take on hand that charge'. The implications of this were of course far-reaching and of the utmost seriousness. Owing to his known affiliations and his presence at Stony Stratford, there were strong grounds for suspicion against Lord Richard Grey, even if the Protector had no undisclosed evidence against him. The act of tyranny was the execution of Thomas Vaughan, who was put to death because his known devotion to the young King would have made him intractable and uncorruptible. His tomb has vanished from Westminster Abbey, but Camden* saw it, in the Chapel of St. Paul, and the epitaph read: Aymer et attender: to love and wait upon.

How soon the news of the executions reached London cannot be said, but when it did, the Marquess Dorset clearly felt that even sanctuary might not afford him complete safety. His uncle Lionel, Bishop of Salisbury, had already emerged and retired to his see; as a bishop, and one who had not been actually charged with treason, he was tolerably secure, but Dorset was in a very different case. According to Mancini, the Protector's spies soon informed him that the Marquess had disappeared out of the sanctuary, and Gloucester, supposing he would be in the neighbourhood, 'surrounded with troops and dogs the already grown crops and the cultivated and woody places, and sought for him after the manner of huntsmen, by a very close encirclement, but he was never found.' Immediately behind Westminster Abbey, open fields with copses and thickets stretched to the skyline. Over this wide area, the soldiers and dogs could not prevent him from disappearing through fields of standing corn as though he had never been.

The impact made by the news of Lord Hasting's death was of course far more astounding and shocking than that of the three executions at Pontefract. The surprise and agitation it had caused had not been entirely allayed by the proclamation, whose inaccuracy had been noted by some. The state of general confusion, in which nothing was positively known but a good deal feared, some of it mistakenly, is set down in the form of a paperful of notes, of which the writer is not identified, found among the Cely Papers†

* Camden, *Kings, Queens, Nobles and Others, buried in the Cathedral Church of St. Peter at Westminster.*
† *op. cit.,* p. 132, no. 14.

'There is great romber in the realm
Chamberlain is deceased, in trouble'.

(A very discreet mention of the execution of Lord Hasting).

'The Chancellor is disproved and not content'. (Rotherhan, already deprived of the Great Seal, had been arrested at the council meeting in the Tower.)

'The Bishop of Ely is dead'. (This was a wild rumour; Morton had merely been arrested at the same time as Rotherham.) A dark cloud of unknowing and dread had settled on the writer.

'If the King, God save his life, were deceased, the Duke of Gloucester were in any peril, if my Lord Prince were, God defend, were troubled, if my Lord of Northumberland were dead or greatly troubled, if my Lord Howard were slain'. The writer is ignorant but apprehensive of the welfare of the King and the Duke of York.

> *There is a tide in the affairs of men*
> *Which, taken at the flood, leads on to fortune.*

At the cost of Hastings' life, Gloucester had now put down the dangerous conspiracy of the Woodvilles; he had secured control of both the Princes; the reinforcements which he had demanded from York were on their way. It is not universally accepted, but at least it is arguable, that he had never meant to go further than this. The preparations for the coronation of Edward V were well known to be going forward; the Lord Chancellor's speech for the opening of Parliament had been drafted; the King's robes of crimson cloth of gold had been made ready, and More said that on the fatal 13th of June, many lords were sitting in council, 'devising the honourable solemnity of the King's coronation', and that the elaborate set-pieces of confectionary for the coronation banquet 'were in making night and day at Westminster', and victual had been killed, 'which was afterwards cast away'. If Gloucester, having secured the office of Protector for the King's minority, as was his legal right, and to the discharge of which there was no-one else so fit as he: if having secured his proper position he had been content with it, he would have had for some six or seven years all the scope he desired; but three historians explain the pressure he was under, to seize the crown. A. R. Myers* has said: 'The Queen's party would now be irreconcilable, and the young King permanently alienated. Richard decided to cut the knot by usurping the crown'. Cheetham† expands the point by saying that the boy, whose attributes had been praised by Mancini, who, on a very frightening occasion, had spoken up for his mother and her family, would prove more formidable as he grew older; and P. B. Pugh,‡ says no doubt

* *History To-Day*, August 1954.
† *op. cit.*, p. 117.
‡ *The Magnates, Knights and Gentry*, XVC England.

Gloucester 'genuinely feared that unless he seized control of the government, he would before long be destroyed by the Woodvilles and the Greys'. 'Hastings,' he says, 'may have joined forces with the Queen's supporters to over-throw the Lord Protector. It was now clear that there was no security for Gloucester unless he became King. Fear may have been as important as ambition in bringing about the usurpation of Richard III.' The removal of Hastings had reduced the Protector's majority on the council to a perilous margin. In Cheetham's words: 'To survive, he must rule, and to rule, he must be King'.

The decision in itself was all in the country's favour. The dire example of the reign of Henry VI, begun when that King was eight months old, the appalling incompetence and the criminal rapine to which the long minority had given scope, ending in a civil war of which the memories were so fierce, that Shakespeare, a hundred years later, found them good theatre still, meant that there would be substantial support for replacing the child of twelve by the hardy, experienced, dedicated Prince who was himself of the blood royal. But how was it to be done? At this point it would appear that Gloucester bethought him of the tale of Edward IV's troth-plight to Eleanor Butler, of which he had never, up till now, appeared to take much, if any, notice. Commines said that Stillington told him of it. It might or might not be true, and if true, it might still be considered as one of those matters which people are willing to put aside; Bacon's opinion of it, as a lawyer, was: 'that fable was ever exploded'.

But a very slight justification is sometimes enough, if there is sufficient force of public opinion behind it. At all events, it had to be tried. With Buckingham's energetic co-operation, arrangements were made with Dr. Ralph Shaa, brother of the goldsmith who was Lord Mayor of London, and famous as a popular preacher. His sermons at Paul's Cross always drew crowds, More said. On Sunday June 22, Dr. Shaa preached on the text: Bastard slips shall not take deep root, and he related to the listening multitude the story of the bastardy of King Edward IV's children; but in his earnestness, he went too far. He said that the Duchess of York had been false to wedlock, and it was known in her family that the only son of the late Duke of York was the Duke of Gloucester; he, said Dr. Shaa, was the only one of his brothers who had a resemblance to the late Duke. It had been intended that at this point the Protector should appear as if by chance in one of the balconies that over-looked the preaching-place, that the spectators might judge this for themselves; but though Gloucester had been willing to stand as a witness to his mother's hypothetical shame and present himself to the crowds as her only legitimate son, owing to bad timing the effect missed its mark. The people, struck dumb by these extraordinary allegations against the venerable Duchess of York, remained altogether silent. The story was repeated by Mancini that when the Duchess of York first heard of Edward IV's marriage to

Elizabeth Woodville, she threatened to accuse herself of adultery, to debar Edward from the throne. If this were true, or even being retailed as true, it is possible that the tale put the idea into Gloucester's head.

The congregation had been so much taken aback, it was felt that Dr. Shaa's accusation of the Duchess had been a mistake. Shaa himself, according to More, was afterwards overcome with shame and would go about only after dark, like an owl. But Gloucester, upheld by his own resolution and heartened by Buckingham, now put off the mourning he had worn ever since his brother's death, and, said Mancini, rode about the streets in purple velvet, attended by a thousand followers. Two days after the preaching at Paul's Cross, Buckingham addressed a gathering of the city dignitaries in the Guildhall. His eloquence astonished them. He rehearsed the ill-doings of Edward IV's reign, the oppressive, unjustifiable taxes, the fact that no desirable woman was safe from the King's licentiousness. He repeated the tale of the marriage that was no marriage; but he now tacked about a little, and touched only distantly on the illegitimacy of the Protector's brothers, saying he would not venture to go further into that matter, because the Protector bore 'a filial reverence for the Duchess his mother', but they would know what he meant, as they'd heard it all from Dr. Shaa. It was plain, Buckingham declared, that Prince Richard of Gloucester had the right to the throne, but he would be extremely loath to accept the crown, as he well knew, none better, what labours of body and mind the trust entailed on anyone who discharged it properly: and here he would remind them that this position 'was no child's office'. In that, he made his one strong point, to those who bore in mind the minority of Henry VI. Still, unwilling as he was, the Duke of Gloucester would be more inclined to undertake these heavy duties, if, said Buckingham, 'you, the honoured citizens of this the chief city of this realm, join with us the nobles in our said request'. '. . . Wherein, dear friends', he concluded, 'what minds you have, we request you plainly to show us'. His words were followed by a deathly silence. The crowd had been much impressed by the Duke's speech—but they said nothing. Buckingham and the Lord Mayor conversed in whispers. It might be, said the Mayor, that as Londoners they were accustomed only to being spoken to by the Recorder of London. Sir Thomas Fitzwilliam had been newly appointed Recorder and was most unwilling to address the crowd on this matter, but the Lord Mayor insisted that he should; he therefore repeated to them the gist of Buckingham's speech but making it clear that he was not adding any persuasions of his own. When he had finished, the hall was still silent, the people standing 'as if they had been men amazed'. Buckingham then spoke very forcibly. It had not been necessary to consult the opinion of the citizens of London; the houses of Parliament could have arranged the matter; but the lords, out of kindness and goodwill to the citizens, had wanted to give them a chance to express their wishes, which it would be very much to their honour and advantage to do in this momentous affair, though that, he said, did not seem to weigh with them. 'Wherefor', he said, 'we require you give us answer one or other, whether you be minded, as all the nobles in this realm be, to have this noble Prince, now Protector, to be your King or not'.

There is no saying how long this might have gone on, but now Buckingham's servants who were standing at the back of the Guildhall, with some of the Protector's followers, were reinforced by 'some 'prentices and lads that thrust into the hall among the press', who suddenly shouted out at the tops of their voices: 'King Richard! King Richard!' and threw their caps into the air. Those who stood in front of them turned their heads round, 'marvelling thereof, but nothing they said'.*

However, next day, June 25, at Westminster, Parliament decided that the Lord Protector should be asked to assume the crown. They had not been taken by surprise like the citizens in the Guildhall, some of whom had last seen the Protector in black clothes, ushering on the child King with gestures of loyalty, to his destination in the Bishop's palace at the top of Ludgate Hill. The idea that the Duke of Gloucester should replace him had been thoroughly canvassed by the Council; most of them took the view that whether Edward IV had been pre-contracted or not, the Duke of Gloucester was a member of that group of hereditary heirs to the crown, among whom Parliament was entitled to choose the one most likely to work the nation's good. Almost anything was to be preferred to a reign in which the Woodvilles would hold the reins of power, or to the civil war which would be needed to unseat them; and of the Duke of Gloucester's capacity to wear the crown, no one was in doubt.

On the day following, June 26, a deputation led by the Duke of Buckingham waited on the Protector at Baynard's Castle. The concourse entered the courtyard and Gloucester appeared at some station above their heads, on a balcony or outer staircase, from which he listened with what appeared to be hesitation and reluctance to the petition Buckingham voiced on their behalf. When he accepted it, there was, this time, no lack of shouting for King Richard. He descended among them. the nobles pressed upon him to take the oath of allegiance and the new King, attended by them, rode to Westminster Hall. There he took his seat in the marble chair of the King's Bench.

Two days later, on June 28, he performed as one of the earliest actions of his reign, a deed of somewhat ominous significance. In the Parliament of May 1474, on the matter of the division of the bulk of the Warwick inheritance between Clarence and Gloucester and their wives, it had been decided that the widowed Countess of Warwick who, by inheritance, was the owner of the estates, was to be 'debarred from her own patrimony'

* More, *The History of King Richard III*.

and to be regarded 'as if she were now naturally dead'. Before the marriage of the Duke of York with Anne Mowbray in 1478, the settlement had created the little boy Earl of Nottingham in June 1476 and Duke of Norfolk in February 1477, to the disadvantage respectively of Lord Berkeley and John Lord Howard. On June 28, 1483, Richard III created Lord Berkeley Earl of Nottingham and John Lord Howard Duke of Norfolk. This appropriation of two of his titles has given rise to some question as to whether, of the two boys, the younger at least might not be dead already. Though an Act of Bastardy made him incapable of succession, it would not affect his occupying titles bestowed on him by the late King. But Burke says: (Vol. XII, pt II, p. 912) 'apparently the new King held that he had lost his titles of Norfolk and Nottingham after the death of Anne Mowbray in 1481, though it is not possible to reconcile such a view with any principle of law', and Garter King-of-Arms Sir Anthony Wagner has said: 'Lawyers are rather apt to think of law as existing independently of any power to enforce it.'

The elder boy's title of King had been taken from him with some show of legality, however specious; the titles of his younger brother were taken with no justification at all. What the state of the two Princes might be at this point, the Londoners were in doubt. On June 25 they were still, it must be supposed, in the Royal Apartments because Mancini says that the lords foregathered at Baynard's Castle, 'whither (the Protector) had purposely betaken himself, that these events might not take place in the Tower where the young King was confined'. Now that Richard had been declared King and was to be crowned in less than a fortnight, it was out of the question that the Princes should remain in the Royal Apartments, waited on as befitted the King of England and his heir-presumptive, the Duke of York. Tradition says that when they were removed from the Royal Apartments, they were placed in the Bloody Tower. This building, it is important to notice, was not so called till the reign of James I. In 1483 it was known as the Garden Tower because its left side gave on to the garden of the Lieutenant's Lodgings. It stands, adjoining the Wakefield Tower which once communicated with the Royal Apartments, immediately behind the Traitor's Gate, separated from it by a path; its front windows command a view of the river. An archway underneath it leads in to the garden, to Tower Green, and the group of separate buildings, chief of them the White Tower, which are comprised within the curtain wall of the fortress. The building above the arch is on two storeys, to which a narrow spiral stone staircase leads up. Though the rooms on each floor were of course much smaller than those the boys had been accustomed to all their lives, the place was not prison-like. They were waited on by several servants (for these were afterwards spoken of as being withdrawn) and as the Royal Apartments were so near, it was easy to bring them clothes, books or playthings. They had bows and arrows with them. The Great Chronicle says that during the mayoralty of Sir Edmund Shaa (that is, before October 29, 1483), 'the children of King Edward were seen shooting and playing in the garden of the Tower, by sundry times'.

Molinet had heard that the little Prince was nimble and merry, the elder one melancholy. A thoughtful and precocious child, Prince Edward may have been so by nature, but the examination of the bones interred in Henry VII's chapel as those of the Princes (*vide infra*) revealed another possible reason for this. The then President of the British Dental Association who was asked to examine the teeth, said: 'There is undoubted evidence of Edward's having suffered from extensive disease, affecting almost equally both sides of the lower jaw; The disease was of a chronic nature and could not fail to have affected his general health. The gums in the lower molar region would have been inflamed, swollen, septic and no doubt associated with discomfort and irritability.'

Mancini relates a circumstance to which enough weight has hardly been given, though Mr. Laurence Tanner in his article* came to the conclusion independently. Mancini says that 'after Hastings was removed', 'the King and his brother were withdrawn into the inner apartments of the Tower proper, and day by day began to be seen more rarely behind the bars and windows, till at length they ceased to appear altogether'. 'After Hastings was removed' is not a precise time and it seems to cover two changes of place; the first, from the Royal Apartments to what has always been agreed was the Garden Tower. Being established here would not properly be described as being 'withdrawn into the inner apartments of the Tower proper'. The Garden Tower as may be seen from various drawings: (i.e. the engraving based on survey of 1597)† is much nearer to the curtain wall than the Royal Apartments were. The fact that the boys were seen playing in the garden suggests that they were not then under close restraint, though within the environs of the Tower. Mancini, after saying they were removed to the inner apartments, adds that there, their servants were withdrawn, the last one 'whose services the King enjoyed', being 'a Strasbourg doctor' who has been identified as Dr. John Argenti. It appears significant in the light of the remarks about the disease of the jaw, that Edward should, up till that time, have been allowed regular visits from a doctor. Argenti said nothing about disease or treatment, but Mancini heard that the doctor reported 'that the young King, like a victim prepared for sacrifice, sought remission of his sins by daily confession and penance, because he believed that death was facing him'. Mancini does not say where the young King was when Dr. Argenti was removed from attending on him, but Laurence Tanner suggests‡ for

* *Archeologia*, LXXXIV, p. 1, *vide infra*.
† *The Tower of London*, Department of the Environment official guide, p. 7.
‡ *op. cit.*

reasons afterwards disclosed, that the Princes had now been lodged in the White Tower. The massive keep was famous for the two great chambers on its first floor: one being the council chamber, the other the chapel of St. John; but the building has another floor above this, and storeys of chambers in each of the four great turrets. From the twelfth century onwards, state prisoners had been bestowed in one part or other of the upper ranges, and when it had been decided that the menace of the boys' existence would best be met by no one's seeing them or being able to say where they were, the upper reaches of the White Tower would seem a natural choice.

It is remarkable that though More and Mancini could never have seen each other's accounts they often confirm each other. One instance is their correspondence over the separating of the King and Lord Rivers; another is the picture they both give of the depressed and hopeless state of the child, no doubt intensified by a lowering illness, which made its impression on the last independent witnesses who saw him; More says: 'The Prince, as soon as the Protector left that name and took himself as King, had it showed unto him that he should not reign, but his uncle should have the crown. At which words, the Prince, sore abashed began to sigh and said, Alas, I would my uncle would let me have my life yet, though I lose my kingdom. Then he that told him the tale, used him with good words and put him in the best comfort he could. But forthwith the Prince and his brother were both shut up and all others removed from them; only one called Black Will, or William Slaughter, was to serve them and see them sure. After which time the Prince never tied his points nor in any way cared for himself, but with that young babe his brother lingered in thought and heaviness.'*

The discoveries made by Laurence Tanner and his colleagues (*vide infra*) showed that the children were four feet ten inches and four feet six and a half inches tall. They were of slender build. The bones of their fingers were very small.

* More, *The History of Richard III.*

177

29

AT the beginning of July the reinforcements arrived from York: about five thousand men. Their accoutrements were rusty and the Londoners who had been afraid that a formidable army might be approaching were not sorry to see their shabby appearance. They were encamped in Moor Fields and Richard reviewed them there. For a man of reserved nature, whose portraits suggest such severe self-repression, Richard was surprisingly alive to the value of theatrical gestures before a crowd; he had shown it when he had the Woodville armour paraded through the London streets, and at Baynard's Castle when he came down from a height to receive the allegiance of his supporters; now he walked bare-headed before the Yorkshire men, graciously acknowledging the ovations of the northerners who loved him.

The coronation was to take place on July 6. The new King's wife had come down from Middleham but she had not brought Prince Edward with her. The fragile son of a consumptive mother, he had been left at home with his attendants. There may have been statecraft in this arrangement as well as anxiety for the child's health. He was ten years old, the age of the younger of his two cousins in the Tower. The sight of him at his father's coronation would have called them abruptly to the spectators' minds and defeated the policy which Richard had now adopted, of complete and deathly silence.

The short notice, from the Parliament on June 25 at which he had been asked to take the crown, to the ceremony itself on July 6, meant that the workmen in the King's Wardrobe were extremely pressed for time. The accounts* read: 'June 27 in the first year of the reign of our Sovereign Lord King Richard III, that Piers Curteys of the King's Wardrobe hath taken upon him to purvey by the third day of July next coming, the parcels ensuing against the coronation of our Sovereign Lord.' Dr. Milles points out that it would have been impossible to provide all the necessary garments in so short a time if some of them had not been made already for the coronation of Edward V. As it was, among the notes of wages paid to tailors, sempstresses and handicraft men 'working on robes and garments in the Wardrobe', the entry occurs: 'given unto

* *Archeologia*, Vol. I, p. 361.

divers skinners by way of reward for their good and hasty expedition of the work, eleven shillings and eightpence'.

For the King to wear when riding ceremonially from the Tower to Westminster, Curteys had provided a doublet of blue cloth of gold and a long gown of purple velvet trimmed with ermine. Several garments had been made for the varied ceremonies of the day itself, among them a long gown of purple cloth of gold, wrought with garters and roses, lined with white damask. This was the Queen's gift to the King. Clothes of silk and gold were given as the King's especial gift 'to divers estates of ladies and gentlemen', including the Lady Margaret Beaufort. The pressure of the time was so great, Curteys had merely written, in one place: "To many divers persons, for to have in haste, by my Lord of Buckingham's commandment, whose names were not remembered, delivered in great haste', such and such lengths of stuff. To the Duke of Buckingham himself, 'for his especial gift' there were issued 'eight yards of blue cloth of gold, eight yards of black velvet'. What the Duke actually wore for the ceremony was so striking that it had come down by word of mouth nearly a hundred and fifty years later. George Buck in his 'Reign of Richard III' said that Buckingham wore blue velvet 'with gold cartwheels burning'.

The procession was headed by bishops accompanying the Cardinal Archbishop; next came the lords who carried the King's regalia. Lord Stanley, the Lady Margaret's third husband, bore the Mace, the Earl of Surrey the Sword of State, the Duke of Suffolk the Sceptre, his son, Richard's nephew, the Orb. The supreme honour was awarded to the new Duke of Norfolk. He walked, carrying the jewelled crown 'between his hands'.

The King walked under a canopy borne by the Wardens of the Cinque Ports, his train supported by the Duke of Buckingham. A bevy of nobles followed. Behind these came the lords who carried the items of the Queen's regalia, and then the Queen herself, surrounded by more bishops, and wearing 'a gold circlet with many precious stones', walking under a canopy which had a gold bell at each corner. Her train was carried by the Lady Margaret Beaufort, Countess of Richmond, Lady Stanley. Two years later, this enigmatical small woman was to attend another occasion of great state in Westminster Abbey, the coronation of her son, Henry VII; meanwhile, the King's procession and the Queen's were followed by a greater throng of noble ladies, knights, esquires and gentlemen than had been present at any coronation on record.*

A carpet was stretched from Westminster Palace to the Abbey and the King and Queen walked over it barefoot. As they stood at the altar, they were said to have been 'naked to the waist'; this meant, of course, that their clothes were opened to the waist, so that they might be annointed on the breast as well as on the head. The long rites were interspersed with

* *Excerpta Historica*, ed. Samuel Bentley, pp. 379–84.

exquisite singing; when the crowns had been placed on their heads, the choir 'sang Te Deum, and the organs went'.* These sounds must have been clearly audible in the Abbots' Place at the east end of the Abbey, where the wretched, furious Elizabeth Woodville lurked with her daughters like a frightened animal. The King and Queen, re-robed in cloth of gold, were led back to Westminster Hall, where the coronation banquet began at four and went on till nine. 'And by that time it was dark night. Anon came into the hall great light of wax torches and torchettes; and as soon as the lights came up the hall, the lords and ladies went up to the King and made their obeisance. And anon the King and Queen rose up and went to their chambers'.†

The act of coronation was of inordinate importance. The Woodvilles had known this when they tried to hurry on the rite for the child Edward V. Richard III had been determined to undergo it himself at the earliest possible time, and this had involved the officials of the Wardrobe in great haste and turmoil. The jewelled crown that the Duke of Norfolk carried between his hands could scarcely have been 'the very rich crown of Edward the Confessor'; the sovereign was crowned with more than one crown during the ceremony, and the Confessor's crown was placed on his head at the supreme moment. The English treasury housed many jewelled circlets, one of which it would seem that Richard III chose to wear; Bacon speaks of his having 'a crown of ornament'; having struggled so hard to gain a crown, he seems to have worn one whenever there was occasion. Such an occasion now presented itself.

The great changes the last three months had seen, the death of Edward IV, the sudden arrest of Lord Rivers whom, it had seemed, nothing could touch, the execution of Lord Hastings, the sudden eclipse of the haughty, resplendent Queen, the obscuring of the two Princes in the Tower, the coronation of Richard III, had created a state of surprise and disturbance which, it was felt, a royal progress was needed to abate.

* Grafton's *Chronicle*, Vol. II, p. 115.
† *Excerpta Historica*, p. 382.

30

RICHARD set out from Windsor on July 20. He had no armed escort; he was accompanied by a throng of bishops, judges and courtiers. The route was to take him to the west then through the Midlands to the north, to York. He visited Reading, Oxford, Woodstock, Gloucester, granting petitions, bestowing benefits and making a highly favourable impression on the people who saw him. He had not the easy, splendid appearance of Edward IV, his manner showed tensely strung nerves, but he had the vitality, the insight, the professional desire to please, which could make a progress a means to kindle loyalty.

At Gloucester he was joined by Buckingham who had left London a few days after the King's departure from Windsor and overtaken the royal cortege at this point.

When Bishop Morton had been arrested at the Council Table he had been first imprisoned within the Tower; it was then a question of what should be done with him; it was not desirable to keep him there indefinitely, but a man of such intelligence needed looking after, and Buckingham offered to keep him under house-arrest in the castle of Brecknock, one of his own residences in the principality of Wales where he himself was now all powerful. Morton accordingly had been sent there under guard, and Buckingham was on his way to join the captive who, though under restraint and technically the Duke's prisoner, was, by intellect, capacity and experience, much the more formidable of the two.

Between Buckingham and the King there was no ostensible cause of complaint. The Duke, ever since he had written to the Lord Protector, three months ago, offering his support, had been demonstrably loyal to him; some of his motive force no doubt had come from his having seen, suddenly, at last, an opportunity to revenge himself on the hated Woodville Queen and her clan, but of his genuine personal commitment to Richard there had been no doubt. Richard had rewarded him nobly and in addition he had granted, as far as he could, the thing for which Buckingham had specially asked. The Earldom of Hereford had been divided between two heiresses of the Bohun family from one of whom Buckingham was directly descended, so that her share had come to him. The other had been married by Henry IV, and her share had been merged in the Crown. This moiety had come down to Henry VI and thus was acquired by Edward IV, who had dowered Elizabeth Woodville on some of it. The legal position needed a revision by Parliament, and Richard had promised that this should be done by the first Parliament of his reign. Meantime he had issued to Buckingham 'a grant provisional till the same shall be invested in him by the next Parliament'. Buckingham had been given the widest authority over Wales, he had been created Constable of England and Great Chamberlain of England, and the moiety of the Bohun inheritance would be his in a matter of months. On the surface, the situation between him and Richard could not have seemed fairer, nor could the aspect of affairs between the new King and the people. In the course of the progress his secretary Kendall had written, in announcing the approach of the royal train to York, that the King had been 'worshipfully received, with pageants, his lords and judges in every place sitting, determining the complaints of poor folks, with due punishments of offenders against his laws'.* The Bishop of St. David's wrote to the Prior of Christchurch: 'I trust to God soon, by Michaelmas, the King shall be at London. He contents the people where he goes, the best that ever did Prince; for many a poor man that hath suffered wrong many days, have been relieved and helped by him and his commands in his progress ... God hath sent him to us, for the weal of all'.† But the whole conspectus of national affairs, bright and dark, seen and unseen, cannot be grasped in its entirety, either at the time or centuries afterwards. Some threat will rise to the eye of the man living at the moment, whose trace has dissolved since it came to nothing; signs which should have conveyed a threat pass unnoticed, their significance becoming plain only through the passage of time. In their meeting at Gloucester, it would seem that Richard and Buckingham may have discussed a problem already recognized by them. Interpreting Richard's actions at this point, Sir James Ramsay has said, speaking of the Princes:‡ 'Richard found that a substantial party might be rallied in their names and that their lives could not be prolonged without imminent risk to his throne'. There were still at large Sir Edward Woodville, his brother Sir Richard Woodville, Lionel Woodville, Bishop of Salisbury, the Marquess of Dorset, and in sanctuary, the Queen, a fecund source of trouble. There were the lords who had been shocked and affronted by the summary execution of their fellow nobleman, Lord Hastings. Beyond the Border were the Scots, and in the court of Duke Francis of Brittany, the sole heir of Lancaster, Henry Tudor. Richard's own Steward of the Royal Household, Thomas Lord Stanley, was the husband of Henry Tudor's mother. The covert menaces were like underground fires in a season of long drought; anyone of them might ignite

---

* Kendall, *op. cit.*, p. 253.
† *Christchurch Letters*, Camden Society, quoted by Kendall, ibid.
‡ Ramsay, James, *Lancaster and York*, Vol. II.

with any of the rest. The most immediately dangerous was the threat posed by the fact of the two Princes being in the Tower.

Richard's characteristic approach to a situation was not cautious vigilance, but sudden action, of which, during his career, he had often proved the benefit, but which meant that he sometimes failed through lack of a patient and level-headed assessment. He did not, it seems, take into account how clear a picture the Londoners had of the Princes. The little Duke of York was a part of the royal household when the King and Queen were at Westminster or Greenwich. He was seen, coming and going, in processions and cavalcades through the streets, on the royal barge going up and down the river. His wedding five years before to Anne Mowbray and the tournament that celebrated it, had been public spectacles. Richard of Gloucester had spent so much of his time in the north that he might have failed to realize the image created by his younger nephew in the public eye, but he himself had accompanied the elder boy into London, presenting him to the enthusiastic crowds as their King, a magnet for the public gaze, fair haired, in a blue velvet riding-gown, surrounded by men in solemn black. The Londoners were kindly disposed to the brothers for the sake of their popular, resplendent father, and the children themselves at twelve and ten years old were still in their touching childhood. The little King, somewhat ailing as he might be, was an intelligent, gracious child, a small boy who appealed to the hearts of the populace and whose future, with his brother's, was a matter of affectionate, anxious concern to them.

Richard had had Hastings beheaded on Tower Green in broad daylight on a log of wood that happened to be handy. Anyone had been welcome to know this and to make what they liked of it; but there was that other tradition, of execution within the Tower itself, which was involved in impenetrable, terrifying secrecy. No one, among the nation at large, knew exactly how the Duke of Clarence had died; it was not positively known how Henry VI had died, while the imprisonment and subsequent removal of Richard II had been conducted in a spine-chilling silence and anonymity. A public execution was accepted, by and large, as one of the harsh facts of existence; the absolute silence that covered a concealed execution created a state of waking nightmare.

It was known that the Princes were in the Tower; it was known also that they were not in the royal apartments; Mancini, writing of the period before he left London, had said that they had been 'withdrawn into the inner apartments of the Tower proper'; and in describing the charm and intelligence of the young Edward V, he had added: 'I have seen many men burst forth into tears and lamentations when mention was made of him after his removal from men's sight, and already there was a suspicion he had been done away with'. The immediacy of Mancini's report gives the reader a start of surprise: 'Whether, however, he has been done away with, and by what manner of death, so far I have not at all discovered'. And concluding with a word on Richard III's coronation, he says, writing in December 1483: 'How he may afterwards have ruled and yet rules, I have not sufficiently learnt, because directly after these his triumphs, I left England for France'.

December was four months away from August, in the first week of which the King arrived at Warwick Castle, to be joined there by his wife so that they might go up to York together. The Queen was frail and sickly, so was their son Prince Edward, and since he was still an only child, it was clear that the marriage would bring no more children. The one precious boy was the object of his father's dynastic ambition. Having a child of his own had inspired him, not with sympathy for other people's children, but with a fierce, exclusive passion to which all conflicting claims must give way. And was Richard III the only member of the ruling circle to argue like this in support of his own family? His brother Clarence had been made a victim of the Woodvilles. He had been guilty of treachery, ingratitude, treason; but the almost unheard-of vengeance, death at a brother's hands, had been wreaked on him, because the Woodville Queen and her relatives had been frightened of losing their place and power. The son of the Earl of Desmond who had succeeded his father, received a letter from King Richard, in which the King told him that they shared a common grief: those who had been responsible for the death of the late Earl and his two sons, were accountable also for the death of the Duke of Clarence.* If there were to be risings in favour of the Queen's children, the firm beginnings of good rule which he had already made might be brought to nothing, and the power of the crown fall into the hands of the debauched, grasping, mindless crew whose influence had injured the late King's reputation and hurried on his untimely death. There was everything to be said for putting an end, once for all, to the menacing existence of two children: except that to do it would be a fearful and abhorrent crime. The decision, it must be safe to say, was not made without agonized mental struggle. Polydore Vergil had never laid eyes on Richard III, but he reported what other people remembered of his mannerisms: 'He did continually bite his nether lip, ever with his right hand pulling out of the sheath to the midst and putting in again, the dagger which he did always wear'.

Ramsay,† compared the dates given by three contemporary chroniclers, to form a rough estimate of the time at which the Princes died. The Croyland Continuator said that the children remained in the Tower when Richard departed on his progress; this was July 20. Rows, in his Historia Regum Anglie, said their deaths occurred three months after Richard III took charge of Edward V, which would imply a date the first week in

* Kendall, *op. cit.*, p. 255.
† *op. cit.*

184

August. Molinet says they were murdered five weeks after they had entered the Tower. The Duke of York was taken there on June 16, five weeks before July 21. Ramsay concluded that the most likely time for the murders to have been committed was the end of July or the beginning of August. Thomas More had heard that the mandate for their deaths had been despatched from Warwick, after the King and Buckingham had parted at Gloucester.

The suggestion, ably argued by Paul Murray Kendall but not finally endorsed by him, is that Buckingham ordered the murders on his own responsibility, with a view, ultimately, to claiming the throne; the advantage of the crime being, first, that it removed the main obstacles, after Richard himself, to Buckingham's own succession, and secondly, that the guilt, when ascribed to Richard, should arouse public indignation and make easy a rising against him in Buckingham's favour; that it was the astute and statesmanlike persuasions of Morton which convinced Buckingham that he would have no chance of successfully asserting his own claim against that of Henry Tudor, and that if he wanted to see the dominating Yorkist king put down in favour of a Lancastrian pretender, he must support Henry Tudor's claim, not try to push his own. The extraordinary *volte face* which Buckingham presently made, in favour of Henry Tudor, which surprised no one more than Richard III himself, whatever its origin, was the reaction of a vain, weak man, and as such, far more difficult to account for than the actions of a strong-minded, consistent character. Kendall's hypothesis as to Buckingham's ambition seems extremely probable but the suggestion that he procured the murder of the Princes on his own initiative is not tenable. Cheetham makes the very strong point that there was no contemporary accusation of the kind against him, and there arises also the question of how he could have done it even if he wished. Kendall suggests that he managed it during the few days when he was in London before overtaking the King at Gloucester, but this does not bear examination. Buckingham was Constable of England; he was not Constable of the Tower. This office was now held by Sir Robert Brackenbury, a follower and friend of Richard III who had been his neighbour at Middleham. Brackenbury would not have obeyed a command of such a fearful nature unless it had come directly from the King, with the most unmistakeable authenticity. Buckingham would have been obliged to forge a warrant with Richard's sign manual, and this would have been putting a lethal weapon against himself into the hands of a King from whom, we are told, his loyalty was already turning. It is of course possible that in those few days after July 20, he took a mandate from Richard to the Constable of the Tower; but Gairdner believed that Buckingham's share of the crime consisted only in 'a guilty fore-knowledge'. Whatever it were, when he left the King at Gloucester, in high summer and in the radiance of his own prosperity and success, he never saw him again. The following

October, the deluging rains had come down, the swollen Severn overflowed the fields, drowning any chance of his rebellion's success, and when he was a captive in Salisbury, sending frantic appeals to the King for a final interview, Richard refused it and ordered his beheading.

31

ON August 29, the King, the Queen and their son entered York. The Prince had been brought to his parents from Pontefract; in view of the taxing celebrations ahead of him, it had been thought best for the child not to ride, and he had made the journey in a litter. The royal entry into York, made through the Micklegate Bar, was magnificent. The streets were hung with tapestries and garlands; the citizens crowded about him in eager welcome; pageants greeted his presence at different stations; among the presents made to him were a pair of silver-gilt basins full of gold marks, while the Queen was given one hundred gold pounds in a piece of gold plate.

Richard had already, earlier in the month, created his son Prince of Wales; now, inspired by the atmosphere of success, he decided that the ceremony of the investiture should take place in York Minster. The Queen and the Prince must have had with them clothes suitable for the occasion, but on August 31, the King despatched his knight Sir James Tyrell to London with orders to the Wardrobe to send up at once 'for us' a quantity of clothes: doublets, short gowns, a hooded cloak of violet in-grained, gilt spurs, forty trumpet-banners of sarsenet and four standards of sarsenet with his cognizance of the Boar.* On Sunday September 7, one of the famous cycle of the York Mystery Plays, the Creed Play, was acted in the Guildhall. On Monday 8th, the King, the Queen and the small Prince walked in procession to the Minster, heralded by forty trumpeters. It was a great day, it was said, for the City of York to see three royal personages wearing crowns in its streets. The Prince wore a gold wreath and in one hand he carried a gold wand; the other hand was held by his mother, who wore a crown. The King himself, said Polydore Vergil, wore 'a notable rich diadem'. As he passed the light on the jewels was reflected in the delight and excitement of the crowds. Grafton said: 'The King was had, in that triumph, in such honour, and the common people of the north so rejoiced, that they extolled and praised him far above the stars.'†

When these rejoicings were over, the royal party separated; the Queen took her son back to Middleham; the King meanwhile established a

---

* Sharon Turner, *History of England*, Vol. III, p. 481.
† Grafton's *Chronicle*, Vol. II. p. 120.

household in his castle at Sherrif Hutton which was to accommodate the Prince of Wales' cousin, Edward, son of the Duke of Clarence, whom Edward IV, in spite of the Duke's attainder, had invested with the earldom of Warwick. This boy was now eight years old. With him was housed another cousin, the nineteen year old John de la Pole, Earl of Lincoln, son of the marriage of the Duke of Suffolk and Edward IV's sister Elizabeth. Richard III appears to have treated both these nephews kindly, the young man and the child; the former was vigorous and able, the latter was neither; Warwick's daughters did not produce healthy children; the little Prince of Wales was alarmingly delicate, the little Earl of Warwick was not quite of normal intelligence.

The fair prospect, so brightly spread at York, did not extend over the whole kingdom. The Croyland Continuator says that the King had scarcely departed from Windsor when 'the people of the southern and western parts of the kingdom began to murmur greatly and to form meetings and confederacies in order to deliver the two Princes from the Tower. Soon, he says, 'it became known that many things were going on in secret and some in the face of all the world, to promote this enterprise, especially by those in sanctuary.' It was urged that the Princesses should be conveyed abroad, so that if any mischance had happened, or should happen, to their brothers, one of them might marry and continue the line of Edward IV. The King's intelligence service was very active. Far out of London as he was, these rumours reached him; he appointed one of his squires of the body, John Nesfield, to put a garrison round Westminster, so firm that as the Croyland Continuator said, it 'enclosed the church and monastery like a camp, so that the Princesses might not be spirited away by sea.'

The policy of deep and absolute silence over the state of the Princes was maintained with extraordinary success. It was known that they were in the Tower and that was all. The number of people attending on them must have been stringently reduced but even so the arrangements for their maintenance must have involved the work of several persons, and these conditions of total secrecy could have been maintained only in the Tower. The suggestion that Richard had had the boys removed to Sherrif Hutton to live with their cousins, but that this never got abroad, is not, in most people's view, a reasonable assumption. Sharon Turner interpreted this massive suppression of information as the policy which Richard III imagined or hoped would in the end cause the idea of the Princes to die away in the public mind, and had it been possible to keep to it over a long stretch of years, it must have caused that idea to become much fainter; but the immediate result was to inflame anxiety and the desire to know the truth.

There are only three known comments from writers actually living at the time, on the public belief that the children had been murdered.

The date of the compilation of Robert Fabyan's *New Chronicles of England and France* is not known, but he died in 1513. He wrote: 'The common fame went that Richard had, within the Tower, put unto secret death the two sons of his brother.' John Rows, who besides the two editions of the Roll of the Earls of Warwick, also wrote a Historia Regum Angliae, said in that work, speaking of the Princes, 'it was afterwards known to very few by what death they suffered martyrdom'. The Croyland Continuator whose additions were finished in 1486, said: 'it was commonly reported that the said sons of Edward were dead, but by what kind of violent death it was not known.'

Sir Thomas More's fragment, *The History of Richard III* is the only work which sets out a detailed account of the murder of the two Princes, and it contains such slips and mis-statements, that present-day amateur historians tend to brush it aside as without value. This is an estimate which in its turn is due for some revision.

More cannot in any sense be regarded as a propagandist for the Tudors. His father Sir John More, a lawyer, and afterwards a judge, was put into gaol after his son Thomas had made a vehement protest in parliament against the taxation of Henry VII. Thomas More himself was executed by Henry VIII for refusing to acknowledge the King as Supreme Head of the Church. More not only never published his History of Richard III, he never finished it. He wrote a Latin version and an English one, the latter, as Professor A. F. Pollard has said,* so much a draft that in some places he had left blanks for names and dates. Among mere slips of detail, he made Edward IV over fifty three at the time of his death, instead of under forty one; the woman to whom the King was said to have been troth-plight is given the name of Elizabeth Lucy, one of Edward's previous mistresses, instead of Lady Eleanor Butler. He says that Warwick was negotiating, at the time of the King's marriage to Elizabeth Woodville, a marriage alliance with the King of Spain's daughter, instead of Bona of Savoy, and, like Mancini, he places the removal of the Duke of York from sanctuary before the execution of Hastings, instead of after. The date of composition has been calculated as 1513. Writing thirty years after the death of Richard III which happened when he himself was six, he made these errors, in an uncorrected draft at that, which did not impair the general reliability of what he had to say. The work is an absorbing piece of writing, of great narrative skill; its vigour and racy simplicity make it, as has always been recognized, the earliest example of great English prose-writing; but it has elements which injure its importance as a historical document and the crucial question arises as to what the grounds may be for accepting the most striking passage of it as historical evidence of unique value.

* Pollard, A. F., *The Making of Sir Thomas More's Richard III—Historical Essays in Honour of James Tait*. ed. J. G. Edwards, 1933.

The very long speeches put into the mouths of Edward IV, Elizabeth Woodville and Buckingham are wished away by the modern reader, since however true in spirit they must necessarily be invention. The explanation put forward for More's method is that he was writing in the classical mode, where literal accuracy of fact was subordinated to an emotional colouring deemed in itself to be accurate. This is further illustrated by the contrast of Edward IV, successful, benevolent, dearly loved and deeply mourned by his subjects, with Richard III 'not letting to kiss whom he thought to kill, pitiless and cruel, not for evil will always but oftener for ambition, and either for the security or increase of his position'; without mentioning the failings of the former or the good features of the latter. But there are two aspects of the work which clearly demand very close attention. One of these is anything which More says about John Morton, Bishop of Ely, in whose house he lived as a page between the years of eight and fourteen, when Morton was Henry VII's Lord Chancellor and Archbishop of Canterbury. More describes him as: 'a man of great natural wit, very well learned and honourable in behaviour, lacking in no wise to win favour.' After the defeat of the Lancastrians at Tewkesbury, Edward IV 'for his steadfast faith and wisdom not only was content to receive him but also wooed him to come, and had him from thenceforth both in secret trust and in very special favour, which he nothing deceived . . . This man . . . had got by great experience . . . a deep insight into politic worldly drifts.' The accounts, both of the Council Meeting in the White Tower at which Richard asked Morton to send for some of his strawberries, which is not found in any other source, and of the conversation at Brecknock between Morton and the Duke of Buckingham, in the middle of which the narrative breaks off, taken together with More's service in the Bishop Morton's house, gave rise to the theory that Morton himself had either written or dictated the Latin version. This has now been rejected; but though More at the age of eight would not have been a receiver of the Bishop's confidential reminiscences, as a very clever child approaching fourteen, he may have had some of them imparted to him, or at least have picked up the information from those who had.

The passage which is of incomparable importance, is the detailed account More gives of the murder of the two Princes, which is not given anywhere else. He makes one palpable error in his description of Sir James Tyrell who, he says, was sent by Richard from Warwick with a mandate to Sir Robert Brackenbury to give up the keys of the Tower to him 'for one night'. According to More, Richard had already sent his commands by his servant John Green to Brackenbury to commit the murders, and Brackenbury had returned word 'that he would never put them to death, though he should die therefor'. When this was reported to the King in his bed-chamber at night, he lamented that he could not find anyone to do him a special service. A 'secret page of his' told him where such a one was to be found, and pointed out to him Sir James Tyrell, an ambitious man, eager to rise, but kept down by Sir Richard Ratcliffe and Sir William Catesby. Whereupon Richard summoned Tyrell and laid the command upon him. The grave blunder here is that so far from Richard's having to have Tyrell brought to his notice, the latter had been knighted by Edward IV after Tewkesbury, Richard had made him a knight-banneret during the campaign against Scotland, and he was Master of the Horse at Richard's coronation. This gross error has been used as grounds for discrediting the whole story of the deed on which Tyrell was employed.

Polydore Vergil, who was working on his English History, under a commission from Henry VII, at what appears to have been the time that More was writing his sketch, and whom, Professor Pollard thinks More may have consulted, says that Sir James Tyrell undertook the murders 'very unwillingly' at the King's command, but he gives no details of the crime. He says none are available. 'With what kind of death these sely children were executed it is not certainly known.' More begins by saying that Richard gave Tyrell a letter to Brackenbury, commanding him to give up to him the Tower keys for one night. This has been criticized as an invention too clumsy for belief but the criticism does not hold water. Polydore Vergil's version of the Constable's refusal of the deed himself makes the position clearer than More's: 'fearing lest he should obey, the same might at one time or other turn to his own harm.' Putting decency aside, the assignment, even on the King's direct command, was, in his view, far too dangerous. When he was told merely to give up the keys, he was not putting himself in peril. More says Tyrell had decided the children should be smothered, and he appointed Miles Forest, one of the jailers in charge of them and already a murderer, and John Dighton, his own horse-keeper 'a big, broad, strong knave'. 'Then, all the others being removed from them, this Miles Forest and John Dighton about midnight (the sely children lying in their beds) came into the chambers and suddenly lapped them up among the bed-clothes—so bewrapped and entangled them, keeping down by force the featherbed and pillows hard unto their mouths, that within a while, smothered and stifled, their breath failing, they gave up to God their innocent souls into the joys of heaven, leaving to the tormentors their bodies dead in the bed. After the wretches perceived them—first by the struggling with the pains of death, and after, long lying still—to be thoroughly dead, they laid their bodies naked out on the bed and fetched Sir James to see them. Who, upon the sight of them, caused those murderers to bury them at the stair foot, meetly deep in the ground, under a great heap of stones.'

Setting aside the error of Sir James Tyrell's provenance, how much confidence can be placed in the rest of this tale, of which More is the only narrator?

In opening the account of the murders, More says: 'For this present matter, I shall rehearse to you the dolorous end of those babes, not after every way that I have heard, but after that way I have so heard by such men and by such means as methought it were hard but it should be true.' This statement has been dismissed as meaning merely that More picked out such elements of gossip and rumour as he chose. This is indeed another way of stating an important truth. Erasmus said that More had the finest legal mind in Europe. When, at the age of thirty-six, he set himself to collect evidence, and to sift it, it is difficult to think of anyone whose findings should be preferred.

The most interesting part of Professor Pollard's essay* is his tracing out those men, who, he says, 'had participated in public affairs while Richard reigned, and were not only alive when More was writing, but were his friends, acquaintances and neighbours.' More's father was one of the judges of the King's Bench, the Bishop of London, Richard Fitzjames had been chaplain to Edward IV and treasurer of St. Paul's under Richard III. The Bishop's nephew, John Fitzjames, a member of parliament and a chief justice, is mentioned in the patent rolls of Richard III. John Roper, of the family of More's son-in-law, was Richard III's commissioner of array for Kent. Fox, afterwards Bishop of Winchester, had been in exile with Henry Tudor and was debarred by Richard III from being appointed to the living of St. Dunstan at Stepney. Christopher Urswick, the go-between in the schemes of the Lady Margaret Beaufort, Bishop Morton and Henry Tudor, escaped abroad and became Henry VII's chaplain, confessor and almoner. Roger Lupton had succeeded to the living left vacant by the wretched death of Dr. Ralph Shaa, attributed to the distress and shame he felt after calumniating the Duchess of York. Sir John Cutte was under-treasurer to Henry VII and More succeeded him in the office. Pollard says: 'Cutte could have given More no little information about Richard III; he was that king's servant and receiver of Crown lands in half a dozen counties.' 'All these men,' he adds, 'were bound in one way or another to Sir Thomas Lovell, who had been attainted in Richard III's only parliament, was Speaker of the House of Commons in 1485, and in 1514, treasurer of Henry VIII's household; his will contains a reference to More.' The most interesting contact from the point of view of More's narrative, was the Earl of Surrey, afterwards second Duke of Norfolk, who, as Sir Thomas Howard, had been sent to accompany Lord Hastings to the Council Meeting in the White Tower to make sure of his arrival, and spoke the ironical words to him when Lord Hastings stopped to pass the time of day with a priest he met in Tower Street: 'What, my Lord, I pray you, come on. Wherefor talk you so long with that priest? You have no need of a priest yet.' And therewith he laughed upon him, as though he would say: 'ye shall have, soon.' It cannot of course be asserted that More gained details of the murder from all or any of these men,

* op. cit.

or that if he had, they were necessarily true; but Pollard's following out his connections with so many people, not only living at the time of the event, but placed in positions highly favourable for gaining inside knowledge, puts More's testimony in a more reliable light than is allowed by his detractors who have not understood his claims to be considered seriously. More's pinning of his story to verbal information, is continuous. He says: 'This have I, by credible information learned, that on the night of Edward IV's death,' one Mistlebrook brought the news to one Pottier, rousing him up in his house in Redcross Street, outside Cripplegate. Whereupon Pottier exclaimed, ' "By my troth, man, then will my master the Duke of Gloucester be King".' Of the 'guilty foreknowledge' of Buckingham, he says: 'When the Protector had both the children in his hands, he opened himself more boldly . . . to the Duke of Buckingham, although I know that many thought that this Duke was privy to all the Protector's counsel even from the beginning.' Of the murders he says: 'Thus I have heard of them that much knew and little cause had to lie.' He speaks of the message sent by Buckingham to the Protector at York, 'as I have for certain been informed'. 'Some I have heard say,' he says, that Buckingham became angry with Richard III before the latter's coronation, because when he asked for the earldom of Hereford, Richard refused it, it being 'somewhat interlaced with the title to the Crown,' with spiteful and minatory words. But some, 'right secret at those days, deny this,' thinking it highly improbable. 'Very true it is,' though, 'that the Duke was a proud-minded man and evilly could bear the glory of another, so that I have heard, of some that said they saw it, that the Duke at such time as the crown was first set upon the Protector's head, his eye could not abide the sight thereof, but he wried his head another way.' More does not accept at its face value every piece of information he received, but his method of assembling them gives the reader the impression that though he may have been mistaken or misinformed, his set speeches apart, he was not inventing.

The part of greatest value of what he has to say is the detailed description of the murders and the source from which it came. According to More, this was a confession from Sir James Tyrell and his servant Dighton when both were in the Tower in 1502, awaiting execution on a charge of high treason for aiding Edmund de la Pole, Earl of Suffolk, in what appeared to be a widespread conspiracy, based in France, and supported by Maximilian, widower of the young Duchess of Burgundy, who had promised to help 'one of King Edward's blood' to recover the Crown of England. Tyrell at this time was governor of the fortress of Guisnes and he was lured from this stronghold by the promise of a safe-conduct which Henry VII shamefully abused. He and Dighton were convicted of treason, and before execution they both made a confession of the manner of the Princes' deaths. The whole story of this confession has been dismissed as worthless, but on grounds which do not stand up to investigation. Why, it has been asked, should Tyrell confess to this crime when he was about to be executed on another charge? The answer is twofold; a desire on Tyrell's part for confession and absolution when on the verge of death and that for reasons not recorded, though Tyrell was executed, his son, who had been charged with him, was not, and the attainders of both of them were reversed: an arrangement so vital to the interests of family inheritance, that if it were offered it would provide adequate inducement.

It is demanded, if Henry VII had gained the proof he was so anxious to establish, that the Princes were truly dead, why did he not publish it when he had it? The answer seems to lie in the date on which it came into his hands.

Tyrell's confession was made in 1502. In 1487 had appeared the first of the 'feigned boys', Lambert Simnel, who claimed first to be the young Earl of Warwick and then altered his identity to that of Richard, Duke of York. After Simnel had been exploded and taken into service in the King's kitchen in 1487, from 1491 until 1499 the Crown was plagued by the career of a much more successful and dangerous imposter, Perkin Warbeck, who also claimed to be Richard, Duke of York. This young man's remarkable appearance, style and wits may have been accounted for by his being a bastard son of Edward IV. He attracted a surprising degree of support from the courts of Spain, France, Scotland and of his supposed aunt, the Dowager Duchess of Burgundy. Whether his impersonation was wholly believed, or entertained as a means of harassing the King of England, the threat he posed was serious. He experienced considerable magnanimity at Henry's hands; the King could legally have put him to death long before he did, since Warbeck claimed the English crown, an act that stood first among those considered to be high treason. What marked his final conviction and execution with shocking cruelty was that Henry VII used it as a means to entrap, convict and execute the hapless young Earl of Warwick. *Agents provocateurs* enticed him into discussing with his fellow prisoner Warbeck some means of escaping out of the Tower. This was erected into a charge of treason, which, in Warwick's case was recognized at the time as an odious and brutal falsehood. The boy, it was said, 'did not know a goose from a capon'. He was led out to execution between two men, as if he hardly understood where to go. The fate of Warbeck was not significant; the rogue and imposter is a constant element of the social scene; but the innocent, and of himself, harmless Earl of Warwick, was yet another victim of the death carried in the veins by royal blood. The motive for destroying him was to take the opportunity when it seemed to offer, of putting down for good and all even the weakest menace of a disputed succession. It was a very dark deed, but once it was done, it was done. It was natural that three years later in 1502, Henry should not want to arouse public discussion once more of the horrible act of nineteen years ago.

More's account of Tyrell's confession states that when Tyrell returned with news of the deed to Richard III, the King was highly content, but he took exception to 'the burying in so vile a corner, saying he would have them buried in a meeter place because they were a king's sons'. This would be consistent with the importance Richard attached to burials in consecrated and dignified surroundings. He had had the corpse of Henry VI taken from Chertsey Abbey and re-buried in St. George's Chapel, and he oversaw the burial of Lord Hastings there, in the spot where Edward IV had said that he wanted his dearest friend to lie. At this point, More committed another of his errors, this time a very serious one. He accepted the story that hearing of the King's wish, a priest of Sir Robert Brackenbury's 'took up the bodies again and secretly interred them in such a place as by the occasion of his death—for he alone knew it—could never since come to light'. Since all the information available to More on this matter was transmitted by word of mouth over a span of some thirty years, it was natural that what had been originally a plan or intention should have become moulded into a definite action. Some intention to remove the bodies had become accepted as the fact of their removal.

Henry did not know where the bodies were. It was this lack of information which made it impossible, in the Act of Attainder passed against Richard III in the first parliament of Henry VII's reign, to accuse him distinctly of having murdered the Princes. The accusation is there, but it is termed: 'the shedding of infant's blood.' When it is declared that if Henry had believed, or even received, Tyrell's confession of the murders and the burial, he would have torn the Tower apart, stone by stone, until he had discovered the remains, it can only be said that people who think so, either have not seen the Tower or have forgotten it. The first statement to be heard was that the burial took place at the foot of an unidentified staircase; the second that the bodies were no longer there.

Polydore Vergil, writing at the same time as More, though saying that Tyrell was responsible for the murders, omits all the details given by More and says only that Tyrell: 'murdered those babes of the issue royal. This end had Prince Edward and Richard his brother, but with what kind of death these sely children were executed, is not certainly known.' This has been held to discredit More's account entirely. Any reliable information available to More, it is argued, must have been available to the King's historian. This is undeniable; the difference between the two accounts is explained by the fact that one was the official version put out with the King's approval, the other a private piece of writing which, in the author's life-time, never saw the light. It may be added that Polydore Vergil's reputation for discreet editing was such that he was accused by English antiquarians of having destroyed cart-loads of documents.

More did not think that Henry VII's policy of silence was entirely sound, especially with regard to the matter of the Princes' deaths, which 'has nevertheless so far come in question that some remain yet in doubt whether they were in (Richard III's) days destroyed or no . . . all things were in later days so covertly managed, one thing pretended and another meant, that there was nothing so plain and openly proved but that yet, for the common custom of close and covert dealing, men had it ever inwardly suspect.'

Bacon, too, thought that Henry would have done better to make an official announcement. John Dighton, who, though he had been arraigned with Tyrell, was afterwards released, Bacon supposed, 'because he spoke best for the king,' was, Bacon said, 'the principal means of divulging the tradition.' When the statements of Tyrell and Dighton had been gained, they were 'delivered abroad', and Bacon thought that Henry VII had been mistaken in not making use of them in any of his official declarations, 'whereby, as it seems, those examinations left the business somewhat perplexed'. He commented in another place on 'the King's manner of showing things by pieces and by dark lights' that muffled rather than explained. But Henry VII, a man of enormous subtlety and astuteness, his faculties sharpened by hard and long experience of the statesman's world, thought his the wisest course.

More had been mistaken in his acceptance of part of the 'divulged' tradition of the burial. Nearly two hundred years later it was proved dramatically that he had not been mistaken in the rest.

In a panoramic view of the Tower made while Sir John Peyton was Governor, from 1597 to 1603, the Great Hall of the royal lodgings is marked: Decayed. During the Protectorate, Oliver Cromwell pulled most of the lodgings down; the remains were left in a disordered, ruinous condition, and in 1674 Charles II directed that their site should be cleared. On the south side of the White Tower, facing the river, to the left-hand corner of the keep, was a rectangular, castellated tower, about twenty feet square and rising some two-thirds of the way up the left hand turret. It was lighted with a pair of lancet windows. This tower, known as 'the fore-building', sheltered a staircase, which was the private way for those in the Royal Apartments to the Chapel of St. John. There were, actually, at this spot, two staircases; one, a spiral stair on the inside of the White Tower, cut out of the eleventh-century wall, which is fifteen feet thick, the other, the external staircase built against the outside wall and covered by the fore-building. This staircase led up to a door on the outside wall, giving on to a landing; from this landing the spiral staircase led up to the Chapel. The workmen employed to clear the White Tower of 'all contiguous buildings',* pulled down the fore-building; they then

* Sandford, *Genealogical History of the Kings of England.*

demolished the external staircase. Under the bottom stair, at a depth of ten feet, they found a wooden chest. In it were the skeletons of two children, the taller one lying on its back, the smaller one on top of it, face downwards.

32

THE bones were laid aside and four years later Charles II commissioned from Wren a white marble urn, with an inscription on it saying that it contained the bones of the two Princes who were put to death in the Tower. The beautiful sarcophagus was placed in the Chapel of Henry VII.

In 1933, the Dean and Chapter of Westminster Abbey gave permission for the urn to be opened and the bones examined by Mr. Lawrence Tanner, Keeper of the Muniments, Professor William Wright, F.R.C.S. and Dr. George Northcroft, President of the British Dental Association. Their report was published in *Archeologia*, Vol. LXXX IV, 1934. It was assumed that during the years between 1674 and 1678, some of the bones had been stolen and the thefts replaced with bones of animals, but enough of the human bones remained for it to be calculated that the elder child had a height of four feet ten inches and the younger of four feet six and a half inches. The collar bones, shoulder blades and hip bones showed that they were of slender build. Their ages, judged from the evidence of the jaws, were stated to have been about twelve and about ten. Prince Edward was born on November 1, 1470, Prince Richard on August 19, 1473. In July 1483 they would have been twelve and eight months and nine and eleven months respectively. If these are the bones of the Princes, their deaths occurred in 1483, and Henry VII is completely exonerated from any share in them, since he did not return to England till 1485. Professor Wright and Dr. Northcroft diagnosed a diseased condition in the lower jaw of Prince Edward, which had progressed so far that it had 'absorbed the inter-dental septum', the thin bone divisions which separate the sockets of the teeth. They said that this condition could not fail to have affected his general health, causing discomfort and irritability.* On the subject of some of the missing bones, Mr. Tanner produced a record that in 1728, the antiquary Thomas Hearne had sent to

* Mr. F. M. Lind, (BDS Lond, LDS, RCS Eng.) gives, as two possible causes of bone loss involving the inter-dental septa: apical abscess of an adjoining tooth where pus has been in contact with the bone, preventing a normal blood supply from reaching the peripheral bone of the jaw; or, chronic gingival infection, where damaged gums allow the invasion of bacteria into bony areas. He adds that poor oral hygiene is the commonest reason for gingival infection.

198

enquire of Mr. Whiteside about some bones of Edward V and the Duke of York 'which Mr. Ashmole had sent to his museum at Oxford'. Mr. Whiteside agreed that they had such bones somewhere or other in the museum 'but Mr. Whiteside did not produce them.' When Mr. Tanner visited the Ashmolean in his search, in spite of all the efforts of the then Keeper, he also was disappointed, but he had discovered the tradition that the bones were very small, 'particularly the fingers'. After the examination the bones were replaced and the urn re-sealed. Some thirty years later, in 1965, the bones of Anne Mowbray, having been recovered, were re-interred in a spot not far from those of the child to whom she had been married. The site of the original burial at the foot of the staircase gives strong grounds for Mr. Tanner's theory that the last phase of the children's imprisonment was in the White Tower. It also shows that whoever performed the burial had the power to ensure that no unauthorized person from the Royal Apartments, or any of the lodgings in the White Tower, came upon the scene till the task was finished. Secrecy and speed were urgently necessary. As part of the general scouting of More's narrative, the idea of a priest's accomplishing single-handed the labour of taking the bodies from such a place has been held up to scorn; but as he was said to be 'a priest of Sir Robert Brackenbury' it must be supposed that whatever help he had needed, he would have been able to command, and that the action was ascribed to him merely because he had organized it. Since it was never carried out, it matters the less, but the whole question of the burial, hard as the work must have been, is sometimes spoken of, as though it were even more of a Herculean labour than it necessarily was. It is imagined by some writers that the diggers faced the bottom stairs, dug down to a depth of ten feet and then dug inwards, so as to make room for stowing the chest under the staircase. Though the chest was found ten feet in the ground, to assume that the hole was originally dug to a depth of ten feet does not allow for subsidence, which, over two hundred years, must have been considerable. The staircase attached to the outer wall of the White Tower would have descended in a procession of steps, each one projecting a little beyond the other. At the base, the steps would form, with the wall and the floor, a triangle of stone. Approaching the staircase from one of its two sides, and digging under the base of the triangle, and inwards, until space was made to push in the chest, would have been heavy work, but not so heavy as if it had been attacked from the front. The upper stairs would be bonded to the wall, but as the flight stretched downwards and outwards, a hollow would be formed, filled, according to masons' practice, with rubble. This would justify the description given to More, of the burial 'under a great heap of stones'.

It must be noted that Paul Murray Kendall submitted the findings of Tanner, Wright and Northcroft to a fresh team of examiners, some of whom demurred as to the age of the elder child, and said that as the skeletons were of pre-pubertal children, it could not be proved that they were not those of girls. As a result of these investigations, Mr. Kendall felt that identification of the bones with those of the Princes could 'only be expressed in terms of probability'.*

The risings in the early autumn of 1483 had originally, it was said, been set on foot to rescue Edward V and his brother; by the middle of September it was generally accepted that the Princes were dead, and the movement had been re-orientated as one to dethrone Richard III and replace him with a young man, known to very few but with a potent name. From the storm centre in Brecknock Castle, it was Bishop Morton who, according to More, wove the conspiracy that was to bring in Henry Tudor. Morton, with great skill, far away as he was in Brecknock, managed a conspiracy in London. Through his influence, the Lady Margaret Beaufort sent her trusted physician, Dr. Lewis, to visit Elizabeth Woodville in sanctuary, and convey the proposition to her that Henry Tudor should marry her eldest daughter, the Princess Elizabeth of York. The scheme was mutually advantageous. The claims to the throne of the Yorkist princess would very greatly enhance those of the Lancastrian pretender, and to be the mother of the Queen Consort would restore something to Elizabeth Woodville of all that she had lost. Though her consent would not have been necessary to the plan, powerless and discredited as she was, it was obviously better to have it than not to have it, and to give her the opportunity of using her influence, should it be necessary, with her beautiful daughter. Whether the account given by Hall of the Queen's agony at hearing from Dr. Lewis of the Princes' deaths, is true or not, the fact that the marriage negotiations were being entertained in September is taken to establish that by that date Elizabeth Woodville had become convinced that her sons were dead. The question of who put out the news so as to get it so thoroughly believed has not been answered. If Buckingham's 'guilty foreknowledge' were a fact, he no doubt imparted it to Morton, who saw in its being spread abroad a really powerful means of turning public anger against the King. What the final intention of the Duke of Buckingham might be—whether he meant to be a loyal subject to Henry Tudor as King of England or whether, having used him as an instrument to get Richard out of the way, he meant then to overcome Henry, is unfathomable; but if he did mean to play them off against each other, he totally underestimated both of them.

The rebellious forces the Duke had been able to inspire were in the Midlands and the west; they included those under Bishop Woodville at Salisbury, those of his brother Sir Richard Woodville, at Newbury in Berkshire, while the Marquess Dorset who had escaped through the fields behind Westminster where the corn stood high, had reappeared

* *Richard III*, P. M. Kendall, Notes to Appendix I.

and was in charge of a contingent at Exeter. A band of rebels collected in Surrey and Kent meant to march on London and join the Duke of Buckingham's army as it approached from Wales. Henry Tudor, with a moderate sum of money and a small fleet given him by the Duke of Brittany, who protected him as a potentially valuable element in European politics, was to land on the south west coast and join forces with the uprising.

Richard had begun to move south, and had reached Lincoln, where, on October 11, he received the astounding news of Buckingham's betrayal. He acted with his usual promptitude and courage. He wished to summon to him the Bishop of Lincoln as Lord Chancellor, but hearing that Dr. Russell was too ill to travel, he wrote requiring the Bishop to send him up the Great Seal, under strong escort. He thanked him, too, for the way his servants had provided for the King and the royal retinue at Lincoln. He added that he had no fear of not being able to defeat 'the malice of him, that had best cause to be true, the Duke of Buckingham, the most untrue creature living'.

He received first-rate support from the Duke of Norfolk who, with his own retainers, cut off at Gravesend the approach to London of the Kent and Surrey insurgents, while the King himself came down with his forces to Leicester. Richard decided that among the various branches of the rebellion, his prime objective must be the army led by the Duke of Buckingham. It is at this point that the certainty of the deaths of the two Princes and Richard's responsibility for them, becomes almost complete. Had he been able then, by sending to London, to produce the boys from the Tower and parade them with suitable ceremony, through the London streets, he would have dealt a staggering blow to the insurrection.

With obvious courage, however, he came on south. In this region also, his supporters had done excellent work guarding passes and destroying bridges, to prevent the passage of Buckingham's army into Herefordshire. Their task was finished for them by a prolonged deluge of torrential rain which caused the Severn to overflow and was known for long after as 'the Duke of Buckingham's Water'. Grafton said: 'Men were drowned in their beds, children were carried about the fields, swimming in cradles, beasts were drowned on hills; the rage of water lasted continually for ten days.'* Buckingham's demoralized forces, drenched and starving, disbanded themselves. Morton, who had set out with the Duke, parted company and fled, first to his diocese of Ely, where concealment in the Fens was easy, then abroad to Flanders. Buckingham, in disguise, sought shelter in the house of one of his servants, who sold him for the price Richard had put on his head.

The King had now reached Salisbury, in what had been a triumphal progress, for no resistance had been offered to him. Here Buckingham was brought. As he was Constable of England, Richard appointed Sir

* Grafton's *Chronicle*, Vol. II, p. 133.

Ralph Assheston Deputy Constable to try him. The wretched man, sentenced to execution, sent impassioned pleas for an audience with the King; they were received in a deadly silence and on November 2 he was beheaded in Salisbury market place.

One detail in his family concerns seems to show the influence of the dread that was immanent in the rumour of the Princes' deaths. Catherine Woodville, the Duchess of Buckingham, had probably had no communication with Elizabeth Woodville since the latter had entered sanctuary six months before, but she was in a position to gain such news of her sister and the latter's affairs as was available to anyone. She must have known at least that Elizabeth had been parted from her sons and that the children were feared or known to be dead. On the execution of her husband she had her five year old son Edward dressed as a little girl and sent, in the hands of trusted family servants, to hiding in Hereford.*

* article: Edward Stafford, 'Third Duke of Buckingham' Dictionary of National Biography, Vol. LIII.

33

THE attempted rising had been an ignominious failure; the insurgents' land forces had been brought to nothing and Henry Tudor, having approached Poole Harbour in his small fleet, had divined the disaster and put out again to sea. But it is not possible to 'look into the seeds of time and say which grain will grow and which will not'. Richard was harassed but hopeful as his good intentions and his capacity gave him the right to be, and he treated the rebels with a magnanimity worthy of kingship. There were less than a dozen executions; no punitive measures were taken against Bishop Woodville, Sir Richard Woodville or the Marquess Dorset. Bishop Morton himself was offered a pardon, but he did not come home to claim it. The widowed Duchess of Buckingham was given an annuity; even that discreet but active conspirator the Lady Margaret Beaufort was not attainted; she was deprived of her title of Countess of Richmond and her lands were taken from her and settled on her husband Lord Stanley, with reversion to other beneficiaries after his death.

Some of this leniency she owed to the fact that Richard valued and trusted to her husband's support. Stanley was given the Garter and the office of Constable of England left vacant after the wreck of Buckingham's fortunes.

The Christmas festivities were held at Westminster with that contrast of brilliance against cold and darkness which makes Christmas the most magical of celebrations. Richard spent money lavishly, and to get it he sold or pawned some of the royal treasures. Edmund Shaa, the late Lord Mayor, gave the King £550 for 275 lbs. of silver plate; among other rich objects, Richard pawned a helmet belonging to Edward IV, 'with garnish of gold, stones and pearl'.* Commines described him at this season as 'reigning with greater splendour and authority than any king of England for the last hundred years'.

But in Brittany, in the cathedral church of Rennes, at daybreak on the morning of Christmas Day, 1483, Henry Tudor swore an oath to marry the Princess Elizabeth of York, eldest daughter of Edward IV, and the Lancastrian exiles around him knelt on the church pavement and did him homage 'as though he were already crowned'.

* *The Great Chronicle*, p. 235.

On January 23, 1484, was opened the only parliament of Richard's reign. The Speaker elected was William Catesby, the King's protégé and friend, who, with Lord Lovell, his Chamberlain and Sir Richard Ratcliffe, Knight of the King's Body, formed the triumvirate of Richard's closest advisors. Their names gave rise the following year to the couplet:

> The Cat, the Rat and Lovell our dog
> Rule all England under a Hog;

Lovell being a name applied to dogs, as Gilbert was to cats, generic animal names, of which the only one now in use is Reynard for the fox.

Bishop Russell had already drafted the speech which as Lord Chancellor he was to have delivered at the opening session of the reign of Edward V. He had now, with some omissions and alterations, adapted it to the present occasion. Its general tone was one exhorting the members of the commonwealth to unite for the common good, and to give their loyal support to the present King. What did the Bishop think had happened to Prince Edward: by common consent, no King, but a human being, a helpless child? Bishop Russell, writing the passages known as the 'Second Continuation of the Croyland Chronicle', finished his addition, he said, in April 1486, adding that the whole of it had been written in nine days. His work is one of the valuable contemporary statements that a belief in the Princes' murders was current during Richard's reign; but when he wrote: 'it was commonly reported that the said sons of Edward were dead, but by what kind of violent death it was not known', it must be supposed that the above passage was the result of rumours which had not reached him when he stood before Parliament on January 23, 1484, and that he then thought the Princes were still living in the Tower.

The silence in which by tacit consent the whole matter of their fate had been shrouded, was in one instance broken. Among the first of the bills introduced was the Titulus Regis which declared that Richard III was the King of England as the 'pretensed' marriage between Edward IV and Dame Elizabeth Grey was void and the children of it bastards. Since this act abolished the claim to the throne of the Princess Elizabeth, Henry VII on his accession destroyed, so far as he knew, every copy of it, but one copy, overlooked, remained in the records then housed in the Tower.

The further legislation reflected Richard's eager determination to be considered a just and beneficent ruler. Among its enactments were laws improving the administration of justice; jurors were to be chosen from men of substance and reputation, so that powerful criminals should not find it easy to over-awe them; when property was sold, it was to be a criminal offence to conceal the fact that part of it had already been sold to another buyer; bail was to be allowed to those arrested on suspicion of felony; when a prisoner was awaiting trial, it was forbidden to loot his property. Sir Thomas Cook would have benefited from this enactment. Serfs on the royal estates were to be enfranchised. The first postal service known in England was set going. The hall-marking of silver was instituted. Many customs duties were lowered, those on imported books were abolished altogether. None was to be levied on those 'bringing into this realm or selling by retail or otherwise, any manner of books, written or imprinted', and there was to be no interference with 'the inhabiting within the realm of writers or illustrators, binders or printers of such books'. One of Richard's most important contributions was not made through parliament. In the previous December, 1483, he had appointed a body, as part of the Council, to sit in the White Hall at Westminster to hear 'The bills, requests and supplications of poor persons', a body which afterwards became the Court of Requests. And when, early in 1484, he was enquiring into the part played by Kentish men in Buckingham's rebellion, he issued a proclamation, saying that 'any man grieved, oppressed or unlawfully wronged', should 'make a bill of complaint and put it to his highness', for the King was 'utterly determined' that all his subjects should live in peace and enjoy their property 'according to the laws of this his land which they were born to inherit'.

Shakespeare's *Richard III* has sometimes been solemnly treated as a work of great moral purpose by which the dramatist means to show, or intends us to understand, certain principles. It may reasonably be doubted whether Shakespeare, at any point of his career, intended or meant anything, except to write a brilliant play that would pack the house. For such success the work had of course to be framed according to public enthusiasm, and in 1592 in the most glorious decade of Henry VII's granddaughter, the presentation of Richard III required an exaggerated darkening. The accusations as to the death of Clarence and the poisoning of his wife were already in being and Shakespeare merely adopted and made the most of them, but for dramatic purposes he invented two major alterations of personality; one, a buoyant sense of humour, a zestful gaiety, of which no trace can be found in the records of Richard's courageous but tense and repressed disposition, and secondly, the cheerfully a-moral nature, summed up in line 30 of the speech with which Richard opens the play:

I am determined to prove a villain.

It was the last thing on which Richard was determined. He was anxious above everything to make a good impression. He used the power well when he had paid its terrible price. It was now decided that the situation of Elizabeth Woodville and her daughters Elizabeth, Cecily, Anne, Katherine and Bridget, must be re-ordered. With the new King on the throne, his son created Prince of Wales, and the first Parliament of the reign in session, the huddling together in sanctuary of Elizabeth Woodville and her daughters aged eighteen, fifteen, nine, five and four, could no longer be tolerated. What Richard said to Elizabeth Woodville and through whose means, is not recorded; the King is most unlikely to have spoken to her himself; the Croyland Continuator says: 'After frequent entreaties as well as threats, had been used, Queen Elizabeth being strongly solicited to do so, sent her daughters from the Sanctuary to King Richard.'

The King swore an oath before an assemblage of 'Lords spiritual and temporal' and of the Lord Mayor and Aldermen, that if the daughters of Dame Elizabeth Grey, 'late calling herself Queen of England', would come to him out of the Sanctuary of Westminster, and be ruled and guided by him, he would, he promised 'see that they be in surety of their lives . . . nor them, nor any of them, imprison in the Tower of London or other prison'. This clause was, plainly, a concession to their acutely apprehensive mother, and says much for what Richard knew and she knew. The oath went on to say that the King would arrange suitable marriages for his nieces to gentlemen born, and that on their marriage he would give them dowries of 200 marks 'for the term of their lives'. And, he said, 'such gentlemen as shall hap to marry with them, I shall straitly charge lovingly to love and entreat them, as wives and my kinswomen'. He further undertook to provide for their mother by paying John Nesfield 'for his finding, to attend upon her, the sum of 700 marks'. He finally promised that if any suspicion or accusation of evil were made to him of them by any person, 'I shall not give thereunto faith or credence, nor therefor put them to any manner of punishment before they or any of them so accused may be at their lawful defence and answer.'*

The significant points in the oath are, the reference to the Tower of London, and that, among the detailed arrangements for the well-being of the Princesses, not one guarantee is given, not one word uttered, about their brothers.

Surprise is sometimes expressed that Elizabeth Woodville should have accepted these terms, but as Cheetham says,† she could safely place every confidence in Richard's promise because he had made it before so wide an audience; the publicity with which he had arranged the ceremony of the oath-taking, whatever had been the fate of her sons, afforded her daughters complete security. The other point sometimes urged, that if she had been convinced of Richard's having procured the Princes' murders, she would never have yielded to his promises or threats, is surely to misunderstand the sort of woman she was. That she suffered agonies from a wound never to be healed, no one will doubt; but though, as regards human compassion, terrible distress places all its victims on one

* *Original Letters Illustrative of English History*, Ed. H. Ellis, 2nd Series, Vol. I, p. 149.
† *Op. cit.*, p. 150.

level, it does not, in the long run, alter their personalities. Elizabeth Woodville, for twenty years, had put first the worldly importance, the material prosperity, the comfort and enjoyment of herself and her family. She was now offered for herself and her daughters, in exchange for for cramped, austere conditions and isolation from all worldly inter-course, freedom, social life and an element at least of the old homage and respect. She had, up to a point, been offered all this before and had refused it; but she had now endured ten long months of privation, humilia-tion and wretchedness, and the hope of rescue and revenge at the hands of Buckingham and Henry Tudor had faded away. While she was in the state of mind produced by these conditions, she received Richard's promise made in form. Her resistance was broken. She not only accepted his assurance; worn out with misery and disappointment, she wrote to the Marquess Dorset, who, having fled abroad after Buckingham's defeat, had attached himself to the court of Henry Tudor in Brittany. His mother advised him to relinquish the latter's cause and come home to make his peace with Richard. This Dorset attempted to do, but he was detected in the act of sidling away, and forcibly persuaded by Henry Tudor's agents to come back.

Early in March 1484, Richard caused to be administered an oath of fealty to his son the Prince of Wales. The Croyland Continuator says that in the Palace of Westminster, Lords spiritual and temporal, with the higher knights and esquires of the King's Household, 'met together at the special command of the King in a certain lower room near the passage which leads to the Queen's apartments'. Here they signed their names to 'a new kind of oath' of adherence to the Prince of Wales, 'as their supreme Lord in case anything should happen to his father'.

But was such kind of oath entirely new? Thirteen years before, in July 1471, Richard had been among those who signed the oath adminis-tered by Edward IV of loyalty to his son: 'I knowledge take and repute you, Edward Prince of Wales, first begotten son of our Sovereign Lord Edward IV, to be very and undoubted heir to our said Sovereign Lord; in case it hereafter happen to you to overlive our said Sovereign Lord, I shall then take and accept you for true, very and rightwise King of England, and faith and truth to you shall bear.' The oath was the same, only the names were different.

The King, taking the Queen with him, set out on a progress to the Midlands by way of Cambridge. There they were welcomed whole-heartedly and among other gifts Richard bestowed a large sum of money towards the completion of Kings' College Chapel. He and the Queen then continued their journey to Nottingham. Here, the castle on its high rock, occupied roughly the centre of England and was the seat most accessible to messengers bringing urgent news from Scotland, or across the Channel. Richard occupied this strategic height knowing that such might be expected from the Scots or from the Channel where Breton vessels were harrying English shipping or from France where Henry Tudor had now found a refuge and from where his invasion was expected at some yet uncertain time.

Richard had demanded an oath of fealty to his son in case anything happened to himself, but it was not he who was the victim of mishap. On April 9, the child died at Middleham Castle. The Croyland Continuator saying that it occurred after a very brief illness, called it merely 'an unhappy death'. Whether he meant that the death caused extreme unhappiness, or that the end itself was painful, can hardly be decided; perhaps the frail child of a consumptive mother died of a lung haemorrhage; but his account of its effect on the parents is vividly clear: 'You might have seen his father and mother in a state almost bordering on madness by reason of their sudden grief.'

Personal grief was only part of Richard's anguish. In the struggle that had endured for twenty-five years as to who should wear the crown, the present and the future were almost equally important. When Prince Edward of Lancaster died on the field of Tewkesbury, his death sealed the fate of Henry VI. Edward IV thought he had left the succession firmly settled but a period of shocks and terrors had set in, of which the English people wanted no more. Richard had achieved much in the way of good government, but if he could not hand on his crown to a son, how well he wore the crown himself might be discounted in favour of a young, able successor whose marriage to a healthful and lovely girl would unite the claims of York and Lancaster and promise undisputed succession.

Richard's situation demanded an heir; but not only was Edward the only child he had; some months later he told Archbishop Rotherham that the doctors had warned him that the Queen's disease was infectious, and he must abstain from her bed. For the brief remainder of his life he spoke of Nottingham as 'the castle of my care'.

34

RICHARD took the most effective step open to him to counter the serious disability of being now without legitimate issue. On the death of Prince Edward the hereditary heir was Clarence's son, the ten year old Earl of Warwick, but this boy was put aside. If he were suddenly to be called to the throne, the accession of a child would inevitably renew old troubles, and his mental condition would recall shuddering memories of Henry VI. Richard therefor chose his other nephew, John de la Pole, Earl of Lincoln, appointing him heir-apparent.

In July 1484, the King's Household in the North was established in Richard's Yorkshire castle of Sherrif Hutton. The chief inmates were Lord Warwick, Lord Lincoln and the latter's brother-in-law, Lord Morley. In the parish church was the tomb with an alabaster effigy lying on it of Warwick's and Lincoln's cousin the Prince of Wales, in his robes and coronet.

An ordinance was drawn out, directing the scale on which food and drink was to be issued for the breakfasts of various members of the household. 'Item: my Lord of Lincoln and my Lord Morley to be at one breakfast; the children together at one breakfast; such of the Council as be present, at one breakfast . . . no pot of livery to exceed measure of a pottle but only to my Lord and the children.'* The mention of children whose allowances of wine or ale were to be larger than those of anyone except Lord Lincoln, has led some people to believe that these were the Princes, living unremarked in Sherrif Hutton and never publicly referred to, in spite of the fact that it would have been so overwhelmingly to Richard's advantage to produce them. One of the children was of course Lord Warwick; another may have been his eleven year old sister Margaret; Professor A. R. Myers, quoted by Kendall op. cit., suggests that by July 1484, the party included some of the Princesses, since they had come out of sanctuary four months previously. The King, in fact, sent Princess Elizabeth to join the household early in 1485.

The castle of Sherrif Hutton had now a particular importance; it was the seat of the King's Council of the North. This institution of Richard's which was to last for a hundred and fifty years, was a branch of the Council

* Harl, Ms. 433, quoted by Kendall, *op. cit.*, p. 407.

at Westminster and replaced by the work of an official body the balance of control hitherto maintained by the great northern landowners, such as Richard himself while Duke of Gloucester had exerted with the Earl of Northumberland. The Council of the North held quarterly meetings at York, assisted by neighbouring magnates and lawyers, to hear complaints, attend to local business and preserve public order. Lord Lincoln was appointed its first President and the King's instructions were that all letters and writings were 'to be made in our name and to be endorsed with the hand of our nephew of Lincoln below, with the words: per consileum regis.' This is a reminder that Sherrif Hutton was not a remote fastness in which people could be immured without the knowledge of the outside world; it was now the official residence of the President of the Council of the North. It would of course have been possible to keep prisoners secretly in a dungeon in any castle, but inmates whose breakfasts were arranged on a settled plan must have been part of a household that was visible to comers and goers, and that the two most famous and mysterious boys in the kingdom could be living openly at Sherrif Hutton without the people of England being aware of it, seems hardly worth arguing.

In spite of public and private cares, the King, it was said, kept the Christmas of 1484 with great magnificence at Westminster. At the feast of the Epiphany of January 1485, he and the Queen wore their crowns 'with remarkable splendour in the Great Hall'. The Queen was dying, but she was the daughter of a soldier and she bore on her head the great weight of gold and jewels which added so much to the brilliance of her husband's state.

In the midst of the feast a messenger arrived from Richard's agents abroad; his rival was preparing to invade in the summer. The King received the news with no trace of fear, only a vigorous satisfaction that the span of uneasy waiting was to be ended at last. Queen Anne died on March 16, the day of a total eclipse of the sun. She was buried in great state in Westminster Abbey at the entrance to the chapel of Edward the Confessor. As her coffin was lowered into the tomb, the King stood and wept.

Now a story appeared as to the truth of which it seems impossible to find conclusive evidence, one way or another. It was said that the King was intending to marry his niece the Princess Elizabeth. Catesby and Ratcliffe, it was said, implored him not to think of it; the hostility the deed would arouse would be fatal to his reputation; it not only ought not to be done, it could not be done, and though Papal dispensations could be procured for marriages within the forbidden degrees, and, it was said, such arrangements were not unknown on the continent, twelve Doctors of Divinity were mustered to explain to the King that the Pope himself could not sanction one between such near relations as uncle and niece. The truth or otherwise of the matter seems to pose an insoluble problem. The Titulus Regis of which Richard himself had been the inspiration, had declared the Princess illegitimate; by the definition of that act, she could not be considered a desirable bride for the King of England. On the other hand, it was clear that the act would be disregarded by Henry Tudor; to him, the Princess was a highly valuable asset in his claim to the crown; none of her younger sisters would be of any use to him as a co-heiress while the eldest sister was living, and if she were married to Richard, she would be completely out of Henry Tudor's reach.

At the same time, Richard was a man of rigid sexual morality; the getting of two bastard children as a very young man before his marriage does not, in the circumstances, undermine his claim to this, and one of the causes of his hatred of the Woodvilles was the sexual licence in which they had encouraged Edward IV. A man of Richard's mental grasp did not need twelve Doctors of Divinity to tell him that a marriage with his niece would be incestuous, and he does not appear a man likely to have been goaded by incestuous passion beyond the bounds of decency and common sense. And yet: inconsistent and implausible as the scheme appears, does not the mere fact that it had arisen even as matter for discussion, confirm that in the last resort, there was nothing, however dark and dangerous, that he would not consider, in the interests of keeping his crown? However, the Croyland Continuator says the feeling of disapproval was so strong that Richard called a council meeting, at which Bishop Russell must have been present himself, to declare 'that such a thing had never once entered his mind', but, the Bishop adds, 'there were some persons present at that Council who very well knew the contrary'. Having made this statement to the Council, Richard then summoned a concourse of Lords, clergy and citizens to the Great Hall of St. John's Priory in Clerkenwell, and announced to them that he had never entertained the idea of marrying his niece; any rumour that he had, was a malicious slander.

Whether, if he did seriously consider it, he could have gained the Princess's consent, seems most unlikely; and though the consent of her mother would have been immaterial, her own would have been absolutely necessary. Grafton, in his continuation of More's *History of Richard III*, says: 'the maiden herself abhorred this unlawful desire as a thing most detestable'. It is strange that Sir George Buc, the earliest defender of Richard III, writing in the reign of James I, should have said that he had seen, among the Howard papers in the cabinet of the Earl of Arundel, a letter from the Princess to the Duke of Norfolk, begging for his assistance in forwarding her match with the King, saying 'the King was her joy and maker in this world and that she was his in heart and thought', and that 'she hinted her surprise at the duration of the Queen's illness and her apprehension that she would never die'. As Buc gave no details about the letter and did not quote any of it in direct speech, and as no one except himself is on record as ever having seen it, the letter cannot be considered as evidence; but from the standpoint of fiction, even, it is interesting that some hundred years later, such an emotion in the Princess was not regarded as having been impossible. Whatever the attitudes of the King and his niece towards each other, early in 1485 Richard sent the Princess to join the household at Sherrif Hutton. This both removed her from the sphere of wounding and injurious gossip and put her in some degree of safety from Henry Tudor should his invasion prove successful.

Bernard André, a Frenchman whom Henry VII employed as tutor to his eldest son Prince Arthur, wrote a History of Henry VII in which he said that the Princess Elizabeth bore a love to her brothers which was 'almost incredible'. She did not find them at Sherrif Hutton.

Throughout the summer the preparations Richard made for the invasion which he knew was imminent were thorough and efficient. His army consisted, it has been said, of about seven thousand men, and he had several capable generals, of whom his unswerving follower the Duke of Norfolk was the chief. Henry Tudor had three leaders, his uncle Jasper Tudor, the Earl of Oxford and Sir Edward Woodville who had given in his allegiance to Henry since his escape from the naval action of 1483. As Henry's army consisted of about three thousand men, of whom the greater number were French mercenaries, released from gaol on condition of taking service with him, there were good reasons why Richard III should have been victorious. That he was not, was owing to the fact that many people, though they had not voiced their sensations of distrust, fear and horror, were willing to see him fall. Considering the greatness of the issue, the number of men engaged on both sides at the Battle of Bosworth was very small. Richard, it has been said, was going to depend for success on the loyalty of a few men in high places. Of these, though the Duke of Norfolk was unalterably staunch, the Earl of Northumberland held off, prepared to offer allegiance to the winner, while Lord Stanley's conduct was from the start, of a highly suspicious cast; he was, after all, the step-father of the king to be. In July, he asked Richard's leave to visit his estates in Lancashire. Richard, who was based on Nottingham Castle, showed the painful state arising from suspicion and ruthlessness. He told Lord Stanley he might go, providing he left his son Lord Strange in the King's hands as a hostage.

On August 7, at sunset, Henry Tudor landed at Milford Haven. He knelt down and kissed the shore. His advance began next day, and to the surprise of all, it was unopposed. He marched uninterruptedly across Wales and into Shropshire. News of his arrival was brought to Richard on August 11, who immediately summoned his leaders to join him with their forces. He was obliged to wait some days while his army collected in full strength;

212

meanwhile Henry crossed the Severn at Shrewsbury and was advancing towards Nottingham. Lord Stanley sent a message saying he was too ill to obey the King's summons, and Lord Strange, hearing this, tried to slip away but was brought back. The young man's life now hung by a thread. Lord Stanley, though too ill to render himself at the King's command, drew up his two thousand men at Atherstone beside the route to London.

On August 19, Richard led his army into Leicester. Holinshed says he rode 'a great white courser'. Kendall quotes an entry in Harl. 433, f. 4, which gives the names of some of King Richard's horses. One of them was called White Surrey.* This must have been known by hearsay. Shakespeare, as usual, picked up every scintillating particle of interest and made this horse, as it might well have been, the white charger on which the King rode into battle.

The next day, Sunday, the royal army moved towards Atherstone and Richard surveyed the terrain. Redmore Plain was crossed by a rivulet, the Sence Brook, which wandered into a marsh; overlooking the plain was Ambien Hill, a height of four hundred feet. Richard determined to dispose his army on the summit.

The Croyland Continuator had heard that on August 20, the night before the battle, the King had bad dreams; he said himself he had 'seen dreadful visions and had imagined himself surrounded by multitudes of demons'. More said he had learned from people who had been in the confidence of the King's chamber-men, that 'he took ill rest a nights; lay long waking and musing, sore wearied with care and watch; rather dozed then slept, troubled with fearful dreams'. If he were habitually a bad sleeper, subject to nightmares, the eve of a decisive battle was not a time for better rest than he had as a rule. When he got up, he neither breakfasted nor heard Mass. At daybreak, he was leading his army to occupy the heights of Ambien Hill. Here he posted it in three detachments one behind the other. Norfolk led the van, he himself commanded the centre, Northumberland lay in the rear.

Richard, in spite of a haunted night, was in a mood of resolute courage. Polydore Vergil says: 'He came to the field with the crown upon his head, that thereby he might either make a beginning or an end of his reign'.

Before the battle was joined, both leaders sent a summons to Lord Stanley, whose two thousand troops were in the end to turn the scale. To Henry's appeal, Stanley replied that he would join him when he saw the time was ripe. To Richard's message which declared that if Lord Stanley did not come in, his son should lose his head, Stanley replied that he had other sons. It was extraordinary that Lord Strange survived the King's receipt of this answer. Possibly a mood of fatalism possessed Richard, in which he felt that nothing mattered except the great issue about to be decided.

* Kendall, *op. cit.*, p. 355.

213

Henry Tudor, on the safety of whose body the whole great enterprise depended, was kept far in the rear, surrounded by a small bodyguard of Oxford's men. It was essential that his own troops should know where he was, and he was identified by a banner of the red dragon of Wales, which his standard-bearer held over his head, as Richard was identified by the crown on his helmet and his great white horse. The battle began with the movement of the Lancastrian troops to the base of Ambien Hill. Norfolk charged down upon them; in the intense struggle, the Yorkist troops were giving ground, and Norfolk, to rally them, drove his way to the front. He was hewn down, and his death turned the struggle into a Yorkist retreat. Richard ordered Northumberland to bring up the rearguard, and the Earl refused. He said he would wait where he was, in case Lord Stanley's troops attacked.

Richard's scouts told him that less than a mile across the plain Henry Tudor was waiting, behind a slight screen of bodyguard. Richard, in a passion of fury and desperation, now saw the battle in terms of personal conflict; the slaughter of either himself or Henry Tudor would mean total victory for the other. With eighty men at his back he charged down the slope and across the plain. A detachment under Sir William Stanley barred the path; the shock of the King's charge carried him and his knights right through it. It must have been at some point after this that Richard's horse was killed under him, but he had got so near to Henry Tudor that he was able to kill the standard-bearer, Sir William Brandon, and then the large-bodied Sir John Cheyney who had come to Brandon's defence. In a pre-Shakespearian play, *The True Tragedy of Richard the Third*, the unknown author makes Richard cry out for another mount. Shakespeare turned this into the tremendous line:

A horse! A horse! My kingdom for a horse!

His star actor, the great Richard Burbage, made such an effect with it, that the keeper of an inn at Market Bosworth used to lead travellers out to the site of the battle, and say: 'Here Burbage cried: A horse! A horse!'

Richard's heroic fight on foot was ended by Sir William Stanley's men re-forming and closing round him before he could reach Henry Tudor. Even the hostile Rows declared: 'he most valiantly defended himself as a noble knight to his last breath'. With him died Sir Robert Brackenbury.

When the King was known to be dead, the battle was at once over. The crown, which the Croyland Continuator says 'was of exceeding value', had rolled from his head; it was picked up and Sir William Stanley placed it on the head of Henry Tudor.

'The coronation ceremony is older than any act of parliament.' This act, on the field where Richard lay dead, carried a force both practical and symbolic. Henry felt this deeply. In his will, he ordered, 'to be placed on the tomb of the Confessor, an image of himself, of wood plated with gold, in armour, holding in his hands "the crown it pleased God to give us with the victory of our enemy at our first field." '*

The power of the crown as a symbol is shown in Camden's *Remains concerning Britain*.† 'When Richard III was slain at Bosworth and with him, John Howard, Duke of Norfolk, King Henry VII demanded of Thomas Howard, Earl of Surrey, the Duke's son and heir, then taken prisoner, how he durst bear arms in the behalf of that tyrant Richard. He answered: "he was my crowned King, and if the parliament authority of England set the crown upon a stock, I will fight for that stock. And as I fought for him, I will fight for you, when you are established by the same authority." '

The previous Lancastrian king differed from his successor in three ways. Henry VI had been weak-witted, quite unable to manage the revenues of the crown, and disastrously in the power of his wife. Henry VII was of exceptional mental ability, his financial capacity amounted to genius, and though he was in essentials a good husband, he was, as Bacon ‡ said, 'nothing uxorious'. His wife's claim to the crown was so valuable in reinforcing his own, that he was jealous of it, and did not have her crowned till two years after their marriage, when their first child Arthur was over a year old. Admired, respected, feared as Henry was, the people's affection was for the daughter of the beloved monarch Edward IV. At her coronation procession she appeared in white cloth of gold, her yellow hair 'at length down her back', crowned with 'a circle of gold, richly adorned with gems'. Groups of children dressed as angels stationed in the streets, greeted her with singing. After the coronation banquet was over, 'the Queen departed with God's blessing and the rejoicing of many a true Englishman's heart'.§

Her privy purse expenses published for the year 1502 show among gifts and rewards made to numerous people, payments to ones who appealed to her from her past: 'To a poor man in alms, sometime being servant of King Edward's IV, 20 pence'; 'To a man of Pontefract, saying himself to lodge in his house the Earl Rivers in time of his death, 12 pence'; 'Three yards of cloth delivered by commandment of the Queen to a woman that was nurse to the Prince, brother to the Queen's Grace'.

Elizabeth died after her seventh childbirth in 1503. She had lain-in in the Royal Apartments at the Tower, and after her death she lay in state in the White Tower, in the Chapel of St. John, for twelve days and nights, watched, with lights burning. Not far distant under a great heap of stones, the bodies of her brothers were lying.

* G. Gilbert Scott, *Gleanings from Westminster Abbey*.
† Quoted by J. D. Mackie, *The Early Tudors*.
‡ Bacon, *The History of the Reign of King Henry VII*.
§ *Leland Collectanea*.

The King's mother-in-law, Elizabeth Woodville, seems never to have been on easy terms with him, though she was allowed to stand godmother to his first child Prince Arthur, and Henry proposed her as a second wife for King James III of Scotland; on one occasion during her daughter's confinement, she was present in state with the Lady Margaret Beaufort to receive the French Ambassador. That she ultimately offended Henry VII is accepted, though the reason for her being lodged for her last years in the convent of Bermondsey, which was under statutory obligation to house members of the royal family, has never been satisfactorily explained; as Bacon said, 'the King had a fashion to create doubts rather than assurances'.

His own mother had now entered the tranquil last stage of her hitherto anxious and repressed existence; and her behaviour sometimes suggested that her reticent and dry manner over the past years had been partly, at least, the result of rigid self control rather than entirely a matter of temperament. Bishop Fisher who became her confessor, and wrote: 'A Mourning Remembrance of the noble Princess Margaret, Countess of Richmond and Derby', praised her kindness and courtesy 'to all that came unto her', her industry, charity and religious observance, but he commented, in astonishment, at her fits of weeping. She wept at her son's coronation and at other ceremonies at which she would have been expected to show lively rejoicing; but now that the long years of strain were ended and she saw on the throne of England 'my good and gracious prince and only beloved son', and could take delight in his family: 'The King, the Queen and all our sweet children', her nature softened as it had hardly done for anyone since the days of her first husband Edmund Tudor. Her son had begun to build his chapel in Westminster Abbey in 1503. When she was dying in 1509 she asked to be buried in it.

The Great Chronicle said of Richard III, 'His fame is darked and dishonoured, but God that is all-merciful, forgive him his misdeeds'. When he died a soldier's death and the crown tumbled from his head, the visual impression on men's minds was so powerful that the putting of the crown on Henry's head seemed tantamount to making him king. The coronation ceremonies and the acceptance by parliament appeared to be confirmations only of what had been already done. The story that the crown was picked up under or off a hawthorn bush is now discarded, but when Henry VII was building his Chapel, it was accepted as true. The east window of the east apsidal chapel contains panes of glass, repeating the motifs of a thorn bush on a blue ground, and a thorn bush with a gold crown poised over it; but these are formal inexpressive devices only. Brayley however, says* that there were several fragments of glass, 'which from their style of colour and ornament, must have been brought from

* Brayley, E. W., *History and Antiquity of the Abbey Church of St. Peter, Westminster*, Vol. II, p. 142.

Henry VII's Chapel' and had now (in 1823), been transferred to windows in the Chapel of Edward the Confessor, especially one piece which had been 'substituted for a martlett in the Confessor's arms'. All the painted glass in the Confessor's Chapel has now disappeared, but Brayley had seen, and was able to describe this piece. It showed the crown with a branch passing through it; an image in painted glass of the English saying to which Bosworth Field had given rise:

Cleave to the crown, though it hang on a bush.

SELECT BIBLIOGRAPHY

Ames, Joseph *Typographical Antiquities*, 1810

Bayley, John *History and Antiquities of the Tower*, 1821

Bentley, Samuel *Excerpta Historica*, 1838

Black, W. H. *Illustrations of Ancient State and Chivalry*, 1840

Brayley, E. W. *History of the Ancient Palace and late House of Parliament*, 1836

Brown, R. A., Colvin, H. M., Taylor, A. J. *The History of the King's Works*: *The Middle Ages*, 1963

Bruce, John *History of the Arrival of Edward IV*, 1838

Buckley, J. C. *The Royal Palace at Eltham*, 1828

Cheetham, Anthony *Life and Times of Richard III*, 1972

Chrimes, S. B. *Fifteenth Century England*, 1972

Collies, J. P. *Household Books of John Duke of Norfolk and Thomas Earl of Surrey*, 1844

De Ros, W. L. L. F. *Memorials of the Tower of London*, 1867

Ellis, Harvey *Polydore Vergil's English History*, 1844

Ellis, Harvey *Original letters of the Kings of England*, First Series 1824, Second Series 1827

Fabyan, Robert *The New Chronicles of England and France*, ed. Henry Ellis, 1811

Gould, S. Baring *Curious Myths of the Middle Ages*, 1869

Gairdner, James *Life and History of Richard III*, 1898

Grafton, Richard *Chronicle at Large*, ed. Henry Ellis, 1809

Hall, Edward *Chronicle*, ed. Henry Ellis, 1809

Halliwell, J. O. *Chronicle of Edward IV, John Warkworth*, 1839

Holinshed, Raphael *Chronicles*, Vol. III, edition of 1807

Jacob, E. F. *The Fifteenth Century*, 1961

Kendall, P. M. *Richard III* (Cardinal edition, 1973)

Kingsford, C. L. *The Stonor Letters and Papers*, 1919

Kingsford, C. L. *English Historical Literature in the Fifteenth Century*, 1913

Lambert, John J. *Records of the Skinners of London*, 1933

Macgibbon, D. *Elizabeth Woodville*, 1938

Mackie, J. D. *The Earlier Tudors, 1485–1558*, 1952

Malden, H. G. *The Cely Papers*, 1900

Mancini, Dominic *The Usurpation of Richard III*, ed. C. A. J. Armstrong, 1936

Mitchell, R. J. *John Tiptoft, Earl of Worcester*, 1938

Myers, A. R. *The Household of Edward IV*, 1959

Nichols, J. G. *Grants from the Crown during the reign of Edward V*, 1854

Nicholas, N. H. *Privy Purse Expenses of Elizabeth of York*, 1830

Owen, H. and Blakeway, J. B. *History of Shrewsbury*, 1825

Pollard, A. F. *The Making of Sir Thomas More's Richard III Historical Essays in Honour of James Tait*, eds. Edwards, J. G., Gallraith V. H. and Jacob, E. F., 1933

Ramsay, James *Lancaster and York*, 1892

Riley, H. T. *Jugulph's Chronicle of the Abbey of Croyland, with Continuations*, 1854

Ross, Charles *Edward IV*, 1974

Routh, E. M. C. *Lady Margaret*, 1924

Rows, John *History of the Earls of Warwick*, ed. W. Courthorpe, 1845–50

Sandford, Francis *Geneological History of the Kings of England*, 1677

Scofield, Cora L. *The Life and Reign of Edward IV*, 1923

Sharpe, R. R. *Memorials of London and the Kingdom*, 1894

Smith, George *The Coronation of Elizabeth Woodville*, 1935

Smith, J. T. *Antiquities of Westminster*. 1809

Stow, John *Annals of England*, 1632

Stow, John *Survey of London*, ed. C. L. Kingsford, 1905

Strickland, Agnes *Lives of the Queens of England: Elizabeth Woodville*, 1870

Thompson, J. W. *The Mediaeval Library*, 1939

Thomson, A. H. and Thornley, I. D., eds. *The Great Chronicle of England*, 1938

Tanner, L. E. and Wright, W. 'Recent Investigations regarding the Fate of the Princes in the Tower', *Archeologia*, Vol. 84, 1935

Turner, Sharon *History of England*, 1814–23

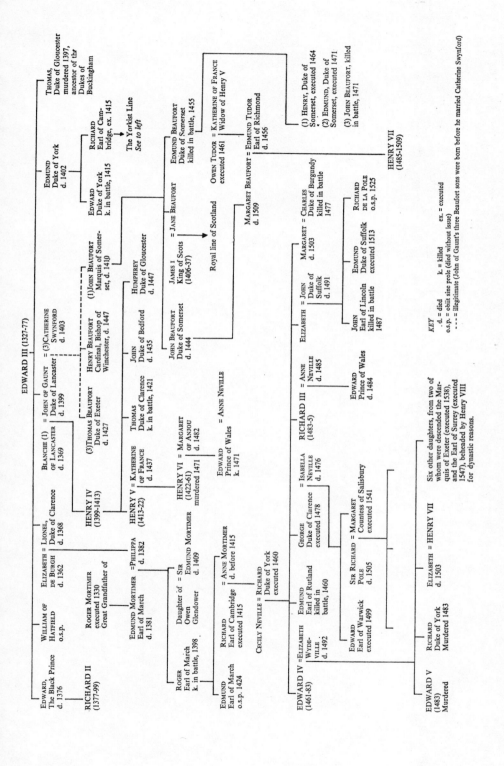

INDEX

Edward V—*cont.*
  popular affection for 183; in the
  Tower 183, 184–5, 188, 199; public
  belief in his murder 188–9, 204;
  murdered ix–xi, 191–3, 195; burial
  195, 196–7, 199; bones 197, 198–200
Eleanor of Aquitaine, 6
Elizabeth, Princess (daughter of
  Edward IV): birth 43; at visit of
  Gruthuyse 87; betrothal to Dauphin
  106, 107, 130; Princess Bridget's
  christening 128; betrothal ended
  134; clothes for 136; portraits 137,
  138; in sanctuary 151; Henry
  Tudor's oath to marry her 203; at
  Sheriff Hutton 209, 212; Richard's
  alleged intention to marry her 210–
  212; claim to throne abolished by
  Titulus Regis bill 204, 211; death
  215
Elizabeth, Queen (Elizabeth Woodville, wife of Edward IV): personality 25–6, 28–31 *passim*, 37, 41, 42,
  43, 45; physical appearance 25, 26,
  28, 29, 30, 37, 41, 42, 45, 115–16,
  137, 138; wife of Sir John Grey 27;
  marriage to Edward IV 28–30;
  influence over Edward 31, 49;
  coronation 33–6, 41, 83; reactions to
  marriage 35–6, 37–8, 41–3, 204, 211;
  household 37; birth of Princess
  Elizabeth 43; churching 43; benefaction 43–4; Princess Mary born
  45, 61; alleged procurement of
  Desmond's death 47–8; revival of
  Queen's Gold 49; birth of Princess
  Cecily 51; in Royal Apartments of
  Tower 61–2; in sanctuary 62–3, 85;
  Prince Edward born 65; reunited
  with King Edward 69; again obtains
  sanctuary in Tower 74, 75; St.
  Eramus chapel established 79;
  enmity to Hastings 81; birth of
  Princess Margaret 83; visit of
  Gruthuyse 87–8; confinement at
  Shrewsbury 97–8, 113; birth of
  Richard, Duke of York 98; family
  favours 99; use of room at The

  Wardrobe 102; elated by daughter's
  betrothal to Dauphin 107; birth of
  Prince George 113; birth of Princess
  Catherine 127; birth of Princess
  Bridget 128; protects property rights
  133–4; clothes for 136; Edward's
  will 141–2, 143; control of fleet and
  treasure 144, 151; seeks sanctuary
  with Abbot of Westminster 151, 152,
  156, 161, 162, 182; Rotherham
  surrenders Great Seal to 152, 155;
  proposal that Princess Elizabeth
  should marry Henry Tudor 200;
  sends daughters to Richard 206–7;
  relationship with Henry VII 216
Ellis, Henry, 75n
Eltham Palace, 32, 86, 128, 135
Ely, John Morton, Bishop of *see*
  Morton, John, Bishop of Ely
Esteney, Thomas Milling, Abbot of
  Westminster, 62, 63, 65, 99–100
executions: public 77, 165, 183; secret
  183
Exeter, Anne, Duchess of 31, 99
Exeter, John Holland, Duke of 48, 99

Fabyan, Robert, 28, 29, 37, 47, 48, 51,
  62, 64, 74, 86, 124, 189
Fastolf, Sir John, 20, 38
Faulconbridge, Bastard of, 74, 75, 80
Ferrers of Groby, John Grey, Lord, 27
Ferrers of Groby, Thomas Grey, Lord
  see Dorset, Thomas Grey, Marquess
  of Rochester
Fisher, John, Bishop of Rochester, 216
Fitzhugh of Ravensworth, Lord, 60
Fitzjames, John, 192
Fitzjames, Richard, 192
FitzLewis, Sir Henry, 134, 169
FitzLewis, Mary, 134, 169
Fitzwilliam, Sir Thomas, 173
Fleetwood, Sir William, 65
Fleetwood's Chronicle, 65
Fogg, Sir John, 49, 52
Forest, Miles, 191
Fortescue, Sir John, 59
Fox, Richard, Bishop of Winchester,
  192

215; mental ill-health 12–13, 14, 69, 78, 215; exile in Scotland 21; imprisonment in Tower 54; released and reinstated as King 64–5; Edward orders return to Tower 69; taken to Barnet 71; escorted back to Tower 71; death of ix, 77, 78; burial 78, 195; memory celebrated in King's College carol service 78

Henry VI, 163

Henry VII: birth 14; brought up by William Herbert 22; in Brittany 79, 182; astrological prediction about marriage 112; plans to join rebels 201; decides against landing at Poole 203; swears to marry Princess Elizabeth 203; would disregard declared illegitimacy of Princess Elizabeth 211; Battle of Bosworth 212–15, 217; coronation 179; policy of silence over Princes' deaths 196; contrasted with Henry VI 215; his will 214–15; relationship with Elizabeth Woodville 216; builds chapel at Westminster Abbey 198, 216–17; Act of Attainder against Richard III 195; André writes History of Henry VII 212; blamed for Princes' murder ix–x.

Herbert, William, Earl of Pembroke, 22, 46, 50, 52, 53

Hexham, battle at, 21

Historia Regum Anglie, 184, 189

'Historic Doubts', 128, 158

History of Richard III, The, 189, 211

History of the Arrival of King Edward IV, 74, 75, 78

Hobbs, William, 138

Holinshed, Raphael, 63, 127, 213

Holland, Ann, 99

Holland, John, Duke of Exeter, 48, 99

horoscopes, 110, 111–12

Howard, John, Duke of Norfolk, 34, 35, 114

Howard, John, Duke of Norfolk (created 1483), 114, 130, 131, 133, 142, 157, 167, 175, 179, 180, 201, 212, 214, 215

Howard, Thomas, Earl of Surrey, 179, 192, 215

Hundred Years' War, 6, 38

Huntingdon, Thomas Grey, Earl of, *see* Dorset, Thomas Grey, Marquess of

illuminated manuscripts, 67, 132

Isabel (daughter of Philip the Good), 6

Ives, E. W., 139n, 153n

Jacob, E. F., 10n, 13n, 50, 77n, 161

Jacquetta of Luxembourg, *see* Bedford, Jacquetta, Duchess of

James III, 127, 129, 133, 134, 216

Jasper of Hatfield, 7

Jesus College, Cambridge, 95

Joan of Arc, 24

John, Sir Hugh, 25–6

John of Gloucester, 90

jousting, *see* tournaments

juridical legislation, 204–5

Kendall, Paul Murray, 145, 182, 184n, 185, 199–200, 209, 213n

King's College, Cambridge, 44, 78: Chapel 126, 207

Kingsford, C. L., 76n, 83n, 88n, 161n

Lambert, John J., 34n

Lancaster, Edward, Prince of Wales, *see* Edward of Lancaster, Prince of Wales

Lancaster, John of Gaunt, Duke of, 5, 6, 11, 13, 14

landownership, 85, 133–4

Langstrother, Sir John, 73, 156

Lannoy, Jean de, 30

Leeds Castle (Kent), 77

Leland, John, 44

Lesser Hall, *see* White Hall

Lewis, Dr., 200

Lewis, Sir Henry, 169

Liber Niger, 135

Lincoln, John de la Pole, Earl of, 188, 209, 210

Lincoln, John Russell, Bishop of, *see* Russell, John, Bishop of Lincoln

Lincoln, Sheriff of, 10
Lind, F. M., 198n
Lingard, John, Dr., 53
Lionel of Antwerp, Duke of Clarence, 5, 11
Little Malvern Priory, 74, 91, 137
London, Bishop of, 65, 68, 69, 132, 155, 156, 166
London Bridge, 1, 33–4, 74, 75, 86
London Chronicle, 6, 19, 22
Lose-Coatfield, 56
Louis XI: seeks English alliance 23, 59, 61, 64; negotiates with Warwick 30, 45; helps Jasper Tudor invade Wales 50; truce with Burgundy 71; anti-Yorkist activities 50, 84, 93, 103, 128; Treaty of Pecquigny 105–106; ransoms Margaret of Anjou 106; death of Duchess of Burgundy 133; Treaty of Arras with Burgundy 134, 135, 141
Lovekin, George, 116
Lovell, Francis, Viscount, 160, 204
Lovell, Sir Thomas, 192
Lucy, Elizabeth, 189
Ludlow, 14–15, 40, 94, 95, 96, 97, 98, 145–6
Lupton, Roger, 192
Luxembourg family, 24, 25
Lyle, Lord, 95
Lynes, Sir Thomas, 119
Lynn, 143

MacGibbon, D., 52n
Mackie, J. D., 215n
Malory, Sir Thomas, 75
Maltravers, Thomas Fitzalan, Lord, 31
Mancini, Dominic, x, 28, 31, 33, 35, 38, 42, 63, 80, 82, 98, 122, 124, 131, 135, 140, 145, 150, 155, 157, 170, 171, 172, 173, 175, 176, 177, 183, 189
Mansion, Colard, 66, 100
March, Edward, Earl of, see Edward IV
Margaret, Princess, 134
Margaret, Princess (daughter of Edward IV), 83, 89
Margaret, Princess (of Scotland), 127

Margaret of Anjou: marriage to Henry VI 8; personality of 8, 9, 17, 64, 74; male friendships of 9, 10, 11–12, 13; tour of Cheshire 14; defeat of Duke of York at Wakefield 16; military activities 16, 17, 18, 21, 63, 72–4; victory at St. Albans 17; flight to Scotland 18; siege of Norham 21; flight to France 21; contrasted with Elizabeth Woodville 26; benefaction 44; plan for Prince Edward to marry Anne Neville 59; defeat at Tewkesbury 72–4; shelter at Little Malvern Priory 74, 91; paraded in London 76, 91; ransomed by Louis XI 106
Margaret of York, Duchess of Burgundy, 35, 42, 45, 46, 48, 50, 61, 66–7, 101, 108, 128, 129
Markham, Sir Clements, ix, x
Markham, Sir John, 49, 50
Mary, Princess (daughter of Edward IV), 45, 138
Maximilian of Austria, 109, 113, 134, 193
Merton College, 110
Middleham Castle, 40, 54, 92, 143, 146, 153, 169, 178, 187, 208
Milles, Jeremiah, Dean of Exeter, 158, 159, 178
Mirror for Magistrates, The, 112
Mitchell, R. J., 47n
Moleyns, Robert Hungerford, Baron, 38
Molinet, Jean, 168, 185
Montagu, John Neville, Marquis, 21, 60, 68, 69, 71
More, Sir John, 189, 192
More, Sir Thomas, 140, 141, 151, 152, 153, 164, 166, 167, 168, 171, 172, 173, 174n, 177, 185, 196, 200, 211, 213: account of Princes' murders 189–92, 193, 195, 199
Morley, Henry Lovel, Lord, 209
Morte d'Arthur, 75
Mortimer, Edmund, 94
Morton, John, Bishop of Ely, 155, 156, 163, 164, 165, 171, 181, 185, 190, 200, 201, 203

Richard III—*cont.*

the crown 171–2; attempts to gain public support 172–4; accepts throne 174; Berkeley created Earl of Nottingham and Howard Duke of Norfolk 175; reviews reinforcements from York 178; coronation robes 178–9; coronation ceremony 179–80, 184; progress to York 181, 184, 187; threat of risings in favour of Princes 182, 184, 188; creates Edward Prince of Wales 187; decision to murder Princes 184; returns to Sheriff Hutton 188; murder of the Princes 190–1, 195; kind treatment of nephews 188; puts down rebellion 201; magnanimous to rebels 203; Christmas festivities 203; sells and pawns royal treasures 203; Titulus Regis bill 204, 211; reformist legislation 204–5; as ombudsman 205; persuades Elizabeth to send daughters 206; swears oath of safe conduct for Princesses 206, 207; oath of fealty to Prince of Wales 207, 208; progress to Midlands via Cambridge 207; establishes King's Household in the North 209; King's Council of the North 209–10; Christmas celebrations (1484) 210; receives news of Henry's impending invasion 210; death of Queen Anne 210; alleged intention to marry Princess Elizabeth 210–12; prepares for invasion 212; Battle of Bosworth 212–15, 216, 217; death 214, 215, 216; Act of Attainder against 195

Richard III, His Life and Character, x

Richmond, Edmund Tudor, Earl of, ix, 12, 13, 14

Richmond, George, Earl of, *see* Clarence, George, Duke of

Rivers, Antony Woodville, Earl: captured by Warwick at Sandwich 27; marries Elizabeth 30; challenges Champion of Duke of Burgundy 33, 38, 45; personality 38–9, 80, 115; governor of Isle of Wight 45; joust

at Smithfield 46, 109; with Edward against Lancastrian rebels 51, 52; inherits earldom 55; to Holland with Edward 60–1; at Burgundy 61, 66; with Queen Elizabeth at Tower 74; puts Faulconbridge to flight 76; projected crusade against Saracens 80–1; appointed Governor of Prince Edward 95–6, 98, 139; pilgrimage to St. James of Compostella 96, 115; translates *The Sayings of the Philosophers* 97, 114–15; diplomatic mission to Charles the Bold 103; pilgrimage to Italy 107; visits Charles the Bold 107; robbed outside Rome 107; suit to Mary of Burgundy put forward by Edward 109; portrait of 115, 116; question of attendance at opening of Parliament 116–17; at Duke of York's wedding 118; celebratory tournament 119, 120; granted incomes from Clarence's manors 124–5; betrothal to Princess Margaret of Scotland 127, 134; translation of French eschatological work printed by Caxton 129; restoration of Our Lady of the Pew Shrine 129; influence on Prince Edward 131–2; marries Mary FitzLewis 134; gift of clothes from Edward 136; letter to Dymmock 139; transfers post of Deputy Constable of Tower to Dorset 139, 144; told of Edward's death 143; prepares to bring new King to London 143, 144–5; purchases armour 153; sets out with King for London 146; at Northampton 146–9 *passim*; arrested 148; despatched to Sheriff Hutton 153; execution 168, 169; bequests 168–9

Rivers, Richard Woodville, Baron, 24, 25, 27–30 *passim*, 38, 45, 49, 51, 52, 53, 55, 62

Robin of Holderness, 51

Robin of Redesdale, 51, 55

Rochester, John Alcock, Bishop of, 95, 105, 131, 137, 155